On Being Unreasonable

Dr Kirsty Sedgman is an award-winning cultural studies scholar based at the University of Bristol. She speaks about her work regularly on radio and television as well as at events around the world, and her research has been featured in outlets from *USA Today* to the *Guardian* to the *New York Times*.

On Being Unreasonable

KIRSTY SEDGMAN

Why Being Bad Can
Be a Force for Good

faber

First published in the UK in 2023
by Faber & Faber Limited
The Bindery, 51 Hatton Garden
London EC1N 8HN

This paperback edition published in the UK in 2024
This edition published in the USA in 2024

Typeset by Typo•glyphix, Burton-on-Trent DE14 3HE
Printed and bound in the UK by CPI Group (UK) Ltd, Croydon CR0 4YY

A CIP record for this book
is available from the British Library

ISBN 978–0–571–36686–6

Printed and bound in the UK on FSC® certified paper in line with our continuing
commitment to ethical business practices, sustainability and the environment.
For further information see faber.co.uk/environmental-policy

2 4 6 8 10 9 7 5 3 1

For Monty, who will probably be very embarrassed
by this book when he's older.

Sorry about that – but in fairness,
you owed me one.

Contents

Introduction

In December 2014 I was sitting on a bench in the jewellery room of London's Victoria and Albert Museum, sweating profusely. My entire upper half, from the top of my head down to my waist, was entirely covered by my thick woollen coat, like a kind of rubbish invisibility cloak. Inside I was struggling to cram my nipple into the mouth of my three-month-old baby, Monty, and achieve what the midwives called 'a good latch'.

I'd chosen that space in the museum because a) it was dark, b) there was something padded to sit on, and c) I was desperate. Monty's cries had revved up fast – from gentle grumbling to lawnmower to XF-84H Thunderscreech* – and people were starting to tut. Around us, a swarm of posh older visitors were busy feigning interest in the jewels sparkling in their cases while muttering to each other about the woman hiding under a coat in the middle of the room, and what is she doing and should we call security?

I don't know how many of you have ever breastfed a baby, but it is brutal. Pre-children, this is how I thought it worked:

1. Cradle baby in arm
2. With other arm, veil maternal bosom in modest cotton cloth

* The loudest aeroplane ever built. I have two little boys – I know these things now.

3. Pop nipple out and point towards baby
4. Breastfeeding achieved!

In reality, in my experience it usually went more like this:

1. Clutching baby, peel nursing bra slowly down—
2. Oh god, turns out bra was the only thing holding milk in! Milk now shooting everywhere!
3. Clutching nipple in one hand and baby's neck in the other, carefullllllly bring them together . . .
4. Quickasaflash, ram nipple into baby's mouth at precise forty-five-degree upward angle so enough breast tissue gets over his hard palate before he clamps dow—
5. OW! NOT FAST ENOUGH! HE'S CHOMPED THE TIP! OW OW OW!
6. Gritting teeth, retreat (to sound of vacuum sucking and skin ripping) then try again . . .
7. After a few goes, finally get position exactly right – then sit through toe-curling pain, absolutely rigid and still for fifteen to thirty minutes so latch doesn't slip and leave nipple white, cracked, and bleeding
8. Repeat steps 1–7 with Boob Number 2.

I didn't realise it at the time but at that precise moment, just a few miles down the road, forty other women were standing outside Claridge's hotel feeding their own infants. No woollen modesty-blankets for them – just a bunch of signs saying things like 'That's what breasts are for, stupid' and 'In future I'll be taking my breast at the Ritz!'

This 'Storm in a D-Cup' was part of a nurse-in protest

organised by breastfeeding campaigners. It had been prompted by an incident a few days earlier, in which a woman tweeted a photo of herself covered in a starched white tablecloth after Claridge's staff asked her to cover up her feeding baby. Her tweet about feeling 'humiliated' by Claridge's request made front-page news after Nigel Farage – that bastion of balanced opinion – said in a radio interview that surely 'it isn't difficult to breastfeed a baby in a way that's not openly ostentatious'.

Thankfully I didn't read about all this until after I'd got home from London, our first real outing from rural mid-Wales since Monty's birth. Until then I'd only ever breastfed at home,* and the whole experience nearly terrified me into never going out in public again. Watching the debates unfurl online, I saw hundreds of my fellow Britons frothing at the mouth over the possibility that they too might one day have to share a restaurant with 'space-hopper udders' and expressing disgust at all those women unceremoniously plonking their breasts on the table left, right, and centre. Um, I know they're often called 'jugs', but I think you're getting a little confused . . .

Peel aside the inflammatory vitriol, though, and underneath there's rather a seductive idea. All we want is for people to be *reasonable.* In the online comments I noticed this exact word showing up again and again. Claridge's baby-concealment actions were very reasonable, actually, when you consider that many people may potentially be embarrassed by the sight of a feeding child. It was unreasonable for the mother to take it

* Pause here for a flashback to sitting on my sofa, stripped down to the waist, my mother-in-law in the armchair opposite watching the midwife forcefully wrestle my painful, swollen mammaries into a sleeping baby's face. Good times.

for granted that everyone would find it acceptable. As most reasonable-thinking people know, breastfeeding can be done discreetly. Farage's statement, too, was totally reasonable – he was only calling for compromise and accommodation on both sides.

For any breastfeeding parents facing a similar dilemma, then, the answer is surely simple. It's just about showing consideration for other people, who might feel uncomfortable at seeing a smidgen of side-boob, a whisper of décolletage.* It's an obvious case of common decency, manners, and respect. Just act *reasonably*, folks! Why is that so hard?

That, as it turns out, is a very good question.

According to the dictionary, being a reasonable person means 'having the faculty of reason', which in turn means 'possessing sound judgment'.[1] This is a meaning that solidified in English around the 1300s, with the word *resonable* derived from the Old French *raisonable*, which in turn comes from the Latin *rationabilis*: from *ratus*, the past participle of *reri*, which means 'to reckon, think'. When applied to objects rather than people, 'reasonable' today can also refer to things that are moderate, fair, or inexpensive: i.e. not extreme or excessive. This information comes from my favourite etymology website, which also tells me that the sense began to shift in Middle English. Initially meaning 'resulting from good judgment', and then 'not exceeding the bounds of common sense', around the

* Of course, many people agreed, a flash of cleavage is perfectly acceptable under normal circumstances, but only when displayed for the consumption of grown men rather than infants. Nice boobs are great, one person commented, but not with a baby hanging off them.

1500s 'reasonableness' came to mean 'fairly tolerably': to act, in other words, in a way that a fair-minded person would be able to tolerate.[2]

Moral philosophers have been commanding us in one form or another to just act reasonably for the past few millennia. Whether it's Confucius in ancient China, or Aristotle in ancient Greece, or the Age of Enlightenment in eighteenth-century Europe, oceans of ink have been spilled debating which beliefs and behaviours are *within reason* and which are beyond the bounds of tolerance. This long history can help us understand what's happening again today.

From Bolsonaro in Brazil to Putin in Russia, Trump in the USA to Alexander de Pfeffel (Boris) Johnson in the UK: right-wing politicians around the world have spent the past few years working harder than ever to encourage visible divisions over hot-button topics. Climate change and immigration, gun laws and gay rights, pro-choice vs pro-life: any public arena for debate has become a kind of Rorschach test for moral judgment. These divisions are playing out especially fiercely within the online realm. Just a quick scroll down my Twitter feed and – yep – there's a cavalcade of police officers charging on horseback towards protesters. But are they deliberately inciting violence at a peaceful protest, or heroically defending democracy from a vicious mob? There's a family of asylum seekers capsized in the ocean, feared drowned alongside their one-year-old child – but what some leap to decry as a human-rights travesty resulting from the wanton destruction of their country by our own, others call the inevitable consequence of an illegal invasion. There's a respected professor campaigning for schoolbooks to teach children the full horrors of slavery

– but are they cynically twisting the past to incite divisions, or simply trying to paint the unvarnished picture of a history which until now has been suppressed?

In the wake of rising populism and virulent misinformation, facing a world that seems to be slipping further and further out of our grasp, we're desperately scrambling to re-establish the boundaries of civic morality on either side of the political divide. No wonder calls to 'just be reasonable' are growing louder and louder. But rather than learning to stand on the same moral ground, what we're seeing is a widening sense of antagonism. All this talk is driving us further apart than we've ever been before.

I study audiences for a living, which means that I spend my days immersed in talk. More precisely: how do people talk about the things they see, read, and hear? Whether it's a play by Bertolt Brecht or a political phenomenon such as the Brexit referendum, I'm endlessly fascinated by how people can watch the same event unfolding but come to understand it in such totally contradictory ways. You'll see throughout this book that I'm spending a lot of time dwelling on the kinds of words people use when they talk about others: whether that's via comments about a newspaper article, or arguments on Twitter, or the things people have said in real-life conversations. That's because I believe that by paying close attention to language use in action – to what academics call 'discourse' – we can understand more about meaning-making in action, as different people come to understand the world, their place within it, and each other. In short: I'm what you might call a valuologist. I believe that the way we talk to each other offers a window into how we construct our competing value systems.

Through studying discourse, my research has examined how human beings can maintain and even strengthen our beliefs in the face of contrary views and evidence.

The short answer to my last question is that we've collected all our experiences together to construct a worldview that often seems to us to be simple common sense. Our personal lived experiences, the culture we consume and the conversations we have, the forms of capital to which we have access (economic capital, cultural capital, social capital, mobility capital), the communities and classes and cultures we're part of: all these things come together to help us build a set of core beliefs. By drawing on varying value *systems*, we reach different value *judgments* about how the world is now and what we'd like it to become. *This* vision seems reasonable to me, so those other people – the ones who disagree – must therefore be unreasonable. Case closed.

Take breastfeeding. Studying this discourse, I noticed that commentators tended to agree in theory that being discreet rather than ostentatious is just a matter of common sense. Yet in practice, each person had a very different idea about what a reasonable level of discretion should look like. Should breastfeeding people simply face the wall? Slink away to the loo? Get out only one boob at a time, rather than whopping out both simultaneously? Should they hide underneath the table, or is it okay as long as they don't leap on top of it and do a shimmy? Precisely how many millimetres of areola are acceptable, I wondered; exactly how many seconds is it okay to leave between unsheathing the bra and getting the baby safely latched? Perhaps, just to be safe, all new parents should stay in solitary confinement for a year? And if everyone has a different opinion about what it means to act reasonably, then *how common can common sense really be*?

This is not a book about boobs and babies. This is a book about behaviour. How do we come to know the right way to act within a whole range of social circumstances, whether that's in real life or online? How do we figure out what's good and bad, acceptable and unacceptable, appropriate and inappropriate, civil and rude? And how can we ever hope to reach agreements in a world where everyone has slightly different ideas about what those things mean?

From whether it's okay for women to apply their make-up on trains to whether pulling down statues is erasing history or correcting its mistakes – these arguments, big and small, are all connected. At their heart is a deep-seated belief in the inherent reasonableness of one's own position, no matter how incorrect, incoherent, or even reprehensible that belief might seem to others. That feeling is what the French poet Jean Gerson in the 1400s called *certitudo moralis*, or 'moral certainty', the sense that certain truths about the world are *beyond reasonable doubt*. What human beings tend to want most of all is for things to make sense: to fit neatly into their own internal reality. When that reality is threatened, people often entrench – or even attack. In debates like these, with both sides so convinced their position is reasonable, how can we figure out what is right?

When it comes to behaviour, the trouble is that rules are a double-sided coin. Sometimes the rules that structure social life are designed to help us moderate our behaviour for the good of everyone, making life better, safer, and fairer for all. Other times, though, the rules have been unfairly wielded as a weapon to disempower and divide, keeping the masses docile, deferent, and in their place. So too with social judgment. At its best, the act of judging other people is a moral imperative, a mechanism for encouraging everyone to work together and moderate their behaviour for the common good. At its worst, laying our own judgments on to others can be simply a way to keep the status quo intact, preserving immoral phenomena like bigotry, inequality, and injustice. Throughout history, the urge to impose strict ideals on to other people has tended to land hardest on those who are most marginalised. As you'll see in the coming pages, this plays out today in all sorts of harmful ways: from angry onlookers trying to ban babies from cafés and aeroplanes, to autistic people getting kicked out of theatres for laughing in the wrong places, to Black families in the USA being arrested every year for celebrating too loudly at their children's graduations. Sometimes, those cries to 'be considerate' of other people are actually failing to consider other people, who are unjustly being harmed by the imposition of rigid rules.

Just like society, this is a book in two halves.

In 'Being Reasonable' we will come to understand the rules of engagement a little better. Where did those dominant norms come from in the first place? How do we learn how to behave? Looking back through history and around the world, I'll uncover how deeply our ideals of reasonableness were embedded within classical ideals of civic democracy, to such an extent that they have been enshrined in international law. How did these laws and belief systems and judgment mechanisms come to root themselves within social life, and whom have they been built to benefit?

In 'Being Unreasonable', I'll ask a more dangerous question. Is there ever a situation where the right thing to do is to break the rules? Modern life works hard to convince us that watching our behaviour and tone – and policing those of others – is what makes us good people. Be civil, we've been told. What's needed is measured debate. Let's have yet more roundtables and panel discussions, in which each side gets equal chance to air their opinion. Destroy sexist and racist ideologies by defeating them in the marketplace of ideas! Sunlight is the best disinfectant! But what if all these powerful appeals to 'be reasonable' are just a smokescreen, holding us back from actually changing anything? What if the best disinfectant for bigotry isn't sunlight after all, but starving it of oxygen? What if exposing a bad idea only spreads it further, while cutting off the attention on which it thrives is the only way to shut it down? This section will argue that we urgently need to face an unpleasant truth. In a world where everything is image, we've risked confusing the appearance of reasonableness with the real thing. In pursuit of those truly morally reasonable ideals – fairness, equality, justice – history tells us that sometimes, under the right sort of circumstances, we need to give ourselves and others permission to act unreasonably.

I wrote this book between the summers of 2020 and 2021 while history unfolded around me. Like millions of people on the planet I sat there day after day, stuck inside with my husband and two small boys, as the COVID-19 pandemic raged. I heard endless arguments about self-isolation and mask-wearing, and whether these were reasonable acts of collective care or an unreasonable infringement of civil liberties. I was there in Bristol when the statue of Edward Colston, the infamous slave trader, was ripped from its pedestal and tossed in the harbour, and I was there again at the subsequent protests against increased policing powers, standing in the dark watching a police car burn. I stared at my computer as, across the Atlantic, Confederate statues began to fall. On the news I witnessed the historic defeat of President Donald Trump and felt a marvellous blossoming relief – then watched with horror as the US Capitol was invaded a few days later. I played on loop the videos of federal officers standing aside, outnumbered and unresisting, when only recently leftist protesters had been shot viciously with tear gas and rubber bullets. I listened as the same people who'd loudly denounced Black Lives Matter protesters as 'undemocratic' and 'savage' began to reason away an armed assault on the very apex of American democracy. I watched respected columnists call for a sensible middle ground, the need for balanced debate between two sides.

Watching all this play out, I kept remembering that famous quotation by George Bernard Shaw: 'The reasonable man adapts himself to the world: the unreasonable one persists in trying to adapt the world to himself. Therefore all progress depends on the unreasonable man.'[3] Then I picked up my laptop and started to write. I wrote about how the political and media establishment routinely permits rich white cis-het men on the conservative side of the spectrum to break the rules of engagement, even when their rationale for dissent has consistently been shown to be invalid, underpinned by appeals to false victimhood and echo-chamber untruths. I wrote about how, for marginalised communities, permission to combat actual verifiable injustice has always been forcefully denied. Of course you can protest – just not like that (or that. Or that.

Or that). And I wrote about how contemporary discourse has become swamped with false equivalences and bad-faith logic dressed up as civil debate.

Balance isn't the midpoint between truth and lies. When the scales of justice are fundamentally unbalanced, trying to 'both sides' everything doesn't work. While some people are fighting to rebalance the scales, others are actively pushing on the weights to keep an unfair system in place. Not everything that can be reasoned is reasonable. Sometimes two wrongs *do* make a right.

At the heart of this book is a central metaphor. This is the language of lines. I'm talking here about the lines that help us separate right from wrong, good from bad, acceptable from unacceptable, appropriate from inappropriate, moral from immoral, civilised from barbaric. Before you read on, let me be very clear. As human beings, *we need these lines*. In fact, as we'll see, this vast global network that we call society only exists because of our ability to draw these lines. We rely on them to function. This isn't *The Purge*.

What we also need, though, is a way to think more critically about *how we draw those lines*, as well as *who gets to draw them*. Where did these ways of being-together come from in the first place? Who have they been actually working for? What happens when we cross that border between reasonable and wrong, and is this really the most sensible way to live?

These are the questions at the heart of this book. *On Being Unreasonable* is about how we navigate social situations in all their messy, cringeworthy, frightening, hilarious awkwardness. It's about the values and assumptions and biases that underpin the way we judge other people, and who the 'we' and the 'others' in that sentence tend to be. It's about manners, civility, propriety, and respect; about morals and ethics and law – all those big words we've come up with, over the centuries, to describe the necessary boundaries for our successful coexistence. And it asks how we might cut through the noise and get back to those old *morally* reasonable values: that true North Star belief in justice, equality, and liberty for all on which vast civilisations around the world were supposedly built. But more than anything else, it's about what it means to think of ourselves as 'reasonable people', with the right to tell others how they should behave.

PART ONE

BEING REASONABLE

1

A Stranger among Strangers

Think about what it means to sit in a steamed-up coffee shop, watching the flow of faces pass by the window. To be swept up in the thrill of a football stadium, the rush of joining in with a wave and getting it exactly in sync with everyone else. To dance in a cramped hot room or a vast festival field, everyone covered in glitter and someone else's sweat on your skin. To spend time in the comfortable hubbub of a restaurant or the silence of a library; to stream around people at the train station, or to sit next to them in hushed pleasure at the theatre, or to manoeuvre your shopping cart around theirs – oh, a wonky wheel! No, please, after you.

Being together, a stranger among strangers, is to exist in a constant state of faith.

In order to be out there in the world with other people, we need to have faith in other people. This begins at the most basic level: the faith that people, by and large, will not set out to harm us. That our bus to work will be free from explosives. That our classrooms and religious congregations won't be disrupted by someone wielding an automatic weapon. That no one will cough on us and spread a deadly virus.

We're beholden to each other in all kinds of smaller, less overtly catastrophic sorts of ways, though, too. Every one of us has a responsibility towards other people. To be considerate towards them, which means considering their needs as well as our own. To try our best not to unduly irritate them, or to get in their way, or to selfishly disrupt their peace. In order to successfully coexist, we all need to do what we can to keep our bodies and sensibilities from encroaching on those of others. We all have to do our best not to rock the social boat, and to keep the currents of everyday life flowing smoothly. To step out of my house each morning is to put my faith in other people: to depend on them to look out for me, and to do my best to look out for them in return. What could be more hopeful than that?

The Shy, Murderous Ape

Human beings are unusually sociable creatures. More than two thousand years ago, Aristotle called us the *zoon politikon*: the 'social animal'. The story of humanity begins with tracing our evolution from living only in familial groups, to forming close-knit communities, to taking up residence among the sprawling civilisations of Aristotle's polis – the people. Today, with cities and other urban areas around the world expanding rapidly, we're increasingly used to living in these mammoth melting pots, where family, friends, neighbours, and other unknown citizens jostle shoulders every day. And it's not just that we *have* to exist around people we don't know. We often do this because we *choose* to. A pre-pandemic study published in the journal *Psychological Science* gathered data from thirty thousand participants to find that when people are feeling sad they are likely to turn to their loved ones for company. When we're feeling happy, though, we become much more likely to seek out strangers, desiring the companionship of an anonymous crowd.[1] We saw this tendency resurge in nations which reacted swiftly to bring the first waves of COVID-19 under control, where lots of people flooded joyfully back into concerts and sporting events, desperate to regain those shared experiences.

This willingness to live among throngs of strangers sets us apart from every other species on the planet. Our complete reliance on non-relatives and people outside our specific social groups is what evolutionary economist Paul Seabright calls a 'remarkable and uniquely human' phenomenon. Of course, we're by no means the only species to engage in cooperative activities. From ants to zebras, the natural world brims with examples of ecosystems relying on a delicate balance of labour divisions among related individuals, as well as symbiotic interspecies relationships. But as Seabright points out, nature contains no other example of a species like ours, which relies on 'elaborate task-sharing' between *genetically unrelated strangers* of the same species.[2] We're the only animal whose very survival depends on a complex system of mutual dependence between people who aren't our families, 99.9999999999 per cent of whom we don't know, and whom we'll probably never meet. If this were a superhero movie, the origin story of humanity would be how we came to develop such an unnatural willingness to hang out with strangers, who should (by the logic of every other species) seem threatening and scary and, well, *strange*!

This is still a relatively recent miracle, the result of an 'extraordinary experiment' that occurred after the end of the last ice age, around ten thousand years ago.[3] That may not seem recent, but if you think about it in the context of the entire almost two-million-year evolution of *Homo erectus* into today's *Homo sapiens*, ten thousand years is like the last minute of our superhero movie. For three hours we see nothing but a bunch of solitary protohumans learning to stand upright, eventually coming together over the final five minutes (representing around fifty thousand evolutionary years) to form small groups of hunter-gathering foragers. Then, just before the credits roll, there would be a few final frames crammed with everything else: with boats and glue and ceramics and bread and mud-bricks and alcohol and leather and plumbing and the wheel and tattoos and puppetry and glass and scissors and C-sections and lighthouses and wheelbarrows and paper and woodblock-printing and chess and suspension bridges and matches and toilet paper and windmills and porcelain and ambulances and moveable type and buttons and eyeglasses and cannons and basically a lot of war stuff here and the printing press and barometers and sewing machines and plywood and vaccines and mechanical computers and electromagnets and lawnmowers and the pneumatic drill and rechargeable batteries and dynamite and light bulbs and a whole bunch more war stuff and penicillin and televisions and radio and nylon and the atomic bomb and space stations and video games and cellphones and the internet.*

Deep breath. All in the last fifty seconds or so. Blink and you've missed it.

What happened ten thousand years ago to prompt such an unprecedentedly rapid acceleration? In Seabright's words: one

* This list of inventions is, unbelievably enough and to the best of my knowledge, in chronological order. According to Wikipedia, anyway.

of 'the most aggressive and elusive species in the entire animal kingdom began to settle down'.

> It was one of the great apes – a close cousin of chimpanzees and bonobos, and a lucky survivor of the extinctions that had wiped out several other promising branches of the chimpanzee family. Like the chimpanzee it was violent, mobile, intensely suspicious of strangers, and used to hunting and fighting in bands composed mainly of close relatives. Yet now, instead of ranging in search of food, it began to keep herds and grow crops, storing them in settlements that limited the ape's mobility and exposed it to the attentions of the very strangers it had hitherto fought or fled.[4]

As the Pleistocene era came to an end, groups in Western Asia started constructing monuments out of wood, stone, and earth around which people began to congregate – often for months at a time.[5] As recently as 2008, a German archaeologist called Klaus Schmidt who was working near the ancient city of Urfa in south-eastern Turkey found enormous carved stones that were placed there eleven thousand years ago, making them more than twice as old as Stonehenge – crafted by people who hadn't even got around to developing metal tools yet.[6] This is the site of the world's oldest remaining temple, called Göbekli Tepe. Its discovery enabled archaeologists to trace the evolution of human cooperation back to its root.

Suddenly, astoundingly, after millennia of avoiding each other, we began willingly to coexist with strangers. Against all odds, it had become a better bet to wait for that figure in the distance to approach you than it was to shoot poisoned darts first and ask questions later. We developed, in other words, a highly un-animal-like ability to *trust*. This might sound like a simple process, but it's probably the most ridiculous thing we could have done. For almost every other organism on this big blue planet, strangers are something to fear.

Trusting strangers used to be an act of suicide. Like living on the edge of active volcanos or scurrying too close to a dinosaur, trust is an instinct which, through millennia of trial and error, our fluffier ancestors learned to avoid. So it is nothing short of a miracle, Seabright notes wonderingly, that a few hundred generations after we first started building settlements, the 'same shy, murderous ape that had avoided strangers throughout its evolutionary history [is] now living, working, and moving among complete strangers in their millions'.[7] Over such a short period of evolutionary time, we have managed to free ourselves of the certainty that stranger means danger, and to begin to have tentative faith in humanity – to believe that other people are (generally, probably, on balance) worth giving the benefit of the doubt.

This new ability to fight our baser instincts and to place our trust in strangers only became possible through the development of what anthropologist Charles Stanish calls 'intense ritualising behavior'. All around the world, at roughly the same time, humans began to construct systems of customs and traditions and taboos designed to organise their social groups and 'to structure people's lives, both political and economic'. Even among 'stateless' societies where the rules of engagement have often been less coercively defined, there developed a universal need for overarching 'norms', which Stanish describes as 'a set of social tools that developed over time to deal with the difficulties of keeping distantly or nonrelated peoples cooperating with each other' by governing how resources were produced, allocated, and exchanged.[8] For example, when it comes to buying goods, some cultures developed a bartering system to mutually arrive at a fair price, whilst in other cultures the norm to ensure fairness is to set a fixed cost which isn't subject to the whims of negotiation. In the 1960s, the US sociologist Harold Garfinkel sent his students into local shops to conduct an 'expectancy breaching' experiment, where they tried to haggle for fixed-price goods – they found that some sales clerks showed anxiety and even anger at this unexpected breach of 'normal' behaviour.[9] So the specificities of these normative systems may differ around the world, but the overarching understanding that humans *need* a system is something that every community has in common.

What does all this tell us? That drawing lines between good and bad, then reinforcing those lines via increasingly complex systems for rewarding fairness and punishing transgressions, was a crucial step in our social evolution. From those early Mesopotamian group-hangs to the Ten Commandments to the etiquette guides of Emily Post: laying down the ground rules of engagement is what allowed us as a species to set aside our instinctual fear, and to create a vast system of mutual cooperation. *Voila!* In just a few thousand years we had become . . . a *society*.

We Live in a Society!

It's the 1990s. Operation Desert Storm has just brought an end to the Gulf War, and the world is reeling. The serial killer Jeffrey Dahmer is about to be caught, and a cyclone in Bangladesh recently killed 140,000 people. In the USA, the average cost of gas is $1.11 per gallon. At home in England, on the other side of the ocean, I am six years old and soon to become obsessed with Beethoven.* Meanwhile, in a nondescript Chinese restaurant in New York City, a balding, bespectacled white guy is waiting to use the payphone.

Eventually he gets to the front of the queue. But when he finally reaches for the handset, a woman snatches it up. He taps on her shoulder and explains politely that he was actually waiting to use the phone – in fact, he'd been standing there patiently for the past ten minutes. The woman waves him away, stating dismissively that she didn't see him, and tells him she won't be long – he can just wait. In tones of rising desperation, he tells her that's not the point – he was here first, so he gets to go next. That's the point. Without missing a beat, she gestures to the handset she's holding and responds that if he really had been there first then he'd be the one with the phone in his hand.

The bespectacled man blinks at her in astonishment and walks away as she starts to dial. Defeated, he stands in the middle of the restaurant and yells at no one in particular the famous phrase: 'we're living in a society!' This means, he adds furiously, that we're all meant to behave in a civilised manner.

* Not the composer; the big slobbery St Bernard from the kids' movie.

You may already have clocked this as a scene from season two of *Seinfeld*, the sitcom created by Larry David and Jerry Seinfeld. Running for nine seasons between 1989 and 1998, the self-defined 'show about nothing' repeatedly came top of the ratings chart, and in 2013 the Writers Guild of America voted it the second-best-written TV series of all time (beaten only by *The Sopranos*).

Here's a dangerous confession to make. I've never seen *Seinfeld*.* But since this particular little moment of micro-conflict first aired some thirty years ago, the scene has become an unmissable part of the cultural landscape, marking a sea change in the nature of television. First aired on 23 May 1991, it is from an episode called 'The Chinese Restaurant', in which Jerry, George, and Elaine try to score a table while they wait to catch a movie. That's it. That's the episode. They wait, and the audience is forced to wait with them, and we're all told repeatedly to hang on 'five, ten minutes' for the pay-off, which predictably comes – 'Seinfeld, four!' – only once the episode is over, the characters have given up and walked out, and the credits begin to roll.

Thirty years later, connoisseurs of the internet may have noticed a resurgence of George Costanza's payphone rant. Today, the phrase 'we live in a society' has become a meme, shared millions of times in varying forms across the web: usually via a George-esque howl of despair over the tendency of modernity to value appearances over substance and selfish self-absorption

* By which I mean I've never seen an episode in its entirety. I've obviously seen little snippets – usually because I've just said the words 'I've never seen *Seinfeld*' near my smartphone or a man at a party, at which point both start frantically trying to recommend me clips.

over consideration for others. Because who among us has never felt the urge to snap and yell 'we're supposed to act in a civilised way!' at someone who breaks the rules: pushing past you in the street; failing to thank you for holding a door open; taking up the whole armrest on an aeroplane? Society has rules for a reason – the idea is that if we wait our turn and take only our fair share then everyone gets ahead equally.

There's a useful Japanese term to describe these collective terms of engagement: *wakimae*, which refers to the ability to keep one's behaviour in line with socially agreed norms. This is a term that can be used both as a noun – *ano hito niwa wakimae ga aru* ('there is observation of social norms in that person') – and as a verb – *ano hito wa wakimae te-iru* ('that person observes social norms'). 'Just like a set of rules you follow when you play a game,' explains the linguist Sachiko Ide, 'you follow *wakimae* in your game of life.'[10]

If we were translating the term *wakimae* into the English language then we might reach for words like 'manners' or 'etiquette' to describe the rules of the game. If we were using Arabic, we might draw on the Islamic concept of *adab*: a word which combines politeness with ideals of humaneness and decency, suggesting that these moral qualities are forged through the refinement of 'seemly' ways of behaving. In Scandinavian societies we find *Janteloven* – the law of Jante. Jante is a fictional town from the 1933 novel *A Fugitive Crosses His Tracks*, in which Danish-Norwegian author Aksel Sandemose gently satirised the Nordic willingness to embrace binding social conformity through unspoken cultural norms: commandments like 'don't show off!', 'don't think you're better than anyone else – you're not!', and so on. In Albanian, the word *sjellja* is like our more general term 'behaviour', but when used alongside honour (*nderi*), hospitality (*mikpritja*), and clan loyalty (*fis*) as one of the four pillars of traditional Albanian law (*kanun*) it means something more like 'right conduct'.

Around the world, in pretty much every language, we can find a cornucopia of words and phrases used to describe the rules of that game of life. But *wakimae* is slightly different, in that it calls attention not just to the game itself, but to how the game should be played. As well as having ideals of good vs bad behaviours, every society also needs a conceptual framework to help its citizens work out which is which in changing social contexts. Illustrating that process in action, in Japanese *wakimae* is the kind of 'discernment' needed to understand and follow implied codes of conduct within a whole variety of shifting settings. In order to follow the rules, we first need to be able to work out *what they are* and when it's appropriate to bend or even break them.

Philosophers and politicians have expended a lot of intellectual energy over the centuries debating what it means to 'live in a society', and how we should figure out what the terms of that bargain should be. In English, those terms have been called 'the social contract'.

The idea of the social contract has been kicking around in the background of philosophical thought for as long as there have been philosophers. As a shared agreement helping us to separate right from wrong, appropriate from inappropriate, acceptable from unacceptable, the social contract has often been seen as society's superglue – the only thing that stops us sliding back into animal anarchy. Under its broad umbrella has been arranged a powerful collective of discrete social institutions – like marriage, and schooling, and the legal system – each with their own regulative and norm-setting rules, that together enforce that insidious picture of a 'normal' kind of person living a 'normal' kind of life.

Crack open a philosophy textbook and turn to the chapter on contractualism, and you'll probably first find references to Englishmen like John Locke or Thomas Hobbes – the latter of whom famously predicted in the 1600s that, without a monarch, society would descend back into a State of Nature where life was 'solitary, poor, nasty, brutish, and short'.[11] Cheerful. You're also highly likely to find the French philosopher Jean-Jacques Rousseau with his 1762 treatise *The Social Contract*, which argued more optimistically that civil society is held in place not by royal force, but by a populace submitting their individual will to the collective will of each other.

This idea can also be found all the way back in the story of Socrates, the Greek philosopher, who in 399 BC was condemned to death by hemlock for corrupting the innocent minds of Athens' youth.* As Plato's story goes, Socrates was visited in prison by a student, who tried to persuade him to

* Socrates' real crime, though, was probably how annoying he was. The 'Socratic method' of education raised the ire of powerful Athenians by teaching bored wealthy kids to use questions to puncture their parents' belief in their superior knowledge of the world: a technique perfected by four-year-olds worldwide ever since. Mummy, what are shadows made of? What does the Milky Way taste like? Who invented bees? Why are you banging your head on the table like that? Mummy? Mummy? Mum? One study found that mothers in particular are hit with a machine-gun fire of three hundred questions per day. Suddenly that hemlock juice isn't looking so bad.

escape Athens and go into exile. Socrates used the idea of a binding agreement to explain why the moral thing to do was to stay in jail and accept an unfair punishment. He argued that the entire weight of human civilisation rests on the shoulders of every individual to faithfully abide by the rules of their society, no matter how unjust those rules may be. By the time you become an adult, Socrates said, you've already made your choice: either you've elected to remain part of the society in which you were brought up, which means implicitly accepting its laws (as well as the consequences for breaking them), *or* you've chosen to opt out of the social contract by removing yourself from society entirely.

Looking beyond the western philosophical canon, we can see that the idea of binding societal agreements goes back even earlier than this. At least two hundred years before Socrates, in fact – all the way back to China in the sixth century BC, when the ancient noble dynasties began to collapse and dozens of small kingdoms started battling it out for imperial domination, culminating in 475 BC with the Seven Warring States. After finally conquering their last enemy more than two hundred years later, the Qin Dynasty emerged victorious and began the impossible task of uniting their feuding rivals into a single military empire. But how could such a diverse collection of ethnic groups and cultural traditions successfully be fused together? Enter China's philosophers. The most influential school of thought was Confucianism, whose founder Confucius had long before argued that unity could be forged by implanting within the populace an internalised system of strict behavioural customs, inspired by the traditional etiquette of the nobility:

the Shang and Zhou dynasties. All the country needed to prosper was for everyone to practise the ancient virtues of *jên*, meaning human-heartedness or benevolence towards others, and *yi*, the ability to feel the right thing to do within any given situation. 'As to how the superior man behaves with regard to others and in view of a situation,' Confucius said, 'he has no particular preference, nor particular prohibition, but only has *yi* as its standard of evaluation.'[12]

But *how* can we feel the right thing to do? Where does that standard of evaluation come from? How do we gain the ability to discern which behaviours will follow the rules and which will break them? To find answers, we need to join the queue.

Queuetopia

Like George Costanza in *Seinfeld*, sometimes you only realise how powerful the social contract truly is when someone has the audacity to break it. I learned this the hard way.

One rainy day a few years ago, I used my lunch break to nip to the supermarket to pick up a colleague's birthday cake. Unfortunately, it seemed that all the other people in the city had also chosen that moment to run errands of their own, because the line snaked all the way back to the door. Our staff meeting was immediately after lunch, so I quickly ran the Sedgman Queue Calculation™ in my head. How many people are waiting? How full are their baskets? How quickly are we moving? I concluded that I would just about be able to get out of there with enough time to speed back to the office, cake proudly held aloft, a sugar-providing hero.

So I joined the back of the queue and waited. We inched forwards. Minutes passed. We inched forwards again. After a good twenty minutes I reached the front of the queue, with just one person ahead of me. Success! And with a couple of minutes to spare – I'm going to make it!

Then, from the crowded store behind, I heard a voice. 'Do you mind if I just . . . I only have to buy this one thing . . . Sorry . . . Would you mind . . .'

I didn't need to turn around. I knew what I'd see. The dreaded queue swimmer, cutting through the bodies behind and leaving a sea of politely furious people in her wake. 'Excuse me . . .' I could hear her getting closer and closer. Oh god. Surely someone will say no and halt her in her tracks?

Except they didn't, and she didn't, and suddenly she was there, standing right behind me and literally breathing down my neck. Normally I'd consider being magnanimous and giving way – but now? This was not the time. I was *not* going to be late. There *would* be cake.

There was, of course, only one reasonable option available – and that was to clamp my headphones tight over my ears and pretend I was too busy listening to music to notice. I figured I could probably just ignore her. After all, she'd done very well, sped past at least twenty other people, she'd only need to wait for me and that guy in front to be served and then she'd be out of here.

But then – oh, the horror! – she stepped next to me. *Next* to me. In a *queue*. Queuing, lest I remind you, is not a side-by-side sport. It's more like bobsleigh – you stay resolutely one in front of the other and try not to make eye contact. This was unprecedented queuing behaviour. I dared a sideways glance:

there she was, staring determinedly ahead as though I wasn't there. I did the same, forcing my face into an expression of gracious unconcernedness (while inwardly boiling with the fire of a thousand furious suns). The cashier opened up, the final person in front moved to pay, and we shuffled forwards in tandem, shuffle-shuffle, still side by side, still pretending not to notice the other, until the only thing in front was open space and the back of the guy who was paying – and then he was finished too, and we both *lunged* forwards like horses at a steeplechase, except that somehow she managed to loop her leg in front of mine and caused me to stumble, and I . . .

I'm sorry. I just need a second.

And I dropped the cake.

Thanks to *Seinfeld*, I know now that what I should have done is to walk away fuming, then loudly announce to the store en masse: 'We're living in a society!' Or perhaps I should have grabbed her by the shiny blonde ponytail and wrestled her to the floor. But the social contract is a powerful force, so instead I just picked myself up and limped off to apologise to a staff member, and to ask if they could find me a birthday cake that was a little less smashed to bits.

So believe me, I have endless sympathy with George's frustration at following the sacred rules of the queue religiously, then having to stand by while someone else breaks them and gets unfairly ahead. After all, nothing says fairness quite like standing in line with your fellow compatriots: everyone restrained by the same unwritten moral code, nobody using physical prowess or superior status or dirty tripping tactics to gain an advantage over others. What could be more egalitarian! Right?

You may be assuming that my fascination with queuing is purely a British pursuit – just as much a part of my cultural heritage as being covered head to toe in freckles, or never quite managing to get the naughty school version of the song 'An English Country Garden' out of my brain,* or that rising panic I feel when I wake up and it's a sunny day – quick, we have to make the most of it before the clouds close over us again! Next to complaining about the weather, queuing is practically our national sport. The most infamous example of an orderly line-standing championship is the Queue (yes, it's earned its very own proper noun) at Wimbledon. At this celebrated annual tennis tournament, the days-long wait for tickets even has its own code of conduct. Rules include: two-person tents are fine but no gazebos; smoking and vaping are strictly forbidden; no ball games after 10 p.m.; and, very specifically: 'Temporary absence from the Queue for purchase of refreshments or toilet breaks etc should not exceed 30 minutes.' When you join at the tail end of the line you get given a Queue Card with its own number and date, and you have to keep hold of it until you reach the turnstile where you can finally exchange it for purchasing a ticket. Anyone found 'adopting unreasonable social behaviour' while in the Queue will be refused entry.[13] All very civilised. The orderly queue has often been celebrated as the epitome of democratic discipline.

But when I researched queuing for this book, I realised it's not so simple. Writing about the history of waiting in line, cultural historian Joe Moran tackles the mythology of queuing

* Picture three hundred kindergarteners lustily singing 'Pull down your pants and fertilise the plants in an English country garden!' and you'll get the idea.

as a symbol of British fair play. As it turns out, this idea is actually a rather modern invention: one that 'began not in a more decorous time of courtesy and consideration in public places,' Moran says, 'but a period of national crisis'.[14]

In the nineteenth century, with rapid industrialisation causing mass migration to urban areas, the more relaxed model of market shopping began to decline and fixed shop retailing became more prevalent.[15] For the respectable shopkeeper, the queue offered a structured way to make everyone wait their turn. But it wasn't until the Second World War, as Moran's book *Queuing for Beginners* tells us, that the myth of British people as champion queuers really took hold – the exemplar of British decency and fortitude, a symbol of everything the troops were fighting for. After all, what's the alternative – a chaotic stampede with children, the elderly, and disabled people getting shoved out of the way? No thanks, guvnor!

Moran explains that, while queuing might seem egalitarian, the long wartime and post-war queues caused by rationing shortages* were actually felt to be highly inequitable. Housewives would join one end of a queue without knowing what – if anything – was on the other end, simply hoping that lots of people waiting meant it might be something good. Older women, disabled people, and those with babies were disadvantaged by their inability to stand for long periods; meanwhile, the rich had the luxury of other people's time and could simply send their waiting staff to wait on their behalf.[16] Queues were also seen as hotbeds for anti-Semitism and class warfare. Organisations like the British Housewives' League saw horrified hordes of white

* Rationing only ended in Britain in 1954.

suburban middle-class mothers arranging 'queue revolts', fuelled by mutterings about working-class shopkeepers failing to 'know their place' and relishing the power to make high-status customers wait. Gleefully, Winston Churchill's Conservative opposition to Labour's post-war government seized on Britons' queue fatigue, linking the queue not to British fortitude but to their mortal enemy – the red peril. 'Socialism,' Churchill announced in 1946, 'meant queueing':

> During a 1949 by-election in South Hammersmith, Churchill again insisted that 'the queues of housewives outside the shops are the essence of Socialism and the restrictive system by which it and its parasites hope to live'. In a pre-election radio broadcast of 21 January 1950, Churchill first used the term 'Queuetopia' to describe a Britain under Socialist rule. [. . .] Churchill's neologism, 'Queuetopia', was widely repeated by journalists and other Conservative politicians like Leo Amery, who contrasted 'the Conservatives' idea of Merrie England' with 'a drab, dead-level, rationed, utility-clothed, licensed, controlled, directed queuetopia'.[17]

So the British haven't always been obsessed with queuing. It's only recently that this became a central part of our national identity. Nor is the rigid order of the queue as equitable as it appears. Today, especially in the USA, long lines outside polling stations are celebrated every election by some commentators as the essence of democracy in action; to others, however, those queues tell a nefarious story of voter suppression and democratic collapse. Whether it's the West African reporter Yomi Kazeem describing a Nigerian system of 'booking' a spot by telling the person in front that you're waiting then trusting others to point out when it's your turn;[18] or an ingenious Thai photo that went viral of a queue made entirely of shoes, their human occupants sitting barefoot around the side of the room having thus marked their position in line; or another viral photo of Finnish people waiting for a bus in the snow keeping a full person's-height of space between them: varying cultures around the world have historically taken very different approaches to waiting. Sometimes, strict discipline and steadfast rule-following can be less civilised than a relaxed good-natured agreement. Sometimes, the demand to wait politely has been a way to keep us docile and in our place.

Really, then, queuing interests me because of its broader socio-political implications. This is a situation where we tend to feel the power of normative expectations intensely, in every inch of our bodies.

Not sure what I mean? Next time you find yourself in a queue situation, try stepping very slightly out of line to grab something. How far away do you dare move before the contract between you and your fellow queuers breaks? How many seconds of absence are you allowed before the line snaps back into shape without you? I tend to adopt a position like an exaggerated lunge: one foot stretched back as far towards the line as possible to signal my continued place within it, body arched away and arm stretching out towards the thing I need to grab – just to make clear that my commitment to the queue remains constant.

This seems silly, but performance is an important part of *wakimae*. I need to show my fellow citizens that I'm able to discern and follow this choreographed societal dance. After all, when it comes to queuing, if we aren't all following roughly the same rules, the controlled crocodile swiftly dissolves into chaos. The power of strangers' expectations is a force that keeps us very literally in line.

The other thing that interests me about queuing is the way it seems, on the surface, to be a pretty straightforward procedure. Get in formation. Wait. Move forwards. Repeat. Simple. Yet under the surface it's actually anything but. When we're queuing, we need to make a series of complicated subconscious social calculations. How straight does the line need to be to signal that there's an order to it? If there's not enough room left to join it, should I wait here or over there? I shouldn't stand too close to the person in front of me, but I also don't want to be too far back either. That risks leading to an awkward confrontation – like when someone slips in front and I have to pipe up: 'Um, sorry, I think I was next?' But precisely how close is too close, and how far away is not close enough?

Behavioural researchers have come up with a series of terms to define the varying circles of space that radiate outwards from our bodies. First there's intimate space, the bubble immediately surrounding us – 'the distance of love-making and wrestling, comforting and protecting', which is usually somewhere between 0–46cm, or roughly the width of a standard PC keyboard. Then there's personal space: around 46–122 cm (about the height of an adult emperor penguin); thereafter, social space: 122–366 cm (exactly the height of two Leonardo DiCaprios placed end to end). Like a Russian doll, these three concentric circles are then enveloped by a much bigger sphere: public distance, starting at the far end of our second Leonardo DiCaprio, which is the space beyond.[19]

As the (surprisingly large!) range between these numbers suggests, the everyday problem we encounter is that these circles aren't set in stone. What seems a comfortable social space for one person is, to another, an uncomfortable or even threatening breach of personal space. This calculation varies according to a whole range of factors – our own social situation, gender, neuro(a)typicality, individual upbringing, generation, and so on, as well as who the other person is. Those four circles of space were first defined by the anthropologist Edward T. Hall in his 1966 book *The Hidden Dimension*. Hall founded the field of 'proxemics', studying the ways cultural elements like social demographics, temperature differences, and population densities influence how we interact with one another. He argued, for instance, that in Mediterranean countries like France, the 'café culture' enabled by a warmer climate has fostered a series of more relaxed interpersonal norms, with Americans abroad reporting feelings of 'sensory deprivation' on their return thanks to the sudden withdrawal of intense eye contact.[20] At that same time, a Canadian psychologist called Sidney Jourard was sitting in coffee shops around the world counting the number of times couples touched: in London, zero; in Florida, two; in Paris, 110; and in San Juan, 180.[21] This is because France and Puerto Rico are examples of so-called 'contact cultures', where people tend to be much more tactile even with casual acquaintances; they also tend to exhibit more expansive hand and arm gestures than those from low-contact cultures. Finally, researchers have even proposed that the sounds of different languages have adapted to their environment. As far back as the 1700s, amateur linguists were speculating that people in warm climates tend to have developed language systems that favour an open mouth, while visiting places like Scandinavia you're more likely to hear clipped guttural sounds. 'The climate rendered their organs rigid and contracted,' surmised the Scottish cartographer John Pinkerton in 1789, 'and cold made them keep their mouths as much shut as possible.'[22]

In the second half of this book I explore more deeply the uneasy relationship certain cultures have with our own bodies and those of others. But for now, suffice to say that all this goes some way towards explaining why I, a Brit, may start to feel like an acquaintance is starting to encroach aggressively on my intimate space if they come closer than three-quarters of a metre (the average man's footstep). Meanwhile, one of my European neighbours to the south might feel like personal space only becomes intimate at around 15cm – not enough room to pass so much as a football in between.

The COVID-19 pandemic forced us to reconsider the rules of engagement for this new and terrifyingly uncertain world. In some ways, public space became a lot simpler to navigate. Socially distanced meant two metres apart – scientifically verified. But the pandemic also threw into sharp relief the problem of relying on our internal proxemic-o-meter to calculate this. Both national bodies and private citizens began to create new visual codes designed to help people measure how far apart two metres actually is. Grigore Lup, a Romanian cobbler, started producing long leather shoes in a European size 75 (UK size 31) – two metres heel to toe. The BBC created a new Snapchat filter called 'Two Metre Peter', which superimposed an image of the famously lanky footballer Peter Crouch lying on the ground. In some villages in India it was reportedly made compulsory to carry an opened umbrella when leaving the house, because two umbrellas nearly touching keeps you in a nicely distanced grid. An art gallery in Poland mowed their garden into a checkerboard pattern (long grass for spacing, short grass for sitting). The Riviere Pain bakery in Miyazaki, Japan, produced a range of extra-long baguettes.

A good way to learn more about social behaviour is to examine what happens during periods of upheaval and change. Whether it was social distancing or wearing masks, this global health disaster showed how differently people from varying social backgrounds experience and make sense of the world. And as Hall hypothesised, when it comes to social space, these variances have always been particularly stark when it comes to how we relate to *strangers*. A 2017 study comparing forty-two countries found that people in Argentina, Peru, Bulgaria, and Ukraine tend to have the most intimate zones of comfort, happy for strangers to stand at a distance of around just 80–90cm. Meanwhile, for places like Romania, Hungary, Saudi Arabia, and Turkey, that comfortable proximity only begins at 120cm – around the height of Danny DeVito. Anglophone nations like Canada, England, and the US, by contrast, fall somewhere in the middle – around 100cm or so.[23] If I can reach out and touch you, and if we both speak English as our first language, then you're probably standing too close.

Let's take a step back. How do we come to learn all this originally? Before the time of Two Metre Peters and very long baguettes, how did we come to know how to behave?

The Rules We're Not Taught to Follow

You probably won't be surprised to hear that a lot of what we know about the world comes from our parents, our immediate communities, and other people close to us. This is what cognitive researchers call 'top-down learning', where we're explicitly taught the rules for social engagement: do this, don't do that, get your hand out of your pants for goodness' sake! In every culture in the world, human beings have always handed down wisdom about what it means to live a virtuous life.

First we had oral traditions, like 'pourquoi stories', passed down from generation to generation. Coming from the French for 'why', a pourquoi tale is a legend that explains why something is the way it is, like how the leopard got its spots, or where stars came from. We can find examples of these kinds of creation narratives all around the globe: whether it's in the Indigenous Australian Dreamtime tradition, or the ancient Filipino folk mythologies known as Alamat, or the Mesopotamian poem *The Epic of Gilgamesh*, which is often considered to be the earliest surviving work of great literature. Carved into soft clay tablets in the Akkadian language then baked, *The Epic of Gilgamesh* is believed to have been composed around two thousand years before the birth of Christ and tells the story of Gilgamesh, the eponymous demigod ruler of the Mesopotamian city-state Uruk, who abuses his citizens and is punished for it. The goddess Aruru creates a man named Enkidu to challenge Gilgamesh. Enkidu is the original wild man of literature: a prototypical 'unworldly innocent with animal characteristics', who throughout the epic becomes gradually tamed and assimilated into civilisation.[24]

The purpose of mythology like this has always been to help guide societies in their quest to understand the world, and to figure out what it means to be an 'ideal' human being within it. Whether it's *Gilgamesh*'s Enkidu, or Ṛṣyaśṛṅga in the Sanskrit epic *Mahābhārata*, or Adam and Eve in the Christian Bible, one way to do this has been to depict characters making that journey from a (simultaneously romanticised and terrifying) State of Nature to civilised humanity. From ancient epics to religious tracts, enduring societies around the world have been built on this kind of morality tale, which tends to offer useful advice about how we might live together *better* – often through depicting imperfect humans undergoing punishment, then amending their deviant behaviour to bring it in line with normative expectations.

Later on, we can see those tentative guidelines for human cooperation being crystallised into formal treaties and legal documents. In 1215 there was the signing of the Magna Carta, which mandated that every citizen – even the king! – should be bound by a common law. Around the same time, the Haudenosaunee Confederacy* confirmed their Great Law of Peace, binding together the nations of Indigenous North America into the world's longest lasting participatory democracy. This agreement was detailed not on paper but via wampum (shell) beads strung together, and is often known as the very first constitution. So that societal impulse to produce formalised guidelines for mutual cooperation has been going on for an extremely long time.

* Meaning 'People of the Long House', the Haudenosaunee were imperially named by the French the 'Iroquois Confederacy', and were originally made up of the five nations of the Cayugas, Mohawks, Oneidas, Onondagas, and Senecas.

We'll come back to all this later. But for now, the important thing to understand is that it's not just official legalese and religious mandates and other formalised codes of conduct that tell us how to act. We're just as guided by the ideals we've internalised about who we are, who we should be, and how we should behave. We are hugely influenced, in other words, by things that go *beyond* words – by the unspoken, the tacit, and the implied.

Every second of every day, our marvellous human bodies are churning away on our behalf, carrying out hundreds of respiratory and digestive and nervous functions of which our conscious minds are largely unaware. Right now, as you're reading this chapter, your digestive system is busy pulverising the food you ate earlier. Your lungs are stripping the air of oxygen, passing it to your heart to pound around your body before returning it to the atmosphere as carbon dioxide. Thousands of times per second, your nerves are sending efferent signals* to your muscles to tell them to make tiny microadjustments – 'tighten muscle X a bit! Rotate joint Y a fraction of a millimetre!' – just to keep you stable and in one place.[25]

As an asthmatic child, I grew intimately familiar with the feeling of suddenly, horribly being forced to pay attention to the laborious process of drawing air in and out of my body: an automatic process that my body usually handled for me,

* 'Efferent signals' are those which are sent by your brain to your body to tell it to perform a reflex, like flinching. In the opposite direction, you also have sensors in your bodies that register outside stimuli, like the heat of a saucepan, and that then send this information via 'afferent signals' to your brain.

without need for effort or thought. This is what's called a closed-loop system. For the most part, these kinds of physical signals pass between our brains and our bodies without our conscious mind needing even to notice it's happening.

It's not that we *can't* draw these things into our sphere of attention, of course. We can always choose to notice, to actively pay attention: to say, 'Hey, brain, stop for a second and think about all the tiny bones and joints and nerves in your clenched hand, working together to keep this book or digital device grasped between your fingers, firmly enough not to let it slip through, but not so hard you damage it. Do you feel that? Amazing!' It's just that for most nondisabled people, most of the time, our physical systems tend to take care of themselves.

The same kind of thing is happening with our cognitive processes, too. In 1974, the Austrian economist Friedrich A. Hayek won a Nobel Prize for his theories about 'spontaneous order' – the understanding that human cooperation is the evolutionary result of our ability to constantly make tiny social adjustments between ourselves and others. Just as my bones, muscles, and nervous system are unconsciously cooperating to keep an object gripped steadily in my hand, I'm also constantly observing and making minuscule adaptations to my *behaviour* in order to minimise interpersonal friction – often without even realising I am doing so at all.

It's tempting to assume that our rational minds act as a kind of conscious command centre, purposefully and knowingly modifying our behaviour at all times to keep us in line with sets of clearly defined rules. But of course that's only part of the picture. As Hayek pointed out, we're also constantly following rules of which we're not even aware. Those constant adjustments of our behaviours are what Hayek calls 'a supra-conscious mechanism' – something that 'operates on the contents of consciousness', and of which we can therefore make ourselves aware if we need to, but which generally passes beneath our conscious radar.[26]

Here's my top-five list of personal supra-conscious rules:

Internalised Rule Number 1

That moment when someone tells me their name and I don't catch it the first time, so I have to ask them to repeat it. How many goes do you get? My internal limit is three – absolutely no more.

'Hi, I'm Rhmmphh, nice to meet you.'

'Sorry, I didn't catch that.'

'I'm Mhrrrimpf.'

'Come again?'

'Fwwnfft!'

'Lovely to meet you.'

Internalised Rule Number 2

That moment when I walk into a shop and realise I've forgotten my wallet. Even if nobody's watching, I still have to engage in an elaborate silent performance: slapping my forehead in dismay, patting down my pockets like I'm frisking myself at the airport, and making a self-deprecating grimace that clearly signals 'Silly me! I'd lose my head if it weren't screwed on.'

Internalised Rule Number 3

That moment when I bid an acquaintance goodbye, and then we both turn to walk the same way down the street. I've developed the highly graceful manoeuvre of converting my initial turning motion into a 180-degree pirouette, walking in the opposite direction for a moment, then hiding in a doorway. Two minutes should do it. There – now I'm free to go.

Internalised Rule Number 4

I will never eat the last biscuit on a plate. Never. Can't do it. In the US, that one lonely piece of food is called the Minnesota Morsel. In the UK we could henceforth call it the Tonbridge Titbit. Spread the word.

Internalised Rule Number 5

When writing a list of rules, always make sure to end on a multiple of five.

Just like my relationship with queuing, these specific examples are all, of course, quintessentially connected to my own upbringing (and also they stopped being supra-conscious when I wrote them down . . .). You've probably got your own – in which case I'd love to hear them! In fact, this entire book could have been devoted to spotlighting varying cultural cues and behavioural norms around the world – but happily, other people have done this for us already. In *Multicultural Manners*, for example, Norine Dresser describes a whole range of cultural practices, from marriage traditions to educational norms, and how these vary from nation to nation. When greeting others, for example, in places like India, Sri Lanka, Bangladesh, and Thailand the custom is to hold one's hands together 'in a prayerlike position and nod'; in Mediterranean countries like France, Spain, Italy, and Portugal the norm is often to kiss on both cheeks; in Latino/a cultures 'the *abrazo* is commonplace – friends embrace and simultaneously pat each other on the back';[27] while the Māori people of Aotearoa use the *hongi*, pressing together noses and foreheads to share each other's breath.[28] In the late 2000s, the banking corporation HSBC launched a big branding initiative calling itself the 'world's local bank', spearheaded by a series of adverts demonstrating other cultural differences in behavioural norms – like how in the USA holding up your palm is an innocent hand gesture meaning 'stop', but in Greece it's the equivalent of raising the middle finger.

This is why, when we go abroad, we'll probably need a guide to the local dos and don'ts if we want to fit in. But growing up embedded within a specific culture means gaining much of our behavioural knowledge from immersion, so that these behaviours seem simply like the obvious right way to be. In his 1890 book *The Laws of Imitation*, French sociologist Gabriel Tarde argued that imitation is 'the essence of the social': that because human beings are an imitative species, learning from copying one another, we take our cues from others around us. Did you ever see that adorable viral video of the cat who grew up on a horse farm and trotted everywhere like he was doing feline dressage? It's called a norm because, when we see others in our social group behaving a certain way, it usually feels normal to behave like that ourselves.

No instruction manual on the planet could ever be detailed enough to specify the exact right thing to do in every single possible social interaction; that would be like the longest choose-your-own-adventure story in the world. Laws, holy books, etiquette pamphlets, peace treaties, and other formal guides: all these things are important, of course. All this writing gives us a kind of instructive frame for how we're supposed to behave. But that's really just an outline. Because at the same time as we're learning through top-down instruction, we're also picking up many more acquired behaviours via 'implicit learning'. This is like how babies learn to speak – 'What do you call this? A ba-na-na. Baa-naa-naa. Can you say ba-na-na?' That's the instructional bit. The real heavy lifting, though, happens through immersion: instinctually absorbing the words we hear into our brains, knowledge acquired independently of awareness.

'Say ba-na-na . . . Baa-naa-naa . . . Oh for fuck's sake never mind.'

'Fuh say!'

'. . . Oh no.'

As for the rest of the picture, we've mostly had to piece it together for ourselves.

Looking back to queuing offers a neat example of how this behavioural immersion works in practice. We may well learn the overarching terms via direct instruction from an authority figure, like a parent or teacher. Stand in line! Stop fidgeting! *No*, darling, stop licking that nice woman's handbag! But for the nitty-gritty specifics – like the precise millimetre at which an acceptable standing distance borders on the criminal – we've probably had to pick up these culturally determined details via immersive osmosis. It's incredible to think about, really: my body as a finely tuned receptor, feeling its way instinctively through the social maze. As Hayek pointed out, the most fundamental rules of the game are those supra-conscious ones: the rules that are beyond our capacity to recognise, that we've absorbed into ourselves without even noticing, and that help us to successfully navigate natural uncertainties in all kinds of situations. It's a kind of social autopilot. And like most automatic processes, we only tend to notice them when things go haywire.

Most people have probably experienced that sickly sensation when your internal social navigation system malfunctions, and you get it slightly wrong. It's like the time my husband Tom and I stripped back the carpet in the bedroom of our first house and restored the original floorboards. For the next few weeks, every time I got out of bed I felt a sudden sharp jolt in my stomach, as my foot carried on falling through the inch of space where I'd expected the carpet to be.

In French, the phrase *faux pas* literally means 'false step'. This is a great description of how it feels to make a social mistake. It's that specific kind of excruciating interaction when you suddenly realise you've misread the situation and followed the wrong social script, but it's too late to get the interaction back on track.

> Like the time I was buying a sandwich in the supermarket, and the cashier asked me if I'd like a drink. 'Sorry, I'm married,' I said. 'It's a meal deal,' he replied. I cringed so much I swear my heart stopped beating for a while.

> Or the time my boss called me on the intercom to ask if I was free to answer a question. I mixed up 'go ahead' and 'fire away' and told him to 'go away', then I cringed myself a redundancy letter out of thin air.

Or the time in a theatre when the woman checking my coat held out her hand, and instead of handing over my jacket I reached out my own hand and shook it. That time I cringed so hard I pulverised my own bones.

. . . You know what I mean. The kind of memory you tend to be reminded of out of the blue, at 3 a.m., when your own personal blooper reel starts playing on loop. *That's* a faux pas.

And they feel so terrible because, on the whole, we're programmed to want to fit in. The fear of breaking supraconscious rules is so strong that the 'the faux pas test' has been used since the 1990s as a key measure to help doctors diagnose neurodivergences such as autism or conditions like dementia.[29] Neurodivergent people, studies have claimed, are more likely to make and less able to detect faux pas than neurotypical people. Meanwhile, autistic scholars have pointed out that this research is often dehumanising, arguing persuasively that autistic people are generally extremely good at following rules as long as their purpose and parameters are clear. In fact, it's the neurotypical tendency to see forthright communication as a rude faux pas which is the real societal problem, and the world would be better for everyone if allistic people could only unlearn the unnecessary expectation of shrouding direct truths within pointless politesse.[30] Debates like this notwithstanding, though, the wheels of interpersonal harmony overall are greased by the general ability to read one another's cues, make minute adjustments accordingly, and figure it out as we go along. Tacit knowledge, internalised codes of conduct, deep-rooted expectations for ourselves and other people: those are the things which are directing most of our behaviour most of the time. These are the threads that bind us together. They can be surprisingly hard to break.

How to Be Together

When the Founding Fathers were establishing America's First Principles, they were heavily inspired by contractualist philosophers like Thomas Hobbes, who believed that if left ungoverned we'd inexorably devolve back to barbaric brutality. In his 'hopeful history' *Humankind*, Rutger Bregman calls this the 'veneer theory' of civilisation: the idea that at any time we are all just one small step (or one big humanitarian disaster) away from letting the mask slip and becoming overwhelmed by our baser instincts, the animal within breaking loose from its cage. It's a common philosophical belief that human nature is inherently self-motivated, and can only be held together by fear – of the monarchy, of government, of the legal system, of the Church, of the police. This is a big mistake. Drawing on sociological evidence from the infamous Stanford Prison Experiment to Hurricane Katrina, Bregman gives us a much more optimistic picture of humanity. We may be prone to moments of unimaginably horrific brutality, but fundamentally we're more disposed to trust one another than we are to harm. The horror, Bregman tells us, is the exception. Not the rule.[31] This is thanks to the social contract.

Looking around the globe, we have seen already that even totally stateless societies have developed their own versions: norms and traditions designed to encourage behaviours deemed communally beneficial and to discourage deviance. We carry those rules of engagement around inside us; we feel them in our bones and embedded underneath our skin; we walk around in the world carrying the weight of society on our shoulders, an inbuilt sense of 'what we owe to each other', as the philosopher T. M. Scanlon (and the TV show *The Good Place*) famously asked,[32] and what we can reasonably expect in return.

This is an idea that has reverberated around the world for the past eleven thousand years, and which is summed up beautifully by the Xhosa philosophy *Ubuntu ungamntu ngabanye abantu* as well as its Zulu version *Umuntu ngumuntu ngabanye abantu.* Meaning: 'A person is a person through other people.'[33] That's why so many citizens came together during the COVID-19 outbreak to communally redesign social space with a new visual language of helpful prompts; that's why the world has by and large done away with the supreme authority of absolute monarchy; and that's why you'll rarely see a queue monitor guarding every single supermarket checkout line. Because humanity, on balance, is more cooperative than it is combative. Our expectations for one another are usually enough to keep us roughly in line. We're living in a society. It's not fear that's been keeping us together, but faith.

And all this is very nice and wholesome and hopeful. Except for one thing. You may perhaps have noticed, reading this chapter, how I've sprinkled in little qualifiers here and there. Generally speaking. Most of us. More often than not. Most of the time.

Lurking beneath the idea of 'behavioural norms' is an uncomfortable truth. That idea of 'normative' behaviour is, in and of itself, fundamentally flawed. At university I teach a class on conflicting value systems, helping my undergraduate students to uncover the layers of history and sociality and biopolitics that have together coalesced to position certain bodies and behaviours as normal, and others as just that: *other*. The very first thing I show my class is a series of slides:

- A Google Images search for the word 'relationship' depicting solely heterosexual couples.
- A photo of a stairwell with the inspirational quotation: 'There's no elevator to success, you have to take the stairs.' (What if you need mobility aids? You fail, I guess.)
- Another photo, this time of a wheelchair ramp that zigzags its way impossibly back and forth across a shallow incline, requiring (I counted!) no fewer than twelve 180-degree turns to traverse a walking distance of about twelve metres.
- A meme illustrating the 'double empathy problem', which is a model developed to reimagine the breakdown of understanding between autistic and allistic people as a two-way process of miscommunication; to fix it, *both* sides need to do empathy work to accommodate the other's communication styles, rather than assuming deficiency on the part of the autistic community alone.
- Another Google Image screenshot, this time for the phrase 'unprofessional hair': a search which made headlines a few years ago for offering up row after row of Black women with their hair worn naturally as it comes out of their heads, or else beautifully braided in traditional styles.
- Finally, a picture of a crash-test dummy based on an 'average' frame, which is to say the frame of an average

man, which was used to test cars up until 2011, leaving women 47 per cent more likely to die in a crash.

Our gender, our ethnicity, our religion, our social class, our sexuality, our body type, our place of birth and current place of residence, whether we're disabled or nondisabled, neurodivergent or neurotypical, cis or trans, and every combination thereof . . . Like it or not, all these factors still – at least to some degree – affect the way we experience, make sense of, and engage with one another within the world. My husband went to a posh all-boys school and he told me how, around the same time as they decided to open the college up to girls, they started cladding the glass stairs with steel panels. He couldn't understand why. Then he saw his new classmates wearing skirts, and he looked upwards and figured it out. So when we're talking about 'normative' bodies and identities, the question we need to ask is for whom have social life and public space been specifically designed to fit, like the most expensive bespoke suit in the world. We cannot keep avoiding the inconvenient fact that the world has historically been organised with only a narrow slice of all of us in mind.

In the rest of this book, we'll be taking a closer look at the social contract in order to think more carefully about who the winners and losers have tended to be in that so-called game of life. As the example of my queue-lunge demonstrates, behavioural expectations are constructed and maintained through social performances: literally, through the way we *act*. And the ability to be seen to act in the 'right way' has historically been determined according to able-bodied, neurotypical, cis-heteronormative, white-supremacist, patriarchal assumptions.

Understanding this is to begin to pay attention to the inequities of being together, out there in the world. Who gets to be seen as 'normal' within varying social situations, and who gets marked out as 'other'? Who gets to take up space and in what ways? Which strangers do we instinctively want to trust, and whom do we instinctually fear? Who can walk down the street holding hands and pass unnoticed and who can't? Who wheels the shopping trolley aside reflexively, and who stands still? Who is made to feel like they don't belong at that library or in that coffee shop? Who disproportionately gets watched, judged, and policed? How can we be together better?

This book isn't a relationship guide. Or rather, it's not a guide to romantic love; plenty more books exist that can tell you how to get the one you love to love you. I've been with my husband since I was nineteen years old, but still I wouldn't dare advise anyone on how to live with a partner harmoniously. Nor am I able to tell you how to forge platonic connections: how to influence friends and win people over, so to speak. Instead this book is about the way we interrelate with strangers at the moment we meet them – both out there in the world and online. It's about how we judge other people, and what happens when we try to control other people's behaviour, and how we negotiate our place within our shared social world. It's about how to reach a richer, deeper, kinder mode of coexistence, and what's been stopping us from getting there.

2

The Disconnection Economy

Today, more than half the population of the world live in urban areas, compared with one in three people in the 1960s. In just three decades' time researchers predict that at least a hundred cities around the world may have populations exceeding five million people.[1] These densely packed urban areas are also growing ever more multiculturally diverse. We have never been closer together than we are today. Welcome to the human stew.

More than half of the world's households also now have internet access, which has enabled us to invent new ways to be together even when we're apart. Called the connection economy,[2] this has been characterised by a millennial explosion in chat rooms and discussion forums and blogs and networking apps. Ever since the very first social media site Six Degrees was launched in 1997, that digital galaxy has been expanding exponentially.

The motto of the connection economy is that 'all of us are smarter than any of us'. This is the internet as global public square, in which knowledge is democratised, minoritised voices are finally given the platform they've historically been denied, and we are all able to make connections and share experiences and form meaningful emotional bonds with people we've never even met. As has been well documented over the past twenty years, the natural end-point of all this increased connectivity has been a global upswell in kindness and goodwill, fostered by the newly nuanced respect we all have for each other's varying cultures and worldviews. This truly is an amazing age.

Okay. You can stop laughing now.

The twenty-first century is a behaviourist's paradox. By every measure, we're currently living in a collective utopia of togetherness. Our new digital technologies allow us to connect with strangers around the globe at the click of a button, and our increasingly diverse neighbourhoods have overwhelmingly been shown to have positive long-term impacts on both the economic and social development of communities, with successful immigrant societies 'creating new, cross-cutting forms of social solidarity and more encompassing identities'.[3] What we *should* be expecting to see is an increase in empathy and mutual understanding, fostered by an unprecedented ability to see the world through strangers' eyes.

What we're actually seeing, though, is a global breakdown of that miraculous, quintessentially human ability to place our trust in strangers – the very quality that my previous chapter celebrated. Trust in politicians, in institutions, in experts, and especially in each other: all are rapidly eroding. The move together was essentially a hopeful one, fuelled by our innate desire for connection; yet somehow we've ended up further apart than ever before.

What went wrong?

Crowds – Wise or Mad?

Imagine going back in time and trying to explain social media to your great-great-great-great-grandparent.

'How it works, right, is every evening I spend hours staring into a tiny window that contains all the anxieties, pain, frustration, and rage in the world. Then I try to go to sleep. Then, eight hours later, I wake up, pick up my little window again, and quickly try to catch up on all the anxieties, pain, frustration, and rage I missed while I was sleeping. Then I eat toast.'

'Why don't you throw the window away?'

'Because my friends live inside it.'

'Do your friends bring you happy news at least?'

'. . . Sometimes they send me pictures of cats.'

A few years ago, a video went viral showing a man on an aeroplane deliberately and repeatedly punching the seat in front. His victim's crime? She'd reclined her seat back on to his legs. In the online backlash, everyone had a different idea of who to blame. In the blue corner: obviously the woman was acting unreasonably – men have longer legs, so they should be allowed to recline but women shouldn't if there's a man behind. In the red corner: reclining seats are made to recline – it was unreasonable of him to expect her not to use the seat as it's designed to be used. As I watched thousands of people take up their positions on the battlefield of public opinion, all I could think was – how did we get here? What makes us so sure our own verdict is the right one? And amid all the noise, how can we figure out which side is actually *wrong*?

This anecdote has stuck with me for lots of reasons, but particularly because it's such a good example of how moments of conflict that happen in public space are increasingly subject to being captured, shared, and furiously parsed online, like real-life moral philosophy trolley problems. Whether the subject is socialism or sourdough bread, every online discussion has become a ticking time bomb, with the potential to explode into furious disagreement at any moment. This descent into acrimony should be familiar to most people who've spent any time on the internet: anyone who's ever strayed BTL (Below the Line) of the comments section on a newspaper article, or posted on Twitter, or glanced at their local community's Facebook feed, or commented on a discussion forum, or downloaded the neighbourhood app Nextdoor. We've even invented a term for it: *reductio ad Hitlerum*, or Godwin's Law – the truism that all online discussions, if allowed to go on for long enough, will eventually end with a comparison involving the Third Reich.

Speaking of Nazis. On 19 October 2020, Sky History channel tweeted a trailer for a new TV show, *The Chop*, hosted by the comedian Lee Mack, featuring a group of carpenters competing to be crowned best woodworker in Britain. In the trailer, Mack introduced us to one of his contestants: Darren Lumsden, a cheerful bald white chappy from Bristol. Hey, that's where I live! Neat! Darren's USP is that he has tattoos covering every inch of his face and scalp. So far, so Bristol. 'Meet the Woodsman,' Mack narrates cheerfully. 'The Bloke-With-All-The-Tattoos. Or Darren, as we like to call him.' Ahhh. Hi, Darren! Feel-good telly at its finest.

Then the internet erupted. Um, Lee? Did you by any chance notice the big number 88 on Darren's cheek? That's Nazi symbolism for the eighth letter in the alphabet: HH, or Heil Hitler. And look, there, that 23/16? That's WP – you know, for White Power? And what about the word HOMEGROWN on his upper lip? To which Sky's response was: 'Darren's tattoos denote significant events in his life and have no political or ideological meaning whatsoever. Amongst the various numerical tattoos on his body, 1988 is the year of his father's death.'[4]

It took the internet no time at all to dig up Lumsden's dad. Not literally, of course, for he was in fact very much still alive. Apparently Sky's rigorous background checks hadn't extended around to the front of Darren's face. Awkward.

These are the swings and roundabouts of the internet. On one hand, our constant networked connectivity has allowed us to capitalise on the so-called 'wisdom of crowds', as explored by James Surowiecki in his 2004 book of the same title. Why is it that the collective aggregation of information by a group tends to lead to better decisions than could statistically have been made by any individual member of that group? Surowiecki gives a nice example in the popular TV quiz show *Who Wants to Be a Millionaire?*, in which contestants who called an expert for the answer got it right almost 65 per cent of the time, but those who asked the studio audience got it right an astounding 91 per cent of the time.[5] This collective wisdom is the premise on which crowd-sourced forums like Wikipedia are based.[6] In modern fables like the Tale of the Nazi Woodsman, we've been able to witness the promised power of the internet come alive: a global knowledge system, rhizomatic like the roots of a tree, interconnected and decentralised, able to fact-check, pinpoint contradictions, and call out wrongdoing at blisteringly fibre-optic speeds.

But on the other hand, we have what's known as the 'madness of crowds': the idea that, when collected together, people are actually *dumber*, more irrational and impulsive and herd-like than any one individual by themselves. In his 1895 book *Psychologie des Foules* (*Psychology of Crowds*), the French polymath Gustave Le Bon drew upon Gabriel Tarde's imitation theory, introduced in the previous chapter, to argue that collective congregation produces a kind of mad contagion in even the most intelligent person. 'Ideas, sentiments, emotions, and beliefs possess in crowds a contagious power as intense as that of microbes,' he wrote. 'This phenomenon is very natural, since it is observed even in animals when they are together in number. Should a horse in a stable take to biting his manger the other horses in the stable will imitate him. A panic that has seized on a few sheep will soon extend to the whole flock.'[7]

The contagion principle is often used to explain why the internet is frequently such an awful place to spend our leisure time. Especially when afforded the anonymising freedom of a fake username, the common argument goes, human beings collected together tend to become vicious, thoughtless, and prone to herd-like 'mobocratic' tendencies: contributing to a horrible surge of anti-Semitism, for example, or making lots of people believe the earth is flat. A 2017 analysis of how to deal with our 'post-truth era' suggested that the 'flexibility and fractionation afforded by social media' allows individuals on both sides of the political spectrum to seek out the information that conforms to their pre-existing beliefs, embracing alternative facts and rejecting expertise when it suits their biases.[8] And yet, for many of us, the internet has also offered genuine human connections in profoundly isolating times.

So which is it, then? Is social media good or bad for us? When collected in crowds, are we wise or are we mad? And if we really are 'social animals', like Aristotle said, why do we often seem to be so bad at playing nicely with other people?

'Tribal Animals'

Blaming social media alone for our contemporary ills is a tempting solution – but, ultimately, a lazy one. There's never been a time in history when a group of people *somewhere* wasn't trying their hardest to dominate another group: that kind of conflict has always been a constant. The other tempting response has been to follow Gustave Le Bon and blame all our problems on our 'humanimal' nature. After all, aren't we really just inherently tribal creatures, led naturally by animal instincts to forge in-groups and out-groups and to attack those who are on the out?

This idea was popularised by a zoologist called Desmond Morris in his massively popular (and massively flawed) 1967 book *The Naked Ape*. Written in just four weeks (it shows), *The Naked Ape* argued that men traditionally go out to work and women stay at home because: 'Working has replaced hunting, but has retained many of its basic characteristics. It involves a regular trip from the home base to the "hunting" grounds. It is a predominantly masculine pursuit.'[9] To which female scientists collectively responded: Oh Desmond. Firstly, you're overlooking the fact that throughout history and across a huge variety of cultures women have been hunters, too, both by necessity and for sport. Secondly, you seem to have forgotten the 'gathering' part of 'hunter-gatherers', which also took women a fair distance from their home base for days at a time and reliably tended to fetch back *more* calories than killing animals with a spear.[10] But don't let facts get in the way of lazy biological essentialism.

Despite the pleas of Indigenous communities to stop using it, the metaphor of the tribe has been annoyingly persistent, deployed to interrogate aspects of everyday life from advertising[11] to fashion trends,[12] and gaining particular traction in the world of politics. During research I came across a book published in 1971 called *The Imperial Animal*, which I was delighted to find was written by two men called Lionel Tiger and Robin Fox,* arguing that democratic elections have been organised around the structure of competing parties because this mechanism feeds our natural hunger to form into competitive tribes.[13] The British politician David Lammy's book *Tribes* uses the metaphor to examine the rising trend of political animosity in recent years,[14] while Seth Godin's 2008 book of the same title does likewise, but focusing on the internet.[15]

The reasoning goes that we evolved in a world of intense competition between different social groups, with loyal members of close-knit communities more likely to survive than those that were more outward-facing and less tightly connected. Therefore, 'selective pressures have sculpted human minds to be *tribal*, and group loyalty and concomitant cognitive biases likely exist in all groups'.[16] I wish I could say that this too is evolutionary nonsense, but sadly it seems like the idea has some physiological basis.

In *Humankind*, Rutger Bregman tells the story of the discovery of oxytocin, commonly known as 'the love drug'.

* Those are exactly the names I'd have chosen if I were, say, a variety of apex predators in a trenchcoat, but they really do seem to be actual human authors – I checked.

Oxytocin is a neurotransmitting hormone secreted by a pea-sized gland at the base of the brain, whose release is prompted by close physical connection like cuddling or breastfeeding, and which promotes feelings of loving sociability. Within the scientific community the discovery of oxytocin led to initial jubilation. Spray it up your nose and we can get rid of animosity forever! Crop-dust the masses and do away with war! But as Bregman explains, that early excitement was later scuppered by the finding that oxytocin strengthens bonds only between people who are already in our in-group. For those outside our social circles, oxytocin actually *intensifies* feelings of suspicion and mistrust.[17]

Like Bregman, though, I believe that leaning too heavily on evolutionary biology as a convenient excuse for bad behaviour misses the point somewhat. 'I didn't mean to do it, your honour – my inner animal made me!' After all, we've moved on quite a way in the generations since Mesopotamia. Far from being helplessly at the mercy of our survival instincts, we are also agentic beings: creatures with a great degree of agency. As we've already seen, humans possess a tremendous prosocial facility to organise dispersed societies around sophisticated rules of engagement. When somebody runs into a burning building to save a stranger, that natural instinct for individual self-preservation is temporarily drowned out by an equally natural communitarian impulse to help and be perceived well by others, whom we then rely on in turn. Of course our interactions are shaped by all those supra-conscious mechanisms we raised in the previous chapter, but crucially, *we aren't beholden to them*. We can learn to recognise our harmful urges and instincts, and to alter our response. We get to *decide* how we live together.

So the problem isn't that we are naturally unable to coexist peacefully. On the contrary: human beings on the whole are generally very good at it. The problem is that we are trying to be together in a world that's designed to pull us apart.

Time Ghosts of the Twenty-first Century

In the 1950s, Welsh academic Raymond Williams coined the term 'structures of feeling' to describe the way historical eras and their aesthetic representations have highly distinctive affective qualities.[18] A bit like the German word *Zeitgeist* (literally 'time ghost'), Williams was offering a way to describe how, as we move out of one moment in time and into another, the world starts to feel differently to us than it did before: an idiosyncratic emotional and physical landscape, redolent of unique textures, sounds, hues, tastes, smells, ideas, and sensations. For me, the structure of feeling of the twenty-first century has so far been characterised by an insidious sensation of being gradually, deliberately incentivised to disconnect from a wider instinct towards human cooperation, and encouraged instead into smaller and smaller bubbles of like-minded people.

Rather than being a social media problem, this is a society problem. Specifically, this is a three-pronged manoeuvre: one which is spurred on simultaneously by our governments, by giant corporations, and by the digital connection economy of Silicon Valley.

First we have to thank the global political movement we know today as neoliberalism. A term coined in the 1930s to describe the free-market project of financial regulation through competition and the promotion of the individual over the collective, neoliberalism properly took off as a political project towards the end of the 1960s. In an interview, David Harvey, the author of *A Brief History of Neoliberalism*, describes it as a counter-revolutionary project designed and implemented by the 'corporate capitalist class'. Feeling 'intensely threatened' by a rising tide of communist and trade-union movements, they 'desperately wanted to launch a political project that would curb the power of labor'.[19] The core neoliberal belief of Reaganomics was infamously summed up by Margaret Thatcher's 1980s sound bite that there was 'no such thing as society' – only individuals and their immediate families.

Ever since, the neoliberal project has continued determinedly to shift the western discourse away from social responsibility and towards personal responsibility, with wide-reaching consequences. Instead of a welfare state we now have individual GoFundMe accounts, mutual aid rebranded as a deadly mixture of personal choice and popularity contest rather than the responsibility of a functioning civilisation. Instead of a fair and equitable labour market we've got hustle culture, which tells us we must 'rise and grind' to get ahead of the competition. Home ownership has given way to tiny rental apartments, individual offices to open-plan workplaces where we share the same air but in a kind of collective solitude, a world of earbuds and smartphones, self-contained little bubbles of WhatsApp, Slack, and Spotify. Instead of a decent social safety net we've been sold a failing vision of rugged individualism, buoyed by billionaires' occasional PR stunts of tax-deductible benevolence. If socialism can be summed up by that famous Marxist slogan 'from each according to their ability, to each according to their needs', then the motto of neoliberalism is more like 'everyone for themselves'.

Second, that prevailing feeling of discord has been hugely exacerbated by the so-called connection economy. In fact, I'd say the term 'disconnection economy' is a better fit. As other commentators have pointed out: the problem isn't digital technology itself so much as how we've designed it to work. 'The internet is a reflection of our society and that mirror is going to be reflecting what we see,' the pioneering developer Vint Cerf argued in a BBC interview back in 2004. 'If we do not like what we see in that mirror the problem is not to fix the mirror, we have to fix society.'[20] Unfortunately for us we didn't listen then. So let's listen now. The problem is neither our naturally divisive urges nor the nature of social media in and of itself, but rather how we're using social media – or perhaps instead the way it's now being used against us. If social media is a mirror then it's like the softly lit kind you get in expensive boutiques, carefully designed to flatter and persuade by showing us a distorted vision of who we want to believe ourselves to be. And this distortion of reality goes beyond mere self-image. Profit-driven platforms are specifically programmed to encourage dissensus and conflict, rather than thoughtfully nuanced forms of dialogue. Twitter algorithms help bad actors turn our hate-clicks into advertising revenue; YouTube shows us things we might like to shout at; companies like Cambridge Analytica have been making a fortune from isolating us into distinct audience segments via our Facebook usage patterns, then selling us to giant corporations with personalised targets on our backs. It's not harmonious discussion that brings in the big bucks. There are gigantic profits to be made from angry debate.

This doesn't apply just to social media platforms, of course, but to more traditional news media organisations, too. Around the same time as we started moving from the community-run public park of the World Wide Web into the corporate-controlled picket fences of Web 2.0, news megaliths began adopting similar strategies for commodifying controversy. Just think about the rapid proliferation in the 2000s of news-aggregation sites, powered by advertising revenue, built to reflect and reinforce the specific values of increasingly niche target audiences. Readers are lured in via the rise of clickbait, for instance: a word that was added to the Merriam-Webster dictionary in 2015 to describe the kind of 'information-gap' headline pioneered by Upworthy, the 'fastest-growing media site of all time'.* A study of clickbait journalism revealed: 'Less than two years after its founding in March 2012, Upworthy had over 80 million unique visitors each month – more than the *New York Times* or *Washington Post*.'[21] Threatened by a tsunami of competition, traditional news organisations have been fighting for survival along with everybody else, exploiting moral panics and actively courting (rather than just reporting on) controversy.

The third and final piece of the puzzle is how entire governments got in on the act. In *This Is Not Propaganda*,

* Clickbait headlines are often written as a question (like 'Is It Ever OK to Have Bad Manners?', the title that once got attached to a BBC article of mine) or else in the format 'Thing Happened to Person – You'll Never Guess What They Did Next!!!' The aim is to strategically withhold information and elicit a knee-jerk emotional reaction – either curiosity or fury – to entice users to opine, (dis)like, and share. Actually reading the article is optional.

Soviet-born British journalist Peter Pomerantsev details how, all around the world, this new technological ability to reduce us all to individually reachable metrics produced scary new phenomena like troll factories and bot farms.[22] Political campaigners immediately began to embrace these fun new divide-and-conquer tools: encouraging our separation into social media bubbles, feeding us competing 'alternative facts', then watching us tear each other apart.

Looked at all together, this is what the writer Richard Flanagan calls the new movement of history: 'The world is being undone before us', and is leading us inexorably towards 'fragmentation on the basis of concocted differences'.[23] Never mind networked connectivity; this feels more like the age of networked hostility.

The problem has been pretty firmly diagnosed, then. In an era that's making it harder and harder just to earn enough to stay alive, we're gradually being incentivised into adopting a mindset of antisocial individualism rather than prosocial communitarian thinking. Silicon Valley is purposefully accelerating that sense of 'detrimental dissonance', which communication theorists see as a characteristic feature of our mediatised public spheres.[24] Intensely niche news-delivery systems are being targeted at increasingly separate like-minded groups, designed to reinforce their specific worldviews, value systems, and behavioural norms. These manufactured tensions are then seeping inexorably back down the internet lines and on to our streets, creeping and winnowing their way into our communities. All this is happening against the backdrop of the 'global village', in which we live and work alongside a much larger and more diverse social community than ever before – bringing us together physically, yet encouraging us psychologically to 'hunker down' in fragmented groups. 'Trust [. . .] is lower, altruism and community cooperation rarer, friends fewer.'[25] No wonder we're in trouble!

Now, let's take a step back and think about the proposed solution. In many ways, it seems pretty obvious. If the villain is that poisonous Venn diagram of capitalism, politics, and technology, which together have conspired to disconnect us into our distinct bubbles and to destroy our sense of communal responsibility – well, then! Surely all we need is to go back to a time when we were all singing from the same hymn sheet? We have to get back on the same page. *We need to re-establish the social contract.*

After all, our evolutionary history conclusively demonstrates that collaboration is fostered when we collectively decide that prosocial behaviour is the norm, while distrustful individualism is seeded through the belief that people are fundamentally, antisocially out to get us. All we need to do, then, is to reinforce a shared expectation that everyone should behave in prosocial rather than antisocial ways, and everything will be fine. Be kind to others. Don't push and shove. Speak calmly rather than shouting people down. Clean up after yourself rather than littering. No manspreading or mansplaining. Empathise with alternative points of view. Do good things; don't do bad things; show consideration for other people; be polite rather than rude. It's simple! If everyone could just be *reasonable*, we'd all get along.

Right?

Living in a Reasonable World

Let's play a game. Go to the 'News' section of Google and search for the phrase 'no reasonable person'. How many statements would you happily disagree with? Here are mine:

> Marco Rubio states that 'No Reasonable Person Can Say Climate Change is a Bigger Threat than Terrorism' – RealClearPolitics.[26] (Meanwhile, the Pew Research Centre recently found that people living in half of the twenty-six countries surveyed do in fact see climate change as the biggest threat facing humanity, compared with under a third for terrorism.)[27]
>
> 'No reasonable person wants to see investors lose money' – Investor Place.[28] (*Sound of guillotine-sharpening intensifies*)
>
> 'If you're in a supermarket, no reasonable person could tell the difference from one turkey or another' – Insider.[29] (Try telling that to a professional chef. Or the turkey's mother.)
>
> 'No reasonable person would ever call Apple a monopolist' – Tim Cook, quoted by CNBC.[30] (HAHAHA!)

Did you find a statement you disagree with? Congratulations! You've just joined the Unreasonable People Club. Population: 7.9 billion.

As someone who studies the construction of value *systems*, I'm endlessly fascinated by the rhetorical manoeuvres people use to explain their value *judgments*. This is good; that is bad.

This is wrong; that is right. This means that I spend a lot of my time examining the twists and turns of how we talk to one another, both in person and online. How do we reach for words to describe indescribable experiences? What might somebody's use of language tell us about the judgment processes they go through to reach varying verdicts about the world? What systems of criteria do they take up in order to describe their beliefs and viewpoints; what senses of self-identity, community identity, national identity do they draw upon; what kinds of knowledge and training do they bring to bear? By paying close attention to patterns of language use, watching as people's discussions evolve and mutate and spill over into new fights entirely, I believe that we can learn more about how different people negotiate their place within our shared social world.

In my work studying arguments, I found the word 'reasonable' appearing over and over again. Commenting in dismay on the fragmenting disarray within political discourse, respectable newspaper columnists and media pundits have been using this term with increasing regularity. Gesturing at everything from climate change deniers to the uproar against 'critical race theory' in schools, there's a common message that we could fix all this if everyone could just stop yelling at each other for one gosh-darned minute and *be reasonable!*

Once I noticed this particular word popping up all over the place, I started wondering: why this term specifically? Why not one of its synonyms: sensible, logical, fair, or appropriate, for instance? The reason, it turns out, is that 'reasonable' isn't any old word. In fact, it goes right to the heart of moral philosophy itself.

As we've already seen, the ability to assess other people's behaviour according to a shared moral code is a societal necessity. The fabric of social life is held together by these implicit agreements, along with the power of communal expectations to enforce them. This means that, in order to live together in the world, we had to develop mechanisms for judging which beliefs and values and behaviours are *within reason* – and which aren't.

On the whole, 'reasonable' has generally been considered a good thing to be. With the Latin word *ratio* meaning 'to reason', it's sometimes been conflated with rationality. From Plato's *Republic* and Aristotle's *Nicomachean Ethics* to Descartes' 'I think, therefore I am', and from China's Confucianism to the Nyāya school of Hindu thought to Islamic *falsafah*: across a huge variety of philosophies and belief systems, cultivating rational judgment has commonly been seen as the way to create morally righteous citizens. Being reasonable means repudiating one's baser instincts in favour of logic and evidence. Being reasonable means weighing up all aspects of a problem before reaching soundly reason*ed* judgments. Being reasonable means being able to recognise right from wrong, good and bad, and being ethical enough to generally make the right decision about where on that spectrum your actions and thoughts should land.

Yes, even your thoughts. Marcus Aurelius Antoninus, Roman emperor from AD 161 to 180, believed that 'the happiness of your life depends upon the quality of your thoughts: therefore, guard accordingly, and take care that you entertain no notions unsuitable to virtue and reasonable nature'.[31] Meanwhile, in the Ptolemaic Kingdom (the ancient Hellenistic state) around

300 BC, the apocryphal Egyptian philosopher Hermes Mercurius Trismegistus supposedly wrote: 'Of the Soul, that part which is Sensible is mortal, but that which is Reasonable is immortal. [. . .] The Earth is brutish, the Heaven is reasonable or rational.'[32]

We can see this division between the reasonable and unreasonable halves of the self emerging all across the ancient world. The Hellenic philosophers divided the soul into animal passions and rational mind. Islamic philosophy used the metaphor of an unruly horse: the *nafs* (or self) in its unrefined state as *al-nafs al-hayawaniyya* signifies man's animal carnal desires, which need to be taken in hand by *aql* (or rationality), possessed by men and angels.[33] In Korea throughout the mid-1500s, Neo-Confucians were engaged in a fierce philosophical dispute called *Sachil Nonjaeng* (the Four-Seven Debate), debating the ancient belief that the four 'moral' emotions of 惻隱 (pity and compassion), 羞惡 (shame and dislike), 辭讓 (compliance and deference), and 是非 (right and wrong) are all cultivated by the mind and are therefore good, while the seven ordinary functions like 喜 (joy), 怒 (anger), and 欲 (desire) stem from the arousal of the body and are therefore evil.[34] Anyone who's ever spent any time with a toddler will probably recognise that internal battle between the nascent ability to regulate their emotions, and the Tasmanian devil of unruly feelings that resides underneath their skin.

'I love you, Mummy.'

'Ahh, what a lovely cuddl— wait, stop, why are you hitting me?!'

'Because I hate you!'

Toddlers: exuding big *nafs* energy all day long.

Luckily, humanity has long been considered uniquely capable of what Islam calls *adab*: the ability to refine our inner dispositions, taming the animal inside us and cultivating a rational ethical self. The ancient Chinese philosopher Mencius argued similarly that everyone is born with a germ of *ren* (compassion or humaneness), along with other traditional Chinese virtues of *yi* (righteousness), *li* (propriety), and *zhi* (wisdom), but that these things need to be nurtured in order to flourish; without this encouragement, a neglected child's goodness will wither.[35] Far from being helplessly at the mercy of tribalistic urges, the ancient world understood what we often seem today to have forgotten – that we all have the ability to cultivate moral goodness so long as we're encouraged and willing to work at it.

As modern child-development professionals have confirmed, this process of moral refinement is an inherently social process. The famous Soviet psychologist Lev Vygotsky demonstrated that we learn to control ourselves by learning from others, with the culture in which we're raised teaching us not just *what* to think but *how* to reason. This implicit knowledge is then reinforced through formal education. Very early on, ancient centres of learning – such as al-Qarawiyyin in Morocco* or the Lyceum in Greece – helped meet the urgent need of determining citizens' rights and responsibilities, by defining how a reasonable subject should think, speak, and behave.

So the ideal of reasonableness runs deep. Seen as a peculiarly human quality, that term was embedded within the very earliest ideals of classical civic democracy and has since become

* Founded in Fez in AD 859 by a Tunisian-born Muslim woman called Fatima al-Fihri, al-Qarawiyyin has often been called the oldest university in the world.

integral to the way we think about moral citizenship itself. This ideal runs so deep, in fact, that over time the word 'reasonable' officially became enshrined within the law.

The Man on the Clapham Omnibus

In 1837, an Englishman called Mr Menlove built a haystack near the boundary of his property. His neighbour, Mr Vaughan, spent the next five weeks warning Menlove that the hay was at risk of spontaneously igniting. Menlove's reaction? He'd 'chance it'. As predicted, the hay burst into flames and the fire roared across the border to Vaughan's land, burning down two of his cottages. When Vaughan took Menlove to court for negligence, Menlove's lawyer tried to appeal that his client shouldn't be held liable due to his 'misfortune of not possessing the highest order of intelligence'. But the court ruled in Vaughan's favour. Menlove 'was bound to proceed with such reasonable caution as a prudent man would have exercised under such circumstances'.[36]

This decision cemented the position that common law judgments should rest not on the mental agility of the individuals involved, but on what an imaginary sensible third party would have done. The legal 'reasonable standard' was born.

The problem with human life is that it's just too complicated for a one-size-fits-all approach. Rigidly explicit guidelines can only take us so far. Just think back to the example of appropriate distancing from Chapter One. Even for those embedded within the same culture, the boundary between intimate and social distance isn't registered as a quantitative shift, with comfort ticking over into discomfort once a precise number of millimetres has been reached. Instead, comfort is experienced within a range of tolerance between X centimetres and Y centimetres.

It's the same with moral judgments. Wouldn't it be great if everything could be clearly divided into black and white chessboard squares, right and wrong sitting neat in their own little boxes? But in reality that's not generally how life works. Morality is more like a colour wheel. On one side you have black and on the other side you have white, but in between there's a whole mess of grey.

After all, lots of things were once rationalised that we now see as reprehensible. The Romans used to enjoy a half-time show of *damnatio ad bestias*, where naked criminals would be strapped to see-saws and slowly ripped apart by lions. In England, you could once go on a fun family day trip to watch convicts get hanged by the neck until nearly dead, then disembowelled and emasculated until very nearly dead, and finally chopped into quarters until definitively dead. What's commonplace changes over time, as values evolve, as well as varying massively between cultures, but these things also shift according to *circumstance*. In wartime, for example, doing a spot of murdering might get you a medal, while normal workplace etiquette tends to frown upon things like stabbing a co-worker for eating your yogurt. Absolutist principles about good and bad are largely incompatible with the full spectrum of human activity. That's why we need *wakimae*: mechanisms for discernment to help us draw that line over and over again within changing social milieus, by working out right from wrong *in context*. It's the same with the law.

As informal agreements gave way to written treaties, lawmakers began to draw on those classical understandings of reasonableness. 'It is an old tradition,' said the philosopher J. R. Lucas back in 1963. 'Plato, Aristotle and St. Paul all insisted on the inability of the letter of the law to exhaust the full content of its spirit, and Aristotle defines a key term of his moral philosophy by reference to what the reasonable man would decide.'[37] Meanwhile, French jurist and sociologist Henri Lévy-Bruhl explained that a 'legal text is rigid, or at least, has only a reduced elasticity. By definition, then, it is incapable of satisfying new needs in a society in constant movement.'[38]

In law as in life, the line between clearly right and obviously wrong can never be as clear-cut as it seems. And this is what the word 'reasonable' gives us: a way to separate black and white from all that grey. '[W]as a killing reasonably provoked? Would advertisements have misled a reasonable consumer? Was a contract offer accepted in a reasonable time? Was a criminal trial reasonably delayed?' Today the reasonableness principle appears within the law of the USA and UK, as well as Australia, Brazil, Canada, China, Egypt, Hong Kong, India, Russia, and Singapore.[39] It's even a fundamental principle of the International Court of Justice, which acknowledges that 'what is reasonable and equitable in any given case must depend on its circumstances'.[40]

In other words: the term 'reasonable' has become central to moral and legal judgment systems because it's a Goldilocks term, introducing that missing element of flexibility to separate too much and not enough from just right. It acknowledges that a fair judgment on any given case will always depend on the peculiarities of that case, and allows juries and judges to apply theoretically rigid rules to situations which, in practice, will actually have infinitely indeterminate variables.

Let's pause for a second to look at some examples. First, imagine you're a junior associate in a law firm. One day a senior colleague calls you into their office for a one-to-one meeting. While you're talking, they repeatedly lean forwards and touch you on the knee, in a way that they may intend as a friendly gesture of collegiality, but which makes you feel objectified and uncomfortable. Could this action reasonably be judged to cross an ethical boundary, or simply to constitute a harmless professional act of support? That's the reasonable standard in sexual harassment trials.

Next, imagine you're the owner of a small business. A customer is suing you because they slipped on ice in front of your store and broke their hip. Is it a reasonable expectation that you should have shovelled and salted the area around your door in order to make it safe for customers? Or, given the time of year, should the customer have understood that icy pavements are an expected winter hazard and have therefore walked more cautiously? That's tort law, which uses 'reasonable care' as the basis for assessing disputes over negligence.

Finally, imagine you're the leader of a country, and your more powerful neighbour is carrying out intensive fishing operations. While the 1958 Geneva Convention on the High Seas recognises the principle of freedom, it also 'posits that this freedom should be exercised "with reasonable regard to the interests of other States"'. Your neighbour insists that they've been acting with reasonable regard to you; meanwhile, you believe that their fishing methods are unreasonably harmful and depleting your stocks. That's where the International Court of Justice steps in, to assess whose version of reasonable is right.[41]

Now imagine you've been asked to draw a verdict on these three cases. How do you decide? In order to figure out a fair judgment in line with the nuances of each situation, lawmakers began to invoke philosophy's mythical creature: the 'reasonable person'. Today, this imaginary figure gets dragged into courtrooms and classrooms all over the world to help jurors and students understand the convoluted messiness of the law. The 'reasonable parent'. The 'reasonable landlord'. The 'reasonable employer'.

Called the Reasonable Person Test, this is meant to make the judgment process a lot simpler. Unlike St Peter at the golden gates of heaven, jurors aren't expected to assure themselves that the person behind the dock is a paragon of virtue, entirely without moral flaws or failings. All you need to do is to decide if this person could be judged to have acted *reasonably*, in that particular set of circumstances, according to the standards of an ordinary sensible onlooker. But who is this reasonable person, really?

In his original form, the reasonable man was absolutely that – a him. In *Vaughan v. Menlove*, the judge's ruling invoked an imaginary 'prudent man'. Two years before, in 1835, the Belgian astronomer Adolphe Quetelet coined the term *l'homme moyen*, the 'average' or 'common' man.[42] Long before Quetelet, though – throughout around a thousand years of jurisprudence, in fact, from roughly 449 BC to AD 529 – ancient Roman law used the figure of the *bonus paterfamilias*, the 'good family man', as the basis for judgments. In the nineteenth century, the popular imagination really picked this idea up and ran with it: the Americans had Joe Bloggs, the 'man on the street'; the English had 'the man on the Clapham Omnibus'; Australians the fella on the 'Bondi tram'.

As legal historian Mayo Moran notes, this figure was a curious creature: at once determinedly ordinary (the everyman who 'mows the lawn in his shirtsleeves and takes the magazines at home'), and simultaneously superhuman, endowed by his commentators with extraordinary abilities – the 'agility of an acrobat and the foresight of a Hebrew prophet'.[43] In the 1920s, *Punch* magazine began to publish a popular series of spoof British legal cases. The very first article was called 'Fardell v. Potts, or the case of the Reasonable Woman', in which a fictional judge rhapsodises about the imaginary figure of the Reasonable Man:

> He is at every turn, an ever-present help in time of trouble, and his apparitions mark the road to equity and right. There has never been a problem, however difficult, which His Majesty's judges have not in the end been able to resolve by asking themselves the simple question, 'Was this or was it not the conduct of a reasonable man?' and leaving that question to be answered by the jury.
>
> This noble creature stands in singular contrast to his kinsman the Economic Man, whose every action is prompted by the single spur of selfish advantage and directed to the single end of monetary gain. The Reasonable Man is always thinking of others; prudence is his guide, and 'Safety First', if I may borrow a contemporary catchword, is his rule of life.

> [. . .] He is one who invariably looks where he is going, and is careful to examine the immediate foreground before he executes a leap or bound; who neither star-gazes nor is lost in meditation when approaching trap-doors or the margin of a dock; [. . .] who never mounts a moving omnibus, and does not alight from any car while the train is in motion; who investigates exhaustively the *bona fides* of every mendicant before distributing alms, and will inform himself of the history and habits of a dog before administering a caress; who believes no gossip, nor repeats it, without firm basis for believing it to be true; who never drives his ball till those in front of him have definitely vacated the putting-green which is his own objective; who never from one year's end to another makes an excessive demand upon his wife, his neighbours, his servants, his ox, or his ass . . .[44]

. . . the list goes on and on and on. Thoughtful, sensible, unselfish, moderate: this man on the Clapham Omnibus became the imaginary benchmark for how an upright moral citizen should behave, as well as a neutral virtuous yardstick by which to judge other people. In the twenty-first century we invented a new version to help figure out the rules and keep us in line. His name is Bill.

Be Like Bill

'This is Bill', reads the caption, next to a rudimentary drawing of a stick figure wearing a woolly hat. 'Bill is on the internet. Bill sees something that offends him. Bill moves on. Bill is smart. Be like Bill.'

There is by now an extremely long list of things that Bill does not do. Bill does not Instagram his meals. Bill does not tag photos of his partner with the hashtag #RelationshipGoals, or tell everyone that he is vegan at every opportunity,* or send pictures of his penis to unsuspecting women. Bill does not boast about his workouts, take pouting selfies, or post 'It's snowing!' when it's snowing and 'It's Friday!' when it's Friday. Bill *never* plays Candy Crush. Bill is smart. Be like Bill.

Bill is a meme. He and his bobble hat started popping up on the web around October 2015, but it wasn't until the following January and the launch of a dedicated 'Be Like Bill' Facebook page that Bill reached full internet saturation. Bill's initial purpose was to lay out guidelines for good internet etiquette, leading by example and providing helpful tips on how not to be irritating online. The meme quickly spawned a raft of alternatives: including Bilal or Bashir in Arabic, Rashid in Malaysian, José in Spanish, Petya in Russian, Qodos in Pashto and Dari (two main languages in Afghanistan), and Juan in Tagalog. 'The idea is very simple,' said the Facebook page's creator. '"Bill" can be anyone who is smart and has common sense and doesn't do annoying things.'[45] With prudence as his guide, Bill is that rare internet creature: moderate and careful, considerate and unselfish, thinking before he acts and informing himself before he speaks. In other words: Bill is the quintessential millennial Reasonable Man.

It's small wonder that, as our world gets ever more fractured and extreme, we can be found reaching back for these old ideals. As historians have pointed out, it's at times of rapid

* The first rule of vegan club: never stop talking about vegan club.

sociopolitical change that we often see a surge of new guides to living virtuously. Whenever a community evolves, its members need to redraw the lines to decide what's acceptable and what's not. Like so many generations before us, we're trying to figure out what can and cannot reasonably be thought, done, and said within this new moral landscape. Bill is just the latest in a long line of imaginary characters that have been invoked to encourage people of a certain time and place to work towards what sociologists call the 'common good': eschewing selfish individualism, thinking before they act, and putting the needs of civic society before themselves. While the rational person – *Punch*'s 'Economic Man' – asks 'Will it benefit me?', the reasonable person asks 'Will it benefit *us*?'

This question goes right to the heart of the disconnection economy. Whether it's swapping your gas-guzzling SUV for a bicycle, or boycotting Amazon in favour of traipsing round the shops, or simply being more careful not to invade someone else's personal space on a plane: the return to reasonableness is again being sold as a panacea for a divided age, encouraging everyone to stop doing what's best for *them*, and instead to prioritise the common good. Which all sounds very nice and virtuous in theory. But here's the rub. For this to work, we are going to have to get a whole lot clearer about what the 'common good' actually means.

In 2020, as the global scale of the COVID-19 epidemic became clear, countries around the world had to redraw the terms of social engagement very quickly in response to evolving scientific advice. In December, as the festive season drew closer, the *New York Times* offered some helpful advice. What really matters 'is that people do as much as they reasonably can to prevent the spread of the disease, not that everyone adhere to the same set of rigid standards'.[46]

Without those rigid standards, though, people reacted in very different ways. Some people took off their clothes at the front door every time they returned home, blasted their mail in the microwave, and ritually disinfected each apple before putting it in the fridge. Others felt that simply washing hands and keeping two metres distance was probably sufficient. Wearing a mask was, for one person, a small price to pay for the sake of public health; for another, it was a suffocating violation of individual civil liberties. Inviting friends over for get-togethers, having a barbecue in the park, going home for Thanksgiving, holidaying in the Caribbean: depending on whom you asked, all these things were either a reasonably proportionate risk or a totally unreasonable act of personal irresponsibility. Rather than helping us all work towards a common goal, the word 'reasonable' began to be used over and over to legitimate the varying decisions of each individual.

My own COVID lockdowns were spent in England, which in January 2021 was announced as having the highest excess mortality rate of any major country.[47] This failure was widely attributed to the government's commitment to providing constantly changing and often contradictory guidelines. Go to work unless you can stay at home, in which case stay at home unless you can't work from home, in which case go to work. Don't go out unless completely necessary, but we'll pay you to go out to restaurants. The economy is the most important thing, except that economic health is directly tied to public health, so your health is the most important thing. Go for walks! Walk with other people! No socialising, though – only exercise! You'd better not be enjoying yourselves, or we'll call the police.

But a defining moment came when the chief advisor to the prime minister – Dominic Cummings, primary architect of Brexit and the man who actually devised the nation's lockdown protocols – broke his own rules on restriction of movement. At the time, the law stated that 'no person may leave the place where they are living without reasonable excuse'. For the rest of us, that was supposed to mean things like hospital visits or going to work or shopping for food, but the wiggle room in that word 'reasonable' – such a useful legal tool! – gave powerful people licence to stretch the rules past breaking point. While suffering COVID symptoms, and contrary to all advice thus far, Cummings and his family fled London and embarked on a four-hour drive to Durham so that his parents could help with childcare. Cummings was only unmasked when he made a family day trip out to a local beauty spot, Barnard Castle, on his wife's birthday. And here's the best bit. Cummings explained that he'd simply decided to take a drive in order to check . . . that his eyesight . . . was safe . . . to drive. 'I believe that in all circumstances I behaved reasonably,' he said in a press conference afterwards.[48] The prime minister defended him in exactly the same way. 'To me, he sounded like someone who was trying to do the best for his family. My conclusion is I think he acted reasonably, legally, with integrity and care for his family and others.'[49]

The nation vehemently disagreed. In the immediate aftermath, a popular UK chain of opticians noted a 6,000 per cent increase in online mentions of their slogan 'Should have gone to Specsavers'. But because of that reasonable clause, Cummings was able to get away with it. Because of that reasonable clause, Britain was later hit by scandal after scandal proving that government ministers had been partying away while everyone else locked down. We're all in this together, apart from the powerful, who aren't. In the longer term, this flagrant flouting of the law was credited by researchers at University College London as the moment the UK lost control of the virus entirely. Prior to this, compliance with restrictions had been very high, with 97 per cent following the strict guidelines. In the immediate aftermath of the Cummings scandal, though, compliance plummeted. 'During lockdown the message on compliance was clear: social restrictions were vital to stop the spread of the virus, so everyone had to play their part; no excuses, no exemptions,' researchers explained. 'But Cummings changed the tone: if you could find a loophole in the rules, it somehow became acceptable (and defensible) to break them.'[50] If you could reason it, it was probably reasonable to do it.

Most worryingly of all: the pandemic exposed how differently people imagined the 'common good' to work. For some, the only equitable response was to adopt a 'leave nobody behind' approach, which meant everyone locking down completely and taking every possible measure for as long as needed to protect those who were most at risk. For others, this was totally over the top: instead, a more utilitarian 'best for the most' approach was deemed fairer, meaning a two-tier system in which people with no known health issues (yet) should be free to go back to normal life, whilst everyone else should be forced to shield in the safety of their homes – possibly forever, if necessary, but without any support.

Around the world these moral debates raged. Is the greater risk to public health a failing economy and the mental distress of forced quarantine, or is this a reasonable price to pay for keeping vulnerable people safe? When it comes to the vaccination programme, should our priority be to uphold everyone's right to individual bodily autonomy, or are mandatory jabs and vaccine passports a reasonable infringement of civil liberties if the result is the protection of those who are most at risk? And *who should decide*?

Shoulda Woulda Oughta

Soon after its launch to fame from the bowels of the internet, the 'Be Like Bill' meme started being widely criticised for its condescending tone and moralistic shaming. You *should* do this. This is the way things *ought* to be. Placing a moratorium on unsolicited dick pics is a good thing, because cyberflashing is actually a sex crime – but why should I be shamed for playing Candy Crush when my enjoyment surely isn't hurting anyone else? Establishing prosocial expectations is clearly the right thing to do in theory, but where in practice should those lines be drawn?

This final question was at the core of the COVID-19 back-and-forth. At its best, those calling for stricter regulations were advocating a communal sacrifice for the common good: entire communities coming together and looking out for one another, everybody shielding everyone else, all of us in the same boat. But at the same time, the pandemic also shone a fresh light on old inequalities. Those able to spend all day in their own back gardens started tattling on people who had spent weeks locked indoors in tiny apartments for using their one hour of government-mandated exercise to sunbathe rather than jog; parents were fined for playing football with their kids; disabled people were yelled at for resting on a park bench in the middle of a walk. The virtuous desire to keep each other safe quickly soured into a puritanical urge to moralise and punish.

The question isn't whether we need rules at all. As Chapter One explained, society needs both formal laws and informal norms to function. I've never had to worry that my children might get smallpox because, in the 1850s, governments around the world made vaccinations compulsory, meaning the virus got all but wiped out overnight. In return, I would happily wear a mask forever if it means that even one clinically vulnerable person feels safe enough to leave the house: that, to me, seems a more than reasonable sacrifice. A libertarian I am not. No, the questions I'm obsessed with are these. When we're living in a world beset by radically divided interests, riven with incompatible moral visions of the common good, *who are the rules benefiting*? Whose standards get to be taken as reasonable, objective, and simply common sense? And whose standards are seen as subjective, irrational, and self-evidently wrong?

I for one have seen this question playing out hundreds of times in the past few years alone. The one where a middle-aged businessman scolds the young single mother who lives next door for letting her children play in their own backyard because they're disturbing his Zoom meetings. Or the one where communities of colour are confronted in their life-long neighbourhoods by white incomers demanding they be quieter or convinced they don't belong. Or the one where the

Australian vegetarian sues her neighbours to get them to stop barbecuing fish, and then nine thousand people sign up for a big community cookout.

When they're designed to protect and serve the most marginalised, rules can be a very good thing indeed. But also, under certain circumstances, there can be a powerful sense of entitlement involved in demanding that other people – with their own ideas about what's reasonable – have to play by *your* rules. In the wrong hands, that 'reasonable person' has become a weapon: an imagined judge, jury, and executioner, whose moral verdicts get wielded unquestioningly against anyone who fails to think and act exactly like them.

In order to understand this phenomenon, we first need to know what happens in our brains and our bodies when we make judgments about other people. Turns out, that legal reasonable standard may not be so objective after all.

3

Uncommon Sense

A couple of years ago I was on an early-morning train. An older gentleman got on and asked the young woman opposite to move out of the window seat he'd reserved. She obediently stood up to let him in. As the man slid into his place, he nodded to the open make-up bag in front of her and said: 'I hope you're not planning to do that here.' This was 8 a.m. and I'd already watched in awe as she'd done ten full minutes of contouring worthy of the finest TikTok artist. As she quietly put the bag back in her rucksack, her face half-finished and full of shame, I got out my own make-up, fixed him with a death stare, and without blinking began to violently draw on new crimson lips. Later on, after I'd given a public talk looking like Pennywise, I realised I probably should have used a mirror. Worth it, though.

This isn't an unusual story; nor is it just a British problem. In 2016, the Japanese rail company Tokyu Corp released a thirty-second etiquette video that begins 'Women in the city are all beautiful. But they are *mittomonai* [ugly to see] at times', and goes on to ask commuters to resist doing their face where people can see them.[1] The year before, the New York Transit Committee put up subway posters for their #CourtesyCounts campaign reading 'Clipping? Primping? Everybody wants to look their best, but it's a subway car, not a restroom', which prompted the strategic ire of cosmetics behemoth

COVERGIRL. Their #ProjectPDA (Public Displays of Application) campaign encouraged women to share photos of themselves applying make-up when out and about. 'We saw the sign and wondered, "What's wrong with applying your makeup in public?",' pondered a video promoting the campaign. 'And is this just an ad on the subway, or a sign of something bigger?'[2]

It's definitely bigger than just an ad. In a recent survey of UK commuters, more than half of women admitted to having done their make-up on public transport;[3] conversely, the BBC found that this is one of passengers' biggest pet peeves.[4] Answering the BBC's survey, one respondent (Michael, 59) was quoted as saying that the sight was so upsetting that he had needed to move carriages. 'I think once or twice I just stared at the person thinking that they would eventually notice and feel embarrassed,' he said. 'That never happened.' Meanwhile, in 2019 the British singer Lauren Byrne made headlines for her response to a man who spent ten minutes tutting and sighing at her train makeover. Eventually told to 'have some self respect love', Byrne reportedly retorted: 'oh I'm so sorry! I didn't realise this was a time travelling train?! [. . .] I'm assuming from your tone that we've travelled back to the 60s where men think it's appropriate to speak to women like shit and tell them what to do for no reason whatsoever???'[5]

Public beautifying is one of those activities about which people tend to have strong feelings one way or another, then. This is how studying discourse can help us to identify the fault lines within seemingly simple moral judgments. As each person argues their case, we can see a tightly choreographed pattern emerging: the 'yes-but, no-because, why-can't, only-if' dance. I call this 'The Reasonable Tango'.*

Yes, but it's unbecoming to see women use the thing they need to use to appear naturally beautiful. No, because it's unfair to expect women to get up an hour earlier than men to conform to the beauty standards that were forced on them in the first place. Why can't you keep it to the privacy of your own bathroom? Why should I have to lock myself in the bathroom to do something that's in no way disgusting? Oh, so I suppose I'm allowed to brush my teeth in public then. Ew, gross, that's undeniably unhygienic – surely we can all agree there's nothing unsanitary about a spot of mascara? Well, as a card-carrying adult human female myself, I'd never dream of applying cosmetics in public; whatever happened to good old-fashioned decorum? Being a stuck-up priss went out of fashion. Okay, but only if you don't use powder – don't want to cause a mushroom cloud hahaha! Okay, as long as it's only lipstick – anything else is just tacky. Stop doing it at all, it's selfish. Stop staring at me, it's rude. Entitled woman! Misogynist! And then from all sides, the inevitable war cry comes: 'IT'S JUST COMMON SENSE.'

But what happens when common sense looks totally different to the person next to us? What do we do when one person's reasonable is another person's rude? When is public censure working for the good of all of us, and when is it forcing only some of us to conform to unrealistic or obsolescent standards?

Here, a warning: in this chapter and those that follow, I begin to dig much more deeply into some of the ways the social

* To be sung to the tune of Tom Lehrer's 'Masochism Tango'.

contract has been used to disempower and wound specific communities. Topics range from the abominable segregation of disabled people caused by 'reasonable accommodations' in disability law, to the victim-blaming of women in cases of sexual and domestic violence, to the ways state brutality is legitimised by 'reasonable use of force': a legal construct which has overwhelmingly been wielded by police against communities of colour, especially Black citizens. To attempt to unravel the skeins of reasonableness without interrogating these intersecting harms would be unethical; to send my reader into this ugly morass without a content warning would be unconscionable.

A Bucket of Water and One Hundred Etiquette Guides

It's 2019, and I'm in the Wickham Theatre, my office building at the university where I work. I'm in the middle of giving a lecture – which because I work in a theatre department means kneeling on the matt-black floor of this black-box space, my head immersed in a bucket of water.

It's that time of year again. The time of year when we invite prospective undergraduates and their guardians to come and get a taste of what student life would be like if they studied theatre with us at Bristol. My lecture is called 'The Audience Contract'. What are the rules of this space? What's permissible and what's not? How do we know how to behave? From their raked seating, my own audience watches as I kneel on the floor, my face fully submerged in water. I've been in there for around twenty seconds so far. Tiny bubbles tickle my face before making a break for the surface. Somewhere off to my left I can hear my friend and colleague, the dance scholar Jess McCormack, moving around the stage. Jess is obediently performing the meaningless task I've given her: picking up crumpled pieces of paper from the floor, smoothing them out, and slowly adding them to a growing pile. Meanwhile, abandoned in my bucket, I feel my lungs beginning to complain. After what seems like an eternity I hear Jess walk up behind me. She places her palm gently on my shoulder. Streaming water, I lift my head up and gasp in a breath. Another. One more. Then I feel Jess's hand leave my shoulder, and I lower my face back into the bucket. We keep repeating this pattern for another five minutes or so.

I borrowed this exercise from a book called *Small Acts of Repair*, which describes the work of the North American company Goat Island.[6] Later in the lecture, I'll get my audience to make 'finger guns' with their hands and shoot me to death, over and over and over, as I throw myself backwards and fall down hard – on my hip, my elbows, my backside – dropping like a stone again and again, until it goes past the point of funny and out the other side, in a scene I've also borrowed (this time from the UK-based company Action Hero). 'What did those exercises make you feel?' I'll ask. 'What did it feel like when you saw my head in that bucket of water? When you "shot" me? When you saw the bruises start to bloom on my knees and my elbows as I fell down? How did it feel?'

'I thought it was funny at first,' somebody usually says, tentatively. 'But then I started to get worried. I knew you weren't in danger, but it felt like you might be putting yourself at risk for us. I mean, I know you were doing it because you'd decided to do it, but I still felt responsible. Like you were only doing it because we were watching. It made me feel uncomfortable.'

'Why didn't you stop me? Why didn't you walk out?'

'Because I couldn't.'

'What was holding you back?'

The answer to this last question is, of course, both nothing and everything. The imagined weight of performers' expectations. The expectations of the rest of the audience. The embarrassment of standing up and shouting out that keeps you frozen to your seat, or else having to do the awkward mid-row bum shuffle to the exit, theatre's humiliating walk of shame. Not wanting to ruin the experience for everyone else. Because that's not what you *do* in a theatre. You don't disturb the performance.

Because, in other words, of the social contract: in this case the version that I tend to call 'the audience contract', those highly specific and culturally determined behavioural norms that govern the live performance space. In the English-speaking world, at least, 'traditional' theatrical events tend to have pretty well-defined rules. Don't eat or drink. Sit down and shhh. No chatting. Do *not* sing along. Keep your elbows to yourselves. Clap at appropriate intervals. Turn! Off! Your! Mobile! Phones! When the famous Shakespearean scholar Glynne Wickham founded our department in the 1940s and made Bristol the first university in the country to offer a degree in drama, he probably didn't imagine future generations of academics using his theatre to dunk their heads in buckets of water. But he did share my belief that studying live performance can be a laboratory space for exploring much bigger social and political questions. Because this lecture I'm giving isn't really about theatre at all. It's about being together in public space, and how we figure out the rules, and why certain ways of behaving have come to be seen as unquestionably correct.

Like I said in the Introduction to this book, I started studying reasonableness when I had my first baby, Monty. At the same time as facing a sea of breastfeeding censure, I also found myself – a professional theatre-goer – suddenly excluded from the theatre. Can't take a crying baby into the auditorium; can't leave him at home without the ability to magically detach my breasts. It just so happened that, at this precise moment, the performance industry was finding itself under siege. Several times a week, it seemed, a new cultural commentator was going on record to complain about bad behaviour in theatres. One day, Benedict Cumberbatch was seen pleading with audiences at the stage door to stop filming him during performances; another day, somebody brought in a bucket of KFC to eat during the interval and faced the wrath of a newspaper columnist; the next, a drunk spectator was seen clambering up on to a Broadway stage to plug their phone into a fake socket on the set. Around these well-publicised disruptions there was also interwoven a cornucopia of smaller gripes: complaints about drinks being slurped, sweet wrappers rustled, people getting up multiple times to go to the loo, the unbearable whiff of cheese and onion crisps . . .

Sitting at home, an exile from my old professional life, I became fascinated by these online diatribes about spectators who needed to be retrained in better behaviour. So I collected together a hundred guides to theatre etiquette and ran them through a linguistics program. What I realised was that, rhetorically speaking, the majority of these guides were framed as an imperious list of dos and don'ts: by which I mean they used what discourse scholars call 'imperatives' ('do X', 'you must do Y') as well as the opposite, negative imperatives or 'prohibitives' ('don't do X', 'never do Y'). Coupled with repeated phrases like 'I think we can all agree that . . .', 'the blatantly obvious boundaries of behaviour . . .', and 'this should be common sense', it became clear that by using this kind of intensely normative language, their authors were intending to promote an extremely rigid separation between those behaviours that were *clearly* acceptable and those that were *self-evidently* bad.

But how obvious are these rules of behaviour actually? How common is common sense? As I read deeper and deeper into the language that was being used, I finally realised what had been bugging me. All these various guides were echoing something I was going through myself, as a sleep-deprived parent. After being completely terrified for weeks by all the conflicting baby advice, I came across a hilarious viral Reddit post (called 'I Read All the Baby Sleep Books') by Ava Neyer, a fellow mother who was similarly trying to make sense of the chaos. 'Naps should only be taken in the bed,' she writes, 'never in a swing, carseat, stroller, or when worn. Letting them sleep in the carseat or swing will damage their skulls. If your baby has trouble falling asleep in the bed, put them in a swing, carseat, stroller, or wear them. Put the baby in a nursery, bed in your room, in your bed. Co-sleeping is the best way to get sleep, except that it can kill your baby, so never ever do it.'[7]

If I were going to plug a whole bunch of theatre etiquette guides into a text generator, it might come up with something similar. Something, perhaps, like this:

I Read All the Theatre Etiquette Guides, by Kirsty Sedgman
Turn your mobile phone off completely and leave it in your bag/at home/on that remote island you own in the North Atlantic. Never leave your phone on vibrate as the relentless buzzing will annoy people, unless of course you need to leave it on vibrate and nobody can hear it, which is fine. As an adult you should be able to go a few hours without masticating some kind of foodstuff, so don't bring snacks or drinks into the auditorium except for a bottle of water, but that might make you need to pee inconveniently so forget the water. Also, they do sell snacks in the theatre so if you're hungry you can buy a bag of sweets, but don't open it until the interval, or else open it beforehand and unwrap each individual sweet so there's no rustling. Even if you're totally silent, the smell can be distracting, so don't eat anything at all – not even ice cream. Quiet snacks are okay – have you tried ice cream? Regarding dress codes, the days of strict formalwear are gone so you can now wear whatever you feel comfy in – even rock up in flip-flops or jeans if you want – except of course there's no place for flip-flops or jeans in the theatre because that would diminish the specialness of the experience for everyone else, so you should buy an outfit that cost at least as much as the price of your ticket. Please go smart casual (perhaps a little black dress or some chinos?), unless you don't want to, in which case don't, except you must. No man buns. No high ponytails. No big hair at all. And don't even think about getting up for a pee unless it's during the interval, in which case okay, unless the interval is short and the line is long, in which case stay put and hold it in. But of course the most important thing is to relax and have fun!

See? Simple! While everyone agreed audiences needed to be taught the difference between acceptable and unacceptable, *where they actually drew that line* varied hugely. Reading between the various guides was like experiencing a kind of mental whiplash: one where everybody was convinced that their own precise preferences were obviously correct, and everybody else was obviously wrong.

So I wrote an academic book called *The Reasonable Audience*,[8] which nerded out about the audience contract in the arts. Over fifty thousand words or so, I carefully examined the historical roots of silent reception, whom it excludes, and why so many audience members today are keen to preserve it. I went on to talk about this research around the world: first at conferences, then on radio and on television, then for outlets like the *New York Times* and the BBC. And what all this gave me was a splurge of angry responses. Why don't I care about those who pay good money for an experience, only to have it ruined by somebody else's self-absorbed disruptions? What I don't realise, silly girl, is that it's actually very simple: it's just about common courtesy and consideration for other people. I'm just a selfish millennial, I'm a bitch who doesn't deserve a job, I'm the reason Trump got elected.

This seemed to me to be a rather ironic set of responses, given that the idea of consideration was right at the heart of my argument. All I was trying to do with all this research was to point out gently how, sometimes, those moral cries to 'be considerate' of other people can lead to an immoral failure to consider other people. Is that woman eating sweets behind me selfish or diabetic? Is that person on their phone playing Angry Birds, or an anxious carer keeping an eye on messages? Has that man who keeps heading to the loo had a few too many pints, or does he have a chronic illness? 'Your piss can wait!' one etiquette article said – but of course sometimes piss *can't* wait. The problem, as I wrote at the time, is that we simply do not know what a stranger may be dealing with, or what the consequences of enforcing these strict behavioural regulations might be.

Along with all those angry messages, I also got a steady flow of messages from people telling me how they'd been shamed out of going to the theatre ever again. A woman with hypoglycaemia who used her phone to keep an eye on blood sugar levels and was asked to leave because of her occasional furtive peeks. A working-class family who talked about going on their first outing to the theatre ever and singing along joyfully to a jukebox musical and being rebuked for it. And don't even get me started on the dog-whistle racism in the fear of 'big hair' – someone told me about how his tiny seven-year-old niece was yelled at by the white man behind her because she was wearing her hair in an afro. Turns out that none of this is quite so simple after all.

Doing this research is how I came to learn more about the 'reasonable person' standard – that objective legal test for determining what it means to act reasonably. But what if that test isn't really as objective or neutral as it's supposed to be?

Who Gets to Judge?

On 12 March 1990, hundreds of demonstrators abandoned their wheelchairs and crutches at Washington DC's National Mall and began crawling up the marble steps. 'The Capitol Crawl, as the event came to be known, underscored the injustices of inaccessibility that the ADA [American Disability Act] was intended to fix.'[9] The ADA, which was signed into law a few months later in July 1990, was supposed to be a big political win, legally enshrining the principle that businesses and public services must make the 'reasonable accommodations' necessary for disabled people to gain full and equitable access to public life. This significant moment of progress came thanks to efforts by activist groups like ADAPT (American Disabled for Accessible Public Transport), whose earliest protests asked for public transport to be equipped with lifts for wheelchair users.

As we saw in Chapter Two, the vagueness of 'reasonableness' is its power. Take reasonable measures. Accept reasonable delays. Apply reasonable care. It's a necessary mechanism for working out a fair judgment according to the nuances of every situation. But its vagueness is also a problem. As Olivier Corten wrote of the International Court of Justice: 'if the use of "reasonable" suggests any form of agreement, it is an agreement on the lack of agreement. Each [party] maintains its own conception of what is reasonable, and will exercise its powers according to that conception.'[10]

When it comes to disability rights, over the three decades since the ADA was brought in, the flexibility encoded in that word 'reasonable' has been used by companies to put off making any kind of equitable adjustment at all. Rather than gaining full access to public life, disabled people have been presented with an endless series of supposedly reasonable compromises. Take the example of public transport. As recently as 2017, some twenty-seven years after the ADA came in, two massive class-action lawsuits were filed to order New York's transit system to install elevators in each subway station. The whole system should be made fully accessible within 'a reasonable period of time'.[11] But what does that mean? Months, years, or decades? Who gets to decide what counts as reasonable?

Definitely not Malaysia Goodson, the twenty-two-year-old woman who died in 2019 after falling down the stairs of a Manhattan subway station while carrying her one-year-old baby in a stroller.[12] Later that year, a Justice of the New York County Supreme Court took the Manhattan Transit Authority (MTA) to task for failing to reach a settlement sooner. '"No money? Find it. You find it for other things," he said to the MTA's three lawyers. "There has to be action, no more talk."'[13] Neither is it the disabled community who gets to decide what timescale counts as reasonable. People with mobility difficulties have shared a ceaseless string of stories about times when they have borne the unreasonable brunt of these delays. Wheelchair users, for instance, are frequently promised the compromise of a railway employee waiting at the terminus with a manual ramp. But when they get to the station, all too often nobody's there to assist. What would you do in that circumstance? Wait for rescue and resign yourself to travelling in the wrong direction for who knows how long? Shout to other passengers for help? Try to navigate the gap on your own, risking a dangerous fall?

These aren't hypothetical questions. Whether it's train stations or banks or supermarkets or schools or restaurants: disability law is littered with moments like these. Disabled people make reasonable requests for the accommodations they need to go about their lives, only to have those requests declined on the grounds that this would be unreasonably expensive or time-consuming. Couldn't you just do your shopping online/

ask someone to carry you/bump up and down the stairs on your backside instead?

This is the problem that disability scholar Jen Slater raises in their 2015 book *Youth and Disability*. Presenting 'A Challenge to Mr Reasonable', the book begins with a blistering letter addressed to our imaginary Reasonable Man:

> What you are not, Mr Reasonable, is the overtly nasty person that it's easy to be angry with. In fact, you could be that person that I occasionally find myself describing as 'alright really'. You are the creation of systems which prioritise certain ways of being over and above others. By functioning around pervasive, market-driven ideas of what is 'good', 'ideal' and 'normal', these global capitalist systems make your life appear as 'reasonable', whereas the lives of others around you are deemed 'unreasonable'. [I]n current political times, the cries to 'be reasonable – we have to draw the line somewhere!' – are heard more loudly, and more harmfully, than ever.[14]

From the 'Reasonable Careers Advisor' who shrugs 'this is just the way it is', to the 'Reasonable Manager' who tells disabled people to 'man up and grow some balls', Slater's work is brilliant at describing how, from the perspective of typically 'normate' arbiters (i.e. those in possession of a body and a mind which society has labelled 'normal'), a seemingly reasonable solution is all too frequently experienced by disabled people as completely, unfairly *un*reasonable.

As someone who's been living with what's called an 'invisible' disability since I was a teenager, and who picked up a brand-new mobility condition during the course of writing this book,

I have some familiarity with Mr Reasonable. Over the years, though – thanks to various medical interventions and a great support system – I've managed to wrestle the more debilitating effects almost completely under control and hidden from view. This means that I've only experienced a pale shadow of the discrimination Slater describes. If the workplace won't change to accommodate me, I have had to figure out how to accommodate capitalism's unreasonable demands on my time and my body – by twisting any so-called weakness into a metaphorical pretzel and shoving it down deep inside, in a way that is fragile, untenable, liable to snap at any moment, but holding steady for now.

I opened this book with a story about breastfeeding because that was a light-bulb moment. There, sitting in my living room with only a tiny uncontrollable infant and thousands of angry commentators for company, too afraid to go out in case I accidentally breached the boundaries of human decency – this was the first time I'd felt the suffocating weight of a public judgment that all my coping strategies couldn't help me avoid. That was when I started really thinking clearly about what it means to act reasonably, and how easy it can be to be judged unreasonable, and how common sense can be uncommon in ways we don't always see.

Because while each breastfeeding commentator offered a seemingly simple solution to my problem, in practice their suggestions presented impossible challenges. Oh, you managed to use a feeding blanket? Good for you – I need to keep my eyes fixed on my kid's mouth at all times or else it's excruciating. You don't see why it's so difficult to feed on the toilet? You try perching completely still for half an hour on a slippery surface, propping up a heavy baby without an armrest. Come to think of it, you try eating your dinner amid the smell of pee. Why can't I just pump at home then take the bottle with me? Because without the ability to feed on the go I'd have to lug around two painfully swollen leaking beach balls strapped to my chest, disrupting my natural milk production in the process. Well, then, in that case, maybe you should just stay home? The World Health Organization advises breastfeeding for two years. In 2019 the global fertility rate was 2.4 children per woman.[15] Are you really suggesting that the only reasonable solution is to lock us inside for half a decade?

And more importantly: if you don't have access to my lived reality, then how can you reasonably judge whether the decisions I'm making are wrong?

Following this line of reasoning, I came to a revelation. What if the problem wasn't me? What if the problem was all those other people – people I'd never even met – who felt like they had the right to tell me what I should be doing with *my* body and *my* baby? Those who felt that they and they alone could confidently advise on what an acceptable level of discretion looks like, without any understanding of my personal circumstances – or, in many cases, without the experience of actually owning a pair of breasts. It's easy to say 'Just grow a thicker skin, then! Stop caring what people think!' – but actually, there's a serious systemic problem that this kind of individualistic rebel-girl mantra cannot fix. A recent UNICEF report found that in high-income countries people are much less likely to breastfeed than in other parts of the world. In places like Madagascar, Nepal, and Sri Lanka, only 1 per cent of babies have never been breastfed. Meanwhile, in European nations like the UK, Spain, and Germany, around one in five babies have never been breastfed. In the USA that number is less than one in four, in France it's around one in three, and in Ireland nearly *half* of all babies have never been breastfed, *ever*.[16] This may be quite literally a 'first-world problem', but within these rich countries it's actually those who earn the least who are the least likely to ever try breastfeeding, with younger and working-class mothers especially affected.

While it is absolutely true that fed is best, and while this phenomenon is the result of a combination of factors, it's also important to acknowledge the problem which many studies have identified:[17] namely, that a big contributing factor is the powerful disincentive of knowing that going out in public means bearing the weight of judgmental eyes.* After all this research, while on maternity leave the second time, I came to think that perhaps the more important line of questioning

* In the anglophone context it's commonly believed that we owe this queasiness to the Victorians, and their determined separation of the private and public spheres. But this division actually has roots in much older traditions: like Aristotle's reflection on the ideal split of Greek society into the home (*oikos*) and the city (*polis*). Throughout the centuries the demand placed on women has been to artificially enhance their bodies in private to appear naturally beautiful, whilst pretending in public that they just woke up like this. See, for example, the *Trotula*, a twelfth-century precursor to the women's-health magazine, which advised that 'noblewomen should wear musk in their hair, or clove, or both, but take care that it not be seen by anyone'. In a world that's been determined to make women despise, disguise, and hide their natural bodies, it's small wonder that some people still see feeding a child or applying a slick of mascara as a scandalous private act. (Reproduced by Monica H. Green, ed. and transl., *The Trotula: A Medieval Compendium of Women's Medicine* [University of Pennsylvania Press, 2001], p. 171.)

is this: What gives *you* the right to suggest that my pain, my inconvenience, and my child's health are a reasonable price to pay for daring to take up my right to lactate in public, in peace, undisturbed by the censure of your scornful gaze? Given that it's actually illegal to treat someone unfavourably for breast-feeding, why do you think that simply averting your eyeballs is an unreasonable thing for you to do?

These questions took me beyond the specifics of parenting. As we've already begun to see, shame and judgment are issues that go way past breasts – to bodies in general, and whose bodies are seen as unruly, and whose bodies are therefore systematically excluded from certain aspects of public life. This is about everyone for whom the simple act of existing in public sees them branded a problem. In my work studying audiences, I came across the work of a wonderful performer called Jess Thom, the self-styled 'Touretteshero' activist, whose verbal and physical tics include hitting her chest and repeating particular phrases (commonly the word 'biscuit'). In her hilarious *Backstage in Biscuit Land* show, Thom talks movingly about how, a few years before, she'd booked to see a show by another comedian, having written to them first to explain her condition and received assurances that she'd be welcome. But during the interval, the venue asked her to move to the sound booth. Apparently her tics had been too disruptive. Audience members had complained. Sitting there at the Machynlleth Comedy Festival, my tiny baby sleeping on my lap, watching the 'relaxed' performance of *Biscuit Land* and feeling – for the first time in months! – like a valued and welcome member of society, I could see with excruciating clarity how that supposedly reasonable accommodation had caused

Thom unreasonable pain. 'Once in the booth I was hit by a wave of humiliation and sadness,' Thom wrote afterwards. 'I started to cry. Part of me wanted to leave and never go to the theatre again.'[18] Instead, she became a performer herself, joking in *Biscuit Land* that she'd been given no other choice. The only place she'd ever be allowed to sit in peace in a theatre was on the stage.

Just like Jen Slater told us, all too often the power to make decisions about whether, when, and in what ways disabled people should be accommodated lies with the normate: those who have never actually needed those accommodations, and who maybe can't really imagine how terrible it feels to be kept out of the flow of everyday life. When it came to breastfeeding, I'm ashamed to say that I used to be one of the 'I don't see why' people. Well, if it were me, I'd simply wear a feeding blanket. I'll just pump and bottle-feed. Why is that so hard? But once I was living the painful, wonderful, awful, nipple-cracking reality, I realised how obviously unreasonable all my naive assumptions had been.

When I started peeling back the layers it became clear how deep the rot within reasonableness runs. Think about all the everyday ways we use the word 'reasonable', in the most banal of scenarios. So-and-so's work was of reasonable quality. Our food arrived within a reasonable timeframe. That item was reasonably priced. Just like the way we figure out proxemic distances from Chapter One, and just like the law in Chapter Two, our mechanisms for making these judgments are imperfect. In my own research, for example, I've found that word coming up again and again in relation to the cost of buying tickets. 'Theatres are usually too expensive,' one person says, 'but this event is very reasonably priced.' Meanwhile, the next person tells me that, as someone on a fixed income, the tickets cost too much. In law as in life, *how* we judge depends on *who* we are. This becomes especially problematic when it comes to judging other people.

There's No Such Thing as a Reasonable Woman

In recent years, critical disability scholars – in tandem with those working in areas such as gender, class, queerness, and race – have collectively begun to push back against the tyranny of Mr Reasonable: that man on the Clapham Omnibus, prudent and logical, designed to be 'an accurate reflection of societal norms', as feminist scholar and law professor Nancy Ehrenreich put it back in 1990. In theory the reasonable standard was meant to be 'the prototypical expression of the law's fairness and objectivity', Ehrenreich's *Yale Law Review* article states, allowing judgments to be made via the gods'-eye perspective of an imaginary neutral individual bereft of race, religion, class, gender, or any other 'non-universal' attributes. In practice, though, with 'judicial definitions of reasonableness often reflect[ing] the values and assumptions of a narrow elite', those supposedly objective judgments are actually steeped in deeply subjective assumptions.*[19]

* This position sounds pretty radical, but it isn't a new idea at all. Remember that *Punch* article from the previous chapter, with its satirical description of the Reasonable Man? The defendant in their fictional case was actually a woman, who'd been out for a lovely day punting on the rivers of Oxford and had accidentally knocked her boat into somebody else. How could she be judged against the usual standard, *Punch*'s imaginary judge mused, when there is no such legal entity as a Reasonable Woman?

Take the example of domestic violence. Jody David Armour, professor of law at the University of Southern California, explains how jurors' 'wrongheaded beliefs' are legally understood to meet the reasonable standard of objective judgment even if these are actually steeped in harmful misunderstandings: like the persistent idea that women who remain in violent relationships 'masochistically enjoy being beaten, deserve to be beaten, or at least assume the risk of beatings', for instance. Meanwhile, the 'accurate and rational beliefs' of the person who has actually experienced domestic violence can only be considered under a subjective standard of judgment.[20]

When it comes to crimes that predominantly affect women, time and time again that objective and neutral Reasonable Man has proven himself incapable of making judgments without falling back on society's most pervasive misassumptions. This is especially evident in cases of sexual assault, a crime which has been experienced by around one in five women and as high as one in twenty men.[21] These statistics get worse again when we add in variables like class, ethnicity, education, economic security, occupation, and location. For example, the World Health Organization states that women living in the poorest places are most at risk, with some countries seeing an approximate one in two women being sexually assaulted in their lifetime:[22] a statistic which seems to be roughly matched by the level of sexual violence experienced by trans and nonbinary people in richer nations.[23] Thanks to law reforms in jurisdictions throughout much of the world, rape reports have been increasing exponentially over the past few decades. However, rape *convictions* have remained relatively static – a discrepancy which has been called the 'justice gap'. Why?

To find the root of that answer, we need to go back in time: to eleventh-century Italy and a Benedictine monk called Peter Damian. In a 1064 letter, Peter sent his fellow clergyman a long list of all the things that he believed women – specifically priests' wives – were like. Ladies: tag yourselves!

- appetizers of the devil
- venom of minds
- poison of drinkers
- toxin of banqueters
- screech-owls
- sword of souls
- hoopoes [a type of bird that's categorised in the Christian Bible as Unclean and Detested]:
- wolves, leeches
- whores, prostitutes, lovers
- mad vipers, who because of impatience of the burning lust of your loves mutilate Christ
- wallows of greasy pigs
- matter of sin
- occasion of ruin
- harem of the ancient enemy
- dens of unclean spirits
- nymphs, sirens, witches, Dianas
- impious tigers, whose bloodstained mouths cannot refrain from human blood
- harpies, who fly around and seize the Lord's sacrifices
- lionesses who like monsters make careless men perish
- sirens and Charybdis, who while you bring forth the sweet song of deception, contrive of the ravenous sea an inescapable shipwreck[24]

Why were women seen as such a threat? The popular history blog 'Going Medieval' explains that in medieval Europe they believed bodies were made up of four 'humours' – blood, black bile, yellow bile, and phlegm – which needed to be balanced in order for a person to be healthy. Men were thought to be naturally hot and dry, while women were seen as cold, wet, clammy creatures. This is relevant, I promise. You see, those hot natures gave men an innate ability to burn any excess or badly balanced humours away, which made them better at warding off illnesses. Just like men, women's humours could become unbalanced – but unlike men, all that cold wetness made women incapable of burning off the bad stuff themselves.[25]

The answer? Sex. More specifically: for women to pursue the poor hapless male of the species in horny droves. While intercourse was believed to drain men of their vital force and produce such deleterious side effects as weakness (sure), trembling (yes), ringing in the ears (only if you're doing it right), and protruding eyeballs (wait what?), women supposedly gained health-giving energies from leeching the masculine essence out of their superior bodies. For as we all know, the more that women 'have sexual intercourse, the stronger they become, because they are made hot from the motion the man makes during coitus. Further, male sperm is hot because it is of the same nature as air and when it is received by the woman it warms her entire body, so women are strengthened by this heat. On the other hand, men who have sex frequently are weakened by this act because they become exceedingly dried out.'[26] That's science, baby. Actually, it's from a book called *De Secretis Mulierum* (*The Secrets of Women*), often credited to a thirteenth-century theologian called Albertus Magnus.

Whether it's innocent sailors being lured under the water by irresistible sirens in Homer's *Odyssey*; warnings of devious incubi given in the *Fang Nei Chi* (*Records of the Bedchamber*) from China's Sui Dynasty, around AD 600; the Roman satirist Juvenal worrying that the lustful dancing of high-born women would 'warm the age-chilled balls' of elderly men;[27] or the Christian mother of all humankind, Eve herself: the fear of the female temptress has ancient roots. Behind every badly behaving man, the story goes, you'll find the corrupting force of a woman, polluting his rational mind with carnal lusts.

What has all this got to do with contemporary cases of sexual assault? Well, legal judgments are supposed to be made solely via 'data-driven' processing, which means arriving at verdicts through objective assessment of evidence alone. But remember, just like life itself, the law is never as tidy as we'd like it to be. The law was built by human beings and is applied by human beings to human beings, whose interactions can't easily be separated along neat moral lines.* That messy necessity of working out who did what to whom within the specific context of how and where and why means that, in practice, decisions tend to be made via what's called 'schematic' processing.

As the authors of *Sexual Assault and the Justice Gap* explain, this means analysing evidence by 'referring to a series of abstract ideas and expectations or "schemata"' – widespread normative assumptions about how we *think* the world works.[28] In cases

* Algorithmic decision-making software is currently being sold to courtrooms as the answer to this conundrum – the idea being that taking the human out of the decision-making process also removes the bias. But who programmes these machines? Human beings. See Hannah Fry's book *Hello World* (Black Swan, 2019) for a robust analysis of the potentials and problems of using algorithms within the justice system and beyond.

of sexual violence, these schemata have been handed down to us by the past few millennia of knotted-up patriarchal repression, that persistent drip-drip-drip of misogynistic ideas about predatory female temptresses who need to be held responsible for their actions, and hapless male perpetrators with promising futures who can never be held responsible for theirs.

In police stations and courtrooms all around the world, we can see the ghosts of those ancient wrongheaded beliefs erupting from the woodwork every single day. But what were you wearing? Couldn't you have reacted differently? Why were you alone (I was walking home from work); why were you there (it was a brightly lit street on the way to my house); why were you out in the dark (it's winter, dusk is 4 p.m.); doesn't the female body have ways of keeping unwanted advances at bay (no); didn't part of you want it (no); did you actually *say*— (I SAID NO).

This is why study after study shows that victims who are seen to subvert the gendered expectations of modest femininity are more likely to be blamed than those who conform. Drinking alone in pubs; wearing short skirts rather than long dresses; being viewed by the court as unattractive; even fighting back physically with fists and knees and teeth, rather than simply shouting demurely for help: those are just a few of the factors that researchers have found frequently lead to shorter sentences for the perpetrator, or even to their being let off the hook entirely.[29]

Clearly, then, it is not just the evidence that matters, but how we make sense of the evidence. The UK's 2003 Sexual Offences Act holds that, in order to return a guilty verdict, the prosecution needs to prove that the suspect 'did not have a reasonable belief that the complainant was consenting'.[30] On a societal level, when it comes to consent, our sense-making abilities are fundamentally shaped by those ancient schemata – those woman-hating, perpetrator-empathising, victim-blaming frameworks of belief. As with many other crimes, the burden of proof lies with the victim to demonstrate the perpetrator's guilt 'beyond a reasonable doubt'. But when you live in a society which has had centuries of practice at giving white men the benefit of the doubt while viewing women with rank suspicion, that burden becomes just too heavy to bear.*

Let's Talk About Doubt

In a fascinating book on the theological roots of reasonable doubt, James Q. Whitman explains how originally 'this familiar rule was not intended to perform the function we ask it to perform today: It was not primarily intended to protect the accused. Instead, it had a significantly different purpose. Strange as it may sound, the reasonable doubt formula was originally concerned with protecting the souls of *the jurors* against damnation.'[31]

As any Horrible Histories reader knows, it's a common contemporary assumption that the past was full of casual bloodshed, with people going round carelessly hacking

* I say white men very deliberately here, because that schemata has worked exceedingly differently when it comes to the simultaneously gendered and racialised interrelations of Black men and white women. At the time of writing, Carolyn Bryant – the white woman who in 1955 falsely accused Emmett Till, a fourteen-year-old Black boy, of whistling at her, then stayed quiet as he was horrifically murdered because of her lies – is still alive, has confessed to lying, yet has never been brought to justice.

bits off each other. Actually, historical evidence of the pre-modern period paints a picture of a people wracked with anxiety. Whitman describes Europe from around AD 1000 as 'an age of fear and trembling',[32] in which the populace were growing very worried about the massive power trip involved in judging other people. Historically, the procedural last resort for judging innocence or guilt had been trial by ordeal – letting God decide. Defendants were forced to carry searing hot branding irons; if their wounds began healing within three days this meant they were innocent. Or in other instances, the defendant was plunged into cold water and if they sank they were telling the truth. In England, by the time the Church outlawed those water and fire ordeals in 1215, the judicial system was already slowly being transformed into trial by jury, those twelve good men and true. And so that ultimate responsibility was ultimately transferred: from the voice of God to the *vox populi*, the voice of the people.

By and large, though, the people who were called to act as jurors were desperately keen to avoid doing so. Not for the same reasons as today, where it's a bit of a nuisance and maybe you have to arrange emergency childcare or risk losing your job if the trial goes on too long. No, they had even bigger things to worry about. Their souls, for example, and the possibility of being damned to hell for all eternity. Especially in the case of 'blood punishments', where a guilty verdict meant mutilation or even execution, accidentally convicting an innocent person posed a perilous danger to the immortal self. Remember St Matthew's famous warning from the Christian Bible: 'Judge not lest ye be judged'? He didn't mean this rhetorically.

Similar fears abounded in many premodern societies around this time: such as medieval Islamic societies, where judges who falsely convicted an innocent person were made to suffer the exact punishment they had inflicted.[33] Or when Buddhism taught that it 'is easy to see the faults of others, but it is difficult to perceive our own faults. A man winnows his neighbor's faults like chaff, but hides his own, as a dishonest gambler conceals a losing dice.'[34] Or in Hinduism, where the Garuda Purana proclaims that the 'vile are ever prone to detect the faults of others, though they be as small as mustard seeds, and persistently shut their eyes against their own, though they be as large as Vilva fruit'.[35] Passing judgment against another was not a thing to be taken lightly.

Whitman argues that the reasonable doubt rule was developed in response to these immortal concerns: particularly the 'disquieting possibility' that a wrongful conviction might lead to damnation. 'It was originally a theological doctrine, intended to reassure jurors that they could convict the defendant without risking their own salvation, so long as their doubts about guilt were not "reasonable".'[36] But how can we be sure that our doubts are unreasonable? Isn't the point of doubting that it means we're not certain at all?

When I was in high school I did work experience for a couple of weeks at a local newspaper, who sent me to the county court to report on any interesting cases. My big break as an investigative journalist! Pulitzer here I come! Sadly this was in a sleepy market town where nothing ever happens, so I suspect it was more a ploy to get me out of their hair than hope of a major scoop. Nevertheless, I spent the fortnight walking diligently from their tiny offices to the courtroom and sitting in the gallery with my little notebook for a few hours, before trotting back again in time to be picked up by my mum.

Twenty years later, I remember precisely nothing about the cases themselves. I think most of them were pretty low-drama. But I do vividly remember one day, in a case where the stakes must have been higher, that there was this feeling just before the verdict – that moment replicated endlessly in procedural courtroom dramas, where a hush falls, and everyone waits breathlessly, the tension thickening in the room like custard. But there's a paradox here. Shouldn't this precise sensation of suspense make us question the idea of reasonable doubt itself? Richard Dawkins argues in *Science in the Soul* that we 'cannot have it both ways. Either the verdict is beyond reasonable doubt, in which case there should be no suspense while the jury is out; or there is real, nail-biting suspense, in which case you cannot claim that the facts have been proven "beyond reasonable doubt".' Dawkins suggests that a better system might instead deliver the verdict like it's a weather forecast: 'Seventy-five per cent probability of guilt, m'lud.' But the 'system insists on certainty,' Dawkins says regretfully: 'yes or no, guilty or not guilty'.[37] This is especially horrifying given that the death sentence is still a reality in twenty-seven out of fifty US states. When you remember that sometimes the judge will send divided juries back until they come up with a unanimous decision, in what world can their eventual verdict truly be said to be beyond a reasonable doubt?

Were I embroiled in a crime, I'd personally want to believe that I could trust a jury of my peers to make an accurate judgment. Unfortunately, studies suggest that jury decisions only have a probability of being accurate anywhere between 75 per cent and 90 per cent of the time.* So those twelve good men and true are perhaps less truly good at making legal judgments than we might hope. What about judges? After all, they're appointed on the basis of being experts in the law, so you'd probably expect that judicial verdicts would be considerably fairer.

Unfortunately, study after study has demonstrated the shocking variation between the verdicts of different judges. One of the earliest was carried out in 1959 by the Pilot Institute of Sentencing in Boulder, Colorado, and looked at disparities in the length of recommended sentences. As one judge at the time remarked, the most startling finding 'was a chart showing the disparity of sentences in income tax cases over a period of 12 years. In one district all of the defendants who were convicted or pleaded guilty were sent to prison; in several districts not one offender was sent to prison. The percentage of those sent to prison in other districts varied

* The most famous study on jury accuracy took place in the 1960s, when University of Chicago law professors Harry Kalven Jr. and Hans Zeisel asked presiding judges in over 3,500 trials across forty-seven states to note down their own verdicts just before the jury was due to rule. Within criminal cases, they found that the judge and the jury agreed approximately 80 per cent of the time – meaning they disagreed on one in every five cases. Surely the agreement rate has got better since their study was published in 1966? Nope – in 2003, the US National Center for State Courts ran a similar study and only found agreement in 77 per cent of criminal cases. 'Those agreement rates,' Bruce D. Spencer explains, 'are quite modest compared to what one would get by chance.' ('Estimating the Accuracy of Jury Verdicts', *Journal of Empirical Legal Studies* 4:2 (2007): pp. 305–329, p. 310.)

widely, from under 5 percent to over 90 percent.'[38] This finding has been echoed by countless scholars since in courtroom proceedings around the world. In another landmark study, the Federal Judicial Center used a 'simulated sentencing' method, asking Second Circuit judges to make sentence recommendations on the exact same hypothetical cases. They found disagreement in *sixteen of the twenty cases* submitted to all the judges.[39] Here are just a few factors that have been found to lead to a disparity:

Judging on a curve. When judicial caseloads are full of 'lower gravity' cases, like shoplifting and other petty crimes, judges are likely to adjudicate more severely and recommend longer sentences. When their caseloads contain a larger proportion of higher gravity cases, they tend to sentence more leniently overall.[40]

Ideology. An 'attitudinal model' is now widely being used to demonstrate what has long been suspected: that the courtroom is not an apolitical space. There is in fact a measurable rift between the decision-making processes of liberal vs conservative judges. 'Simply put,' scholars of the US Supreme Court summarised in 2002, 'Rehnquist votes the way he does because he is extremely conservative; Marshall voted the way he did because he was extremely liberal.'[41] While this correlation has been identified throughout the judiciary, a recent study found that the influence of ideology gets strongest at its very highest levels, showing up particularly within the Supreme Court and the court of appeals.[42]

Partisan solidarity. Just like the rest of us, judges are subject to 'group polarisation', which is when like-minded people push each other further and further to a shared extreme. For example, when sitting on three-judge panels with one Democrat and one Republican, judges considering disability discrimination cases were found to side with the plaintiff an average 45 per cent of the time for Democrat nominees and 29 per cent of the time for Republican nominees. For Republican judges, that 29 per cent dropped to 17 per cent when they were sitting with two fellow Republican appointees, and jumped to 38 per cent when they were totally outnumbered by Democrats. For the Democrats, that 45 per cent rose to 50 per cent with two other Democrats, and then dropped to 35 per cent when outnumbered.[43]

What they ate for breakfast. I'm not kidding. An Israeli research project examined thousands of parole decisions against the time of day they were made, in relation to the two daily food breaks Israeli judges are given. They found that the percentage of favourable rulings dropped from around 65 per cent to nearly zero within each session, then returned abruptly to 65 per cent after a break. Researchers concluded that 'judicial rulings can be swayed by extraneous variables that should have no bearing on legal decisions'.[44]

Back in 1881, in a famous paragraph, Supreme Court Justice Oliver Wendell Holmes Jr. wrote: 'The life of the law has not been logic, it has been experience. The felt necessities of the time, the prevalent moral and political theories, intuitions of public policy, avowed or unconscious, even the prejudices which judges share with their fellow-men, have had a good deal more to do than the syllogism in determining the rules by which men should be governed.'[45]

Rather more poetically, in a BBC radio lecture a hundred years later, the Scottish judge Lord John McCluskey said: 'The law, as laid down in a code, or in a statute or in a thousand eloquently reasoned opinions, is no more capable of providing all the answers than a piano is capable of providing music. The piano needs the pianist, and any two pianists, even with the same score, may produce very different music.'[46]

When we make judgments about other people, then, those judgments will be totally different depending on who we are. But even more problematically still, how we judge also depends on who *they* are – the ones who are being judged.

This Is Your Brain on Bias

In cases of police violence, the question of culpability is decided according to whether a reasonable person would have felt threatened in the same way as the defendant. That's the infamous Get [Cops] Out of Jail Free card: the 'reasonable use of force'.

In the United States, until 1985 the law allowed officers to use any force necessary to execute a felony arrest. The Supreme Court (*Tennessee v. Garner*) then ruled that deadly force may not be used unless 'it is necessary to prevent the escape and the officer has probable cause to believe that the suspect poses a significant threat of death or serious physical injury to the officer or others'.[47]

Four years later, in 1989, the Supreme Court (*Graham v. Connor*) introduced the standard of 'objective reasonableness', to help account for the on-the-spot calculations that police officers often have to make. Is the subject resisting arrest or possibly armed, and if so could my life be in danger? Are they attempting to flee, and if so would others' lives be endangered? All this information may need to be processed in a fraction of a second in order for officers to decide what constitutes a necessary amount of force in any given situation. The objective standard was meant to be a way to help juries figure out whether a reasonable person, confronted with that exact scenario, would have made the same decision in the moment.

In order to understand why this is such a problem, we need to turn again to underlying schemata. In this case, it's because centuries of white supremacy have congealed into enduring beliefs about the link between skin colour and threat. The eminent sociology professor Patricia Hill Collins has spent her career explaining in painstaking detail how the discrimination against African American people has been rooted in racist stereotypes spread through the vast international system of colonialism and enslavement:

> Because Black men did hard manual labor, justifying the harsh conditions forced upon them required objectifying their bodies as big, strong, and stupid. White elites apparently found men of African descent to be more threatening than women because they believed that Black men were naturally violent. [. . .] This combination of violence and sexuality made Black men inherently unsuitable for work until they were trained by White men and placed under their discipline and control. To explain these relations, White elites created the controlling

> image of the buck [. . .], a human animal that had achieved partial domestication through slavery. [. . .] Taming the beast in order to produce the buck involved domesticating Black men's predilection for violence, placing their brute strength in service to productive manual labor, and directing their natural albeit deviant sexuality toward appropriate female partners. In this fashion, White elites reduced Black men to their bodies, and identified their muscles and their penises as their most important sites.[48]

This global smear campaign spread like wildfire, searing into the western consciousness a bigoted and biologically essentialist false distinction between 'civilised' white invaders and the people they wanted to dominate. As Collins points out, these 'controlling images' were gendered: while Black women were forced into narrow stereotypes like 'mammies' or 'jezebels',[49] Black men were specifically portrayed as a threat to the (equally powerful and powerfully racist) counter image of the vulnerable white woman. This potent schema of Black masculine danger vs white feminine purity was then used as validation for the horrors of enslavement, and continues to underpin the ongoing oppression of Black people today.

In 2017, research published by the American Psychological Association conducted a series of seven experiments involving around a thousand participants from across the United States.[50] Participants were shown a series of colour photographs of men's faces. Some of these photos were of Black men, others white, but all the individuals in the photos were of the same height and weight. The study's participants were then asked to estimate the 'height, weight, strength, and overall muscularity' of these men in real life. 'We found that these estimates were consistently biased. Participants judged the black men to be larger, stronger and more muscular than the white men, even though they were actually the same size,' the lead author explained. They also found 'that men with darker skin and more stereotypically black facial features tended to be most likely to elicit biased size perceptions', with this size bias operating even when the participant was Black themselves. Finally, white participants tended to believe 'that the black men were more capable of causing harm in a hypothetical altercation and, troublingly, that police would be more justified in using force to subdue them, even if the men were unarmed.'[51]

No wonder a recent survey found that a Black man serving time for sexual assault is nearly *four times more likely to be innocent* than a white sexual assault convict, or that Black people are five times more likely to end up in prison than white people for the same offence.[52] Black people are also much more likely on average to be stopped and searched by police officers,[53] to be denied bail and given longer prison sentences by judges,[54] as well as to be put on death row and executed once there.[55] Meanwhile, perpetrators who are accused of murdering or otherwise harming Black people tend to be convicted at starkly lower rates than those whose victims are white.[56] Researchers even found that Black boys as young as ten are regularly 'adultified' by the criminal justice system: i.e. they are likely to be perceived to be older than their white peers, lacking in childhood innocence, and therefore ready to be held responsible if they commit a crime.[57]

This persistent schema of Blackness as threatening continues to have hugely violent consequences because of how it shapes police officers' and juries' perceptions of danger. Throughout much of Europe, people who have been racialised as white experience much lower levels of police attention than communities of colour despite generally lower crime rates among these groups.[58] While no western country is innocent, this disparity is particularly starkly evident across North America. The *Washington Post*'s database of police shootings shows that these have remained relatively constant since 2015, at around one thousand people per year (1,055 in 2021). Of these, white people have been killed by police at a rate of 16 per million. For Hispanic suspects, that goes up to 28 per million; for Black people, 39 per million. Year after year, the US police force kills Black people at more than twice the rate of white people.[59] Remember George Floyd, 2020, Minneapolis, Minnesota, handcuffed to the ground as his murderer Derek Chauvin knelt on his neck. Remember Atatiana Jefferson, 2019, Fort Worth, Texas, shot in front of her nephew through the window of her own home. Remember Stephon Clark, 2018, standing in his grandmother's driveway in Sacramento, California, holding a mobile phone, which officers mistook for a weapon. Remember Tamir Rice, 2014, twelve years old, in Cleveland, Ohio, playing in the park with a toy gun, which officers mistook for a real one.

In all these cases, the objective standard meant asking one simple question. Would a reasonable person, within these same set of circumstances, have made these same mistakes? Would a reasonable person faced with a playing child, a woman in her own home, a man helpless on the floor, have felt similarly threatened, have outnumbered and overpowered their victim, have pulled out their own weapons and opened fire?

Law professor and sentencing expert Jelani Jefferson Exum says that it's in cases like these, where police use deadly force, that the law's 'nearsighted approach to reasonableness' is most devastatingly evident. Here, those reasonable judgments about 'the suspect-victim's "dangerousness"' and 'acceptable police conduct' have been 'built upon a foundation of racial biases that all in society unfortunately share'.[60]

It's not just in the use of force that police bias shows its face, of course. Officers also have the power to detain people they deem suspicious, thanks to laws like the 1968 US Supreme Court ruling which allowed officers to conduct frisks of people on the street without a warrant, and the UK's similar 1980s stop-and-search legislation. The authors of a systematic review of global detainment explain that, in theory, no one should be stopped unless a police officer has 'reasonable suspicion' they are involved in wrongdoing. 'But what does this mean in practice? On what objective criteria should suspicion be based? How accurate and reliable should suspicion be before it can be described as "reasonable"?' As the authors go on to show, just like the evidence on police use of force, the literature on stop-and-search 'is replete with police officers' comments about intuition, hunches and general signals of disreputableness which would not satisfy a neutral observer':

> Often suspicion is linked to more general views about marginal communities and stereotypical beliefs about their criminal behaviour. [. . .] It is well established in a number of contexts that 'categorical suspicion' based on the social category to which the individual belongs is often used as the grounds for

> a stop. The use of cues of this sort has the effect of making suspects out of entire communities.[61]

Hundreds and hundreds of studies and reports and testimonies have shown how spurious the reasons given for these reasonable suspicions can be. In this one systemic review alone, excuses range from claiming that a suspect 'looks like they shouldn't be here' to saying they were listening to 'ethnic music' to blaming them for looking 'foreign' or 'dirty'. And yet we persist in calling these abhorrent prejudices 'reasonable'.

Let's take a step back for a second. How do our brains process these biases? In *Blindspot*, the American psychologists Mahzarin R. Banaji and Anthony Greenwald describe the results of a Dartmouth University study. This found that, when we're thinking about ourselves, the brain engages a specific cluster of neurons, located in the ventral region of the medial prefrontal cortex (or mPFC). This by itself isn't particularly shocking – except that a Harvard study then found that thinking about people whom we see as 'like us' *also* activates those same neurons. Meanwhile, thinking about people who are 'not like us' activates an entirely different set of neurons (in the dorsal rather than ventral region of the mPFC). 'The brain, it turns out,' Banaji and Greenwald write, 'engages two different clusters of neurons in thinking about other people, and which cluster gets activated depends on the degree to which one identifies with those others.'[62]

The invention of brain-imaging technology has confirmed what social psychologists have known for decades. While our collective human survival relies on that global network of interconnections detailed in Chapter One, people nonetheless have a self-harming tendency to retreat into imagined in-groups of diverse and multifaceted individuals, and to lump everyone outside together under harmfully reductive stereotypes. Called the 'out-group homogeneity effect', if left unacknowledged it can foster feelings of hostility towards anyone we see as unlike ourselves.

Thanks to our brains, bias has the potential to seep into every aspect of our everyday life. The good news is that it isn't a done deal – studies are beginning to recognise that 'empathy is not an all-or-none phenomenon'.[63] With the human mind capable of a high degree of flexibility, people may be able to retrain their brains to activate the 'like us' neurons for those whom they have previously labelled 'not like us', if brought face to face with their common humanity.* But the bad news is that the carceral system in general has not faced up to the biased schemata underpinning the judgment process. Not even close.

Whose Reasoning?

The ancient Chinese philosopher Chuang Tzu once gave an answer to the question 'Are we arguing?' He said:

* See also the findings from domestic violence studies examining what happens when women kill their abusive partners in self-defence. When jurors 'are asked to base their assessment of reasonableness not on the hypothetical "reasonable person" but on their understanding of the subjective situation of the defendant, they arrive at different verdicts', and are far more likely to vote to acquit. (Jennifer Temkin & Barbara Krahé. *Sexual Assault and the Justice Gap: A Question of Attitude* (Bloomsbury, 2008), p. 68.)

> Arguments cannot really be settled. Suppose I argue with you and you win, are you really right and am I really wrong? And if I win, am I really right and you really wrong? Or is one of us right and one of us wrong? Or are both of us right or both of us wrong? And if I and you can't settle the argument between us, others will be equally in the dark. Who can tell us what is right? If the judge shares your opinion, how can he decide which is right? And if he shares both our opinions, how can he decide who is right?[64]

Two and a half thousand years later, the law is only now beginning to ask these same questions. The paradox of the legal 'reasonable person' is that they are a utopian figure: someone who by definition cannot be racist or sexist or classist or homophobic or ableist, and who must judge everyone according to equal moral standards in order to be considered reasonable. But because we live in a world 'saturated with derogatory stereotypes',[65] as Jody David Armour puts it, nobody can reasonably consider themselves to have actually reached the plane of true moral reasonableness – elevated above the quagmire, a neutral font of objective wisdom, completely and blissfully free from society's all-too-human flaws.

So why do we persist in using this as a foundational legal standard? Because it's a way to legitimise as objectively correct a position that is inherently subjective and 'subject to challenge', Olivier Corten explains. The word 'reasonable' 'provides legitimacy to the international legal order as a whole, by presenting an image of a closed, coherent and complete legal system'. Embedding reason within the heart of common law, he says, was designed to suggest 'an ideal of unity and community of values that is particularly remarkable in an international society which is very loosely integrated, and which is characterised by decentralised centres of power and acute cultural and political differences'. The result has been 'a true occultation: it masks persistent contradictions regarding the meaning of a rule, behind a formula which leaves open the possibility of divergent interpretations'.[66]

And that, in a nutshell, is the problem of reasonableness in everyday life. In an increasingly international society, calling our own viewpoints reasonable is a way to 'occult' – or eclipse – contradictions, alternative viewpoints, and divergent interpretations under the utopian ideal of unified community values. This leaves no room for disagreement: because if our own viewpoints are the ones that are simple, obvious, and objectively common sense, anyone with alternative opinions must therefore be *unreasonable* – rude, wrong, and not to be trusted.

What's not in doubt, of course, is the need to have these kinds of shared community values. Without shared values, in fact, there can be no community at all. To return to the example of public transport, some good rules might be: if you're able-bodied then you should give up your seat for pregnant and disabled people. Don't spread yourself too wide: keep to your own personal space rather than impinging on others' bodies. Use headphones if you're going to watch a video, rather than letting your personal soundscape impinge on others' ears. If you're applying make-up, make sure it doesn't go near anyone else's nose or clothes. Wear deodorant so you don't smell bad, but don't overdo the perfume (an asthmatic's plea!). In all these examples, the goal is to encourage people to adhere to prosocial norms – those rules of engagement that really do make social life nicer and safer and more sociable for everyone. I'm not contesting these fundamental principles at all.

What I am querying, though, is whether any of this is as simple as it seems. In practice, drawing those lines can often be anything but simple. After all, when does insufficient deodorant turn into too much scent? When does protecting one's personal space turn into fat shaming? If consuming food on a short journey is just selfish gluttony that unnecessarily assaults other people's noses, at what precise length does that journey need to last before eating a meal becomes an acceptable necessity? What about reasonable exceptions, like people with diabetes and other hidden conditions – should they be allowed to eat in public and, if so, how are we meant to tell who is who? What about the potential for 'access friction' – for example, where conditions that make the sound or smell of eating unbearable may conflict with another's legitimate need to eat?* Which kinds of food are acceptable, and where's the boundary between a meal and a snack, and whose food is considered unreasonably smelly, and on and on and on?

* People who have a condition called hyperosmia can experience severe migraines in response to just the slightest whiff of food. Those with misophonia experience intense sensitivity to sounds – commonly chewing – which can swamp them with painful waves of anger, disgust, and a strong physiological desire to fight or flee. In the same vein: certain theatres have started making 'relaxed performances' the norm – but while these can be great for many autistic audiences and people with conditions like Tourette's, who may need to vocalise their reactions, they are less ideal for other neurodivergent people and those with hearing loss, who may need total silence. This is what 'access friction' means. It's really not simple at all.

When we use that word reasonable, we need to learn to ask ourselves: *Whose reasoning* are we talking about?

In the next half of this book I dig a lot deeper into that tug of war between consideration and moralising – between the right of certain people to go about their lives without being subjected to unreasonable disruptions, and the right of other people to exist in the world without being subjected to unreasonable judgments. As to why being judged is such a terrible thing, we only have to pay attention to how minoritised people have talked and written (in so many different ways and for so very long) about the stultifying power of The Look.

In her book *Shrill*, for example, the comedian Lindy West recounts her experience of being a plus-size woman in capitalism-size aeroplane seats, and being met with gross revulsion by a fellow passenger with whom she then has to share a flight.[67] For the website Motherly, Diana Spalding opens her hilarious open letter about parental judgment: 'Hey there. Yes, you! The stranger who just gave me the hard stare followed by the eye roll as my kid was having an epic melt down in the grocery store. Yes, I *did* see the look you gave me, and now I'm going to make it weird.'[68] Couples in same-sex relationships talk about getting The Look for walking down the street holding hands; people in wheelchairs describe being hit by The Look when trying to navigate crowded restaurants; for people of colour, The Look is such a regular occurrence that Procter & Gamble made a short film about it, depicting just one day in the everyday life of a Black man in corporate America being surveilled with white-eyed suspicion everywhere he goes.[69] The Look might not sound like much but, like all microaggressions, its function is to gradually and inexorably grind its recipients down: death by a thousand cuts, a thousand tiny moments of being made to feel too much or too visible or too out of place. And of course, behind every Look lingers the ever-present threat of violence.

It's evident that public censure can be a useful tool in the construction and maintenance of those necessary prosocial norms. Shame isn't itself morally wrong. In fact, when witnessing dangerously self-serving behaviour or acts of bigotry, calling out deviance may well be a deeply moral act. The desire to be seen in a positive light – and the fear of social reprisal! – can be a powerful force keeping us together. As a set of formal and unwritten guidelines for communal behaviour, the theoretical concept of the social contract is undeniably a good thing, helping us to balance our own needs against our collective responsibilities to each other. We live in a society! But in practice, in so many ways, the terms of engagement we have today are fatally flawed. Produced by white upper-class men for the primary benefit of white upper-class men, many of the reasonable standards we take to be neutral common sense have been designed to protect western ideals of individualised property ownership above all else. As more recent writings within philosophy have shown,* the social contract has been used historically to facilitate the exclusion, the subjugation, the

* First, Carole Pateman's *The Sexual Contract* (Stanford University Press, 1988) established the use of the social contract in women's patriarchal subjugation; then, Charles W. Mills' *The Racial Contract* (Cornell University Press, 1997) built on Pateman's work to interrogate the racialised dimension. Both are essential reading for anyone wishing to understand more.

violent oppression of non-normative bodies and minoritised communities in ways that continue to reverberate still.

Whether we like it or not, we live a society which has always allowed men to take up space while insisting that women make themselves as small as possible. We live in a society which continues to deny disabled people their basic human right to equity and dignity, because capitalism has deemed it cheaper and easier to design the lived environment to suit the normate. We live in a society where queer people still have to plan their travel exhaustively to avoid discomfort or even danger; where people of colour continue to be violently surveilled and policed; where the gentrification of cities has been pushing working-class families inexorably further and further to the margins. We are living in a fundamentally unreasonable world.

But what can we actually do about it? That's where I'll be taking you next.

PART TWO

BEING UNREASONABLE

F*ck Civility

In the winter of 2020, I took part in a BBC radio debate about the value of debate. In the dying days of the Trump presidency, as he roared impotently and gnashed his teeth on Twitter and began finally to fizzle away, I sat there and politely argued about the pros and cons of arguing politely. What we need, my fellow panellists said, is to bring civility back to civic life. We're living in a time, they said, where the individual is king. We've forgotten how to listen to each other, they said, how to care about other opinions, how to treat our fellow humans with decency and respect. We need to relearn, in short, how to be civilised. 'Yes,' I said. 'Yes, that's a good point. Yes, but.'

That's why I'd been asked on to the programme, after all. My job was to be the academic. The 'yes, but' woman. Yes, I too believe that manners are important. Yes, I agree that late-stage capitalism is incentivising us to abandon collective responsibility in favour of individual gain. Yes, I think that civil discourse is generally a good thing to promote. Yes, but. *Isn't it more complicated than that?*

In the late 1930s, a Jewish refugee from Nazi Germany called Norbert Elias published his famous sociological study *Über den Prozeß der Zivilisation.*[1] Later republished in English as *The Civilizing Process*, Elias' two-volume magnum opus analysed 'conduct books' (European guides to manners) published between the thirteenth and eighteenth centuries, and found within their pages evidence of a rising sense of revulsion towards the human body, with its messy fluids and inconvenient urges. This 'expanding threshold of repugnance', Elias wrote, was characterised by sensations of embarrassment and shame, as well as a growing belief in the superior ability of European nobility to discipline their physical self via the restraining influence of reason.[2] The overall result was a gradual codification of strict behavioural standards: what Elias called 'habitus', the kind of individual habits that seem like they're just second nature, but are actually informed at that supra-conscious level through lifelong societal conditioning. Manners, Elias suggested, can be both good and bad.

Before we leap to the defence, let's hear Elias out. On the one hand, healthy societies need mechanisms for encouraging their citizenry to think about the needs and desires of communities as a whole, prioritising empathy and consideration over entitled narcissism. This ideal can be found embedded in the original meaning of the word *civilité*, from the Old French (with Latin roots in the word *civilis*), meaning 'relating to citizens'. But on the other hand, as Elias pointed out, manners have also historically been a tool used by powerful people to produce artificial status hierarchies. We can see this definition of manners in the root of the word 'etiquette' – also from the Old French, this time the word *estiquette*, meaning 'to attach' or 'stick'.

Let's start with *civilité*. This idea was first popularised within Europe by the biggest selling book of the sixteenth century. It was a little handbook called *De Civilitate Morum Puerilium*, usually translated into *On Civility in Children*, published in 1530 in Latin by the Dutch humanist Erasmus of Rotterdam, then republished in 130 editions and twenty-two languages over the following three hundred years. Written to aid the education of young noblemen – the heirs of Europe's titled aristocrats – Erasmus' treatise advocated a shift away from absorption in the self to consideration of others. As Elias points out, the first step in this process was *observation*, encouraging young noblemen to look about themselves and think about the needs of other people. Don't spit on the floor, use a handkerchief. Don't stick your hands in a communal dish of food unless you've washed them first. If you need to fart, step away from the table. Similar advice to the kind I impart today, sitting at the dinner table with two little boys. As the doyenne of impeccable behaviour, Emily Post herself, once wrote: manners are simply 'a sensitive awareness of the feelings of others'.[3] So in that sense, civility is absolutely a moral quality, designed to bring us together by encouraging people to be more observant, thoughtful, equitable, and kind. What's not to like?

Now let's look at the word 'etiquette'. In Europe, this term also became synonymous with manners around the 1600s, in the court of King Louis XIV of France, who used a series of small cards or 'estiquettes' stuck around the palace of Versailles to advise visitors on the rules of courtly behaviour. As courtiers became embroiled in increasingly bitter rivalries over status, these choreographed rituals became increasingly intricate and difficult to learn. How wide the servants opened doors for you, for example, would depend on your rank; meanwhile, noblewomen may have reportedly been free to relieve their bladders in the palace hallway wherever they walked, but woe betide anyone who failed to wear the extravagant *grand habit* of traditional court dress.

To go back to the dining table metaphor: if consideration means an ethical urge to stop everyone from sticking dirty hands in food and poisoning everyone, then etiquette is more like the serried ranks of cutlery at a posh banquet. It has nothing to do with caring about others, and everything to do with figuring out who belongs at the table – and who doesn't.

Long before Erasmus, ancient societies around the world were wrestling in similar ways with the relationship between manners and morality. Writing about the *Tahdhīb al-Akhlāq* (a tenth-century AD translation of Aristotle's *Nicomachean Ethics* into Arabic by Ibn Miskawayh), for example, Margrit Pernau of the Max Planck Institute for Human Development explains how uncivilised people were those without knowledge and feeling: characterised by 'the lack of those emotions, which draw people together. Barbarians are *be-rahm* (merciless), *be-dard* (unable to feel compassion), and *sang-dil* (stone-hearted).' The ethical cultivation of the self known as *adab* required *tahzib* ('polishing [. . .] of the habits and the inner being') through the development of *narm* (soft) and *latif* (pleasant) emotions: things like feelings of 'compassion and generosity when faced with human misery', as well as the willingness to stand up against injustice.[4] Much, much earlier, more than two thousand years BC, *The Maxims of Ptahhotep* set out links between moral virtues (like honesty tempered by discretion) and deference norms (like how to behave in the presence of people from higher social ranks). Manners have *always* been caught between scruples and status.

The point I'm making isn't that cultures outside Europe have exotically mystical systems of knowledge and behaviour. That in itself is an orientalising mode of thinking. My point is that, up until around the late seventeenth century, lots of nations had been wrestling in roughly similar ways with the complicated link between manners and morality. Then the global system of European colonialism disrupted everything. By studying those European etiquette texts, what Elias noticed in the rhetoric of 'civilisation' was a relentless disconnection of manners from those ideals of *moral* decency – values like honour, generosity, and compassion. Instead, the tone shifted towards urging everyone to cultivate the *appearance* of decency in order to avoid social embarrassment and shame. From then on, becoming 'civilised' began to mean a systematic process of repression: a process of suppressing mind, body, and emotions beneath a stiff-upper-lip veneer. This process began in the western world with strict ideals of 'courteous' behaviour being formulated within the nucleus of the royal court, then slowly permeated outwards throughout 'polite' society, and then outwards again via those global systems of imperial capitalism, until the entire world became changed by it.

Empire apologists argue that this change was for the better, but history tells a different story. The coming pages of this book focus on that story.

We're now at the scorpion's tail of Elias' civilising process. As always, the important question isn't whether ideals like 'manners', 'civility', 'courtesy', or 'respect' are inherently good or bad. The real question is: when are those ideals genuinely being used to make the world a more ethical place, and when is a facade of mannerly propriety actually disguising immoral acts – unfairness and discrimination happily excused, so long as everything *seems* nice and decorous? In reimagining the social contract, the challenge now is to avoid mistaking the outward trappings of civility for those *truly* civilised ideals of compassion, consideration, and care.

Or at least, this is what Elias argued. Almost a century ago now, in fact, he pointed out that society tends to cling to reasonable appearances – crisp uniforms, cultured mannerisms, a love of high art, Hitler's neat little moustache – most fiercely at times of stark moral conflict. Think about the honeyed gentility of the American South, where smiling courtesy provided cover for simmering racial violence. Think about the buttoned-up laced-down aggression of the white imperial invader, sitting on their verandas in the Indian sunshine sipping tea. Think about the polished performances of the Nazis, with all their approving 1930s newspaper articles about impeccable manners and rarified tastes in art and dress.

Now, connect all this with the contemporary state of op-ed journalism. Think about the propensity of centrist commentators to focus on the dapper outfits and old-fashioned good manners of modern-day white supremacists. Eugenicists are cool again, apparently, and so are rampant misogynists, so long as we make sure to keep things *polite*. Be respectful when they tell you they think you shouldn't exist. Smile as they strip away your rights. Because as we all know, when it comes to social justice, every new bit of progress has happened because someone asked nicely.

Over the final half of this book, I'm going to argue that this reasonable rhetoric of 'agree to disagree!' and 'let's all be civil!'

is the enemy hiding in plain sight. All talk, no action – that's the reasonable way. I'm going to ask what would be different if we had listened more carefully to the people who've spent centuries explaining that claiming the moderate middle ground is never the answer. In fact, it's the problem – a phenomenon that's been pulling our politics further and further to the right. Far from establishing a common ground on which to build a better world, what if all we're achieving with our polite debates and what-about-isms is to widen social rifts and give legitimacy to evil ideas, allowing them to be dragged further into the mainstream?

The final three chapters take a deep dive into these questions by tackling three big interrelated topics. With a nod to what came before, my aim is to understand when the notion of civility has been used throughout history to bring us together, and when it's been deliberately deployed to tear us apart.

Beginning with 'Neighbours Behaving Badly', I interrogate the idea of 'civil behaviour', and the battle that's currently raging around how we should live together in close proximity with other people. To what extent should shared social spaces welcome acts of collective joy, noise, and play – a world of block parties and community cookouts and children happily playing games in the street? When should public life be carefully controlled, and who should have the power to control it? In 'Where We're Going . . .' I look at the long history of 'civil disobedience', and the wrongheaded idea that the disruptions caused by civic protest movements are too great a price to pay for civic justice. And in 'Whatever Happened to Public Reason?' I turn to the idea of 'civil debate', asking why talking things through rationally gets offered as the solution when so often it seems to fix nothing at all.

Finally, I conclude with my key takeaway from all this research. For too long now we've been wrestling for the soul of reasonableness on an uneven playing field. Drawing moral lines between two sides and then trying to find a balance between them only works when both sides are equal to begin with. If we're serious about rebalancing the scales, we need to learn to think critically about relations of power.

4

Neighbours Behaving Badly

When you have kids, everyone warns you about the ordinary things. Dealing with various bodily fluids. Never having enough batteries for all the plastic spewed around your house. The brain-numbing repetition of hide-and-seek. All the crying – theirs and yours. Tiny fingers reaching under the bathroom door like in a horror movie. Red sauce everywhere, like in a horror movie. Years of sleepless nights.

What nobody warned me about, though, was the parenting performance. Oh dear, my toddler is crying on this plane because he's exhausted and bored and his ears hurt. I guess I'll now make pointless shhh-ing noises for the next hour, maybe bounce him up and down a bit while grimacing apologetically at my fellow passengers and mouthing *sorry! sorry! so sorry!* None of this will do anything to ease the baby's discomfort, or to stem the misery spilling out of his tiny mouth. All it will do is maybe go some small way to mollifying my fellow passengers, who are currently in the middle of putting on their own performance. If I'm lucky this will be a show of resigned understanding; if not, I'll get to be an audience of one to an ensemble of irritation, replete with sighs and eyeball rolls and tut-tut-tuts. Hopefully, my demeanour of cowering penitence will demonstrate that *I really am doing everything I can* and that *I care about your inconvenience* and that *I'm not just an inconsiderate asshole, promise!* Where is my Oscar?

One particularly memorable instance happened when I was still desperately trying to claw a career out of thin air and a collapsing job market, having ill-advisedly gained a baby and a PhD within a few weeks of one another. I'd recently got home from a conference overseas where, instead of carry-on, I'd had to wrangle my nearly one-year-old solo for a six-hour red-eye. Monty refused to sleep through any of it, and I was left with nothing to do except watch in dismay as his usual cheery demeanour increasingly turned manic, before shattering into exhausted wails with an hour left to go.

The journey out had been a breeze. It was a midday flight, and Monty had cooed delightfully on my lap for a while before passing out milk-drunk for the rest of the journey. This prompted several people to comment, as I filed off the plane, on what a *good* baby he was and what a *stellar* mother I must be to keep him so quiet. For a perennial people-pleaser this kind of praise is catnip. Obviously he made up for it on the way home – no accolades for me then. Instead, as we got ready to leave our seats after landing, an older man sitting several rows behind loudly commented: 'See, this is why we didn't bring our kids on holiday until they were grown.' With Monty wriggling like a greased eel clamped under one of my arms, I grabbed his changing bag down with the other, turned my back, and burst into tears.

A couple of weeks later I was catapulted back into that memory when I read about another mother being accosted by another angry man – this time in a café. She'd taken her toddler out after a sleepless night of teething pains and was struggling to keep him calm, but at least she was now dealing with it caffeinated, and a guy in a suit marched over to tell her off. Then the

Reasonable Tango began. Yes, but she chose to have kids; other people decided not to procreate precisely because they don't want to deal with the noise. No, because people with kids have the right to go out of their house for some human interaction; being a new parent can be intensely isolating. Well, he has the right to enjoy his drink in peace – she should stick to mother-and-baby groups. You can't lock all the people who procreate in a soundproof box – being in public means dealing with the public, and it's not her fault babies cry. It's certainly not *his* fault her baby was crying! Forcing others to conform to your strict standards is selfish and unfair; ever heard of headphones? Forcing others to deal with the result of your bad decisions is unfair and selfish; you chose this responsibility, so deal with them at home alone. It's just about being a bit more tolerant. It's just about manners, consideration, and respect.

I keep writing out the arguments in full like this, but that's because the rhetorical patterns really are that predictable. Both sides believe they are fighting a moral battle. One side is fighting for the right to spend time in public without being exposed to disruptive annoyances; the other for the right to exist fully and equitably in public at all. Given this disagreement, was there any reasonable way for me – a new mother with high-functioning anxiety disorder and a strong desire to never cause a scene – to coexist peacefully with other people in the world?

That's when I came across a couple of useful terms to help me understand all this more deeply. Firstly, from the field of human geography, the term 'spatial hegemony' describes an ongoing power struggle over the rules of engagement in shared social spaces, like an aeroplane or a café or a public park. Secondly, coined by Black and Chicana/o Studies expert Gaye

Theresa Johnson, the term 'spatial entitlement'[1] defines how those with more social power have always presumed themselves morally qualified to set those rules for everyone else.

In relation to parenting, since the 1980s particularly, children have been subject to a rising tide of concern. On one hand, the end of the latch-key era and the emergence of 'stranger danger' saw the sudden intensification of a moral panic about children's vulnerability to external threat. On the other hand, adults became increasingly worried about the potential for children to *be* a threat, with popular concerns about the unruliness of youth within increasingly densely populated areas. These 'contradictory concerns' show how 'public space is being produced as a space that is "naturally" or "normally" an adult space', as geographer Gill Valentine puts it.[2] This has produced an atmosphere in which *any* child tends by default to be seen as an abnormal intrusion, needing to be constantly monitored, regulated, and controlled.

I read about this while on maternity leave with my second child, Sully. I spent a lot of that period thinking about that sickly exhausted feeling I got every time I had to leave the house, and the mental effort it took to prepare. Not just the practical things, like bundling Sully up in clothes and coats and the carrier, but to prepare for my parenting to be inevitably flayed by judging eyes. As a society, we have offloaded the overwhelming bulk of responsibility for childcare on to women, while at the same time expecting women to run around doing the majority of household errands in a way that doesn't inflict the children they have to bring with them on anybody else. And I found myself writing this:

whether in restaurants or theatres, on public transport or at academic conferences: the attendance of small children has disrupted my ability to fit invisibly into public life. When in their presence I am always at risk of being (and being seen as) a disruptive presence within other adults' worlds. [. . .] The consequence of having children is often exclusion; more specifically, the uneven exclusion of *women* from public space, and particularly professional life. When I am unable to attend a conference because of childcare difficulties, or when I miss out on a performance event, or when I bundle the kids into the car rather than braving the train, or when I decide to eat at McDonald's rather than at my favourite adult restaurant: my absence is positioned as a reasonable sacrifice, a renunciation of my individual desires for the benefit of the many. By this I mean those reasonable people who would prefer to eat their meal and have a nice conversation without watching a small child mangle a plate of spaghetti. Those who just want to read the news in peace while travelling from A to B, and not be required to share their space with sticky humans bellowing *Let it Go*. Those who want to present their research or perform their pivotal scene to a room rapt in silent absorption, along with those on the other side of the stage, who desire to sit in rapt silence and absorb. Within all these scenarios there are always those who benevolently propose reasonable exceptions ('as long as they are totally silent/are not too loud/you make an effort to quiet them/you remove them if they get out of hand') – and yet [. . .] what seems a reasonable level of disturbance to one is wholly unreasonable to another.[3]

This all got me thinking again about shame, and about judgment, and about The Look I described at the end of Chapter Three. But it also made me consider the broader power dynamics involved in labelling somebody else a disruptive presence. Who historically has been allowed to exert control over shared social space, and who has been seen as in need of controlling? What does it mean to set reasonable limitations over things like noise and mess and other societal disruptions, and who gets to decide? What if we allowed ourselves to envision a better, kinder, more inclusive way of life?

It was just as I was starting to really wrap my head around this, back in the height of the COVID-19 pandemic, that I idly downloaded a new app designed to bring neighbours together. Suddenly, I found I had a perfect digital window seat to watch that battle of spatial entitlement playing out 24/7 in front of my eyes on a much bigger scale – our neighbourhoods. Only recently released in the UK a couple of years earlier, that social media platform is called Nextdoor.

'When Neighbors Start Talking, Good Things Happen'

2 November 2017. 'Howdy, neighbors.' A Seattle citizen posts a carefully worded message asking football fans to please reconsider lighting fireworks whenever their local team, the Seahawks, scores a goal. They have a terrified dog, and every Sunday they have to watch him hide under the bathtub whenever a firework or celebratory cannon goes off nearby. Maybe we could 'chill out on the booming noises, please? Thanks!'

3 November. A couple of people reply in agreement. Their dogs are getting upset, too. One person suggests substituting the cannon for an air horn? Another complains they've seen people setting off fireworks in their backyards and told them off over the fence, and even called the police a few times, but nothing's helped. 'I'm completely sick of my neighbors,' they say.

6 November. The backlash begins. It's not a big deal. It's tradition. This is a free country. Most people love it. They're just dogs! Get over it, buy earmuffs, quit whining. It's awesome. At some point someone is called insensitive. Somebody else is called an ass.

17 November. The man who was called an ass calls a neighbourhood meeting. 'December 5 at seven thirty – the White Center Library meeting space. All of your ideas and stories are welcome in this time of great division. Let's participate in active community building. There is strength in numbers. See you there.'

6 December. The day after. 'Well, that was a mess,' somebody posts. The man who was called an ass ruefully agrees: 'So it went bad. Yelling, scuffling, all in the library. [. . .] Police were called, threats were made, citations were handed out. [. . .] My hope is that we all learned something about each other, and with education there is hope. My fear is last night was just a microcosm of all that is wrong with our society, and it's going to get much worse before it gets better. I hope I'm wrong.'*

* See the website Lapham's Quarterly for a thorough record of the dispute as it unfolded ('Neighborhood Football Match', 2017: www.laphamsquarterly.org/rivalry-feud/neighborhood-football-match).

The slogan of the Nextdoor app? 'When neighbors start talking, good things happen.' Launched in 2011, Nextdoor is the world's largest and fastest growing private social network for neighbourhoods, offering members of specific communities a way to connect with each other. To get an account, Nextdoor users first need to verify their real home address. They're then allowed to join the residents' group for that community and can start asking questions, getting to know one another, and exchanging local know-how in ways that are meant to strengthen neighbourhood bonds. As of June 2022, Nextdoor had expanded to cover more than 285,000 neighbourhoods in eleven countries across the UK, Canada, Europe, and especially the USA,[4] where one in five households were active on the app, and where the *New York Times* found a 70 per cent spike in usage just after COVID-19 sent everyone into lockdown.[5] At the time of writing, Nextdoor's plans for total neighbourhood domination are continuing apace.

An isolation-busting lifeline to some users, for others the site has been a breeding ground for disconnection and mistrust. Nextdoor has become particularly famous for its ability to escalate local conflicts, the crème de la crème of which are regularly documented in an ongoing Twitter feed called @bestofnextdoor. Here are some of my favourite examples:

1. The Case of the Cheese Bandit. This one began when an outraged resident posted a picture of a single slice of American cheese resting on the windscreen of their car, apparently for the second time that week. The real culprits, they explained, were the garbage parents who'd

raised such garbage kids. The police had already been called.

2. The Case of the Obscene Pumpkin Vandal. Posted around Halloween, this was a nefarious bandit who crept around at night removing uncarved pumpkins from stoops and carving phallic symbols into them. 'I will also be speaking to the police,' the victim said, 'as this was a planned vandalism that clearly took some significant time.' That kind of crime could incur a stiff penalty, one bystander warned. Sounds like someone has a boner to pick.
3. The Case of the Unstoppable Erotica. 'I just now heard my printer running mysteriously by itself and it turned out to be printing (unstoppably) many sheets of "erotica" i.e. soft porn,' this user exclaimed. 'It would be pretty bad if this came into a house with children,' they pointed out, asking 'do you know who to report it to?' The purple-prose police, perhaps?
4. The Case of the Late-Night Mailbox Farter. This one is pretty self-explanatory, but just in case: 'Someone keeps farting in my mail box late at night, I can hear it outside the window and I smell it every time I check my mail,' the post reads. 'This is getting old and is extremely childish, my bills and coupons smell so bad I can't even pay them or use them at the grocery store, anyone in my neighborhood keep an eye out for the brown eye. I will catch the flatulent phantom.'
5. And finally, The Case of the Cursèd Dog, in a post titled simply 'Cursing at my dog?' 'Whoever just told my dog to "Shut the F### up" needs to come to my house and

> speak to me or my husband directly.' That's biting talk. Sounds like they're looking for a barkument. No need to be so pugnacious. Can't we be a bit more neighpawly?

While many posts are genuinely helpful (and some of the others are almost definitely fakes), Nextdoor has also given dedicated curtain-twitchers a forum on which to unleash their inner amateur detective. And this is where it gets a lot less funny. Many contributors famously share a faulty radar for suspicious behaviour, obsessing over the most banal of occurrences: like the neighbour who gets reported to their landlord for leaving their own house too many times a day, or the vehicle driving around slowly in the morning that's eventually revealed to be a newspaper-delivery van.

I opened this book with the miracle that is our ability to trust strangers at all. But just like how the 'reasonable suspicions' of police officers have been proven to be tainted by racist bias, the ability of ordinary civilians to judge which strangers should be trusted is fundamentally compromised. This has been pointed out by the 'feminist killjoy' scholar Sara Ahmed in her book *Strange Encounters*, which examines the phenomenon of the Neighbourhood Watch: a network of residents who collectively police their own local areas. Ahmed explains that this kind of community self-policing rests on the ability of ordinary citizens to identify anyone or anything that is out of the ordinary. But how do we figure out what 'ordinary' and 'suspicious' look like? Ahmed argues that those seemingly common-sense judgments are actually more about sensing the difference between ourselves and others. Within the middle-class suburban neighbourhoods which are most likely to have a Neighbourhood Watch, Ahmed argues, it's the 'white, male, middle-class, heterosexual body' that tends to be viewed as 'a body which is *at-home* or *in-place*', unmarked by the strangeness that is afforded everyone else.[6]

The brain-wiring I described in Chapter Three that leads us to form imagined in-groups and enemy out-groups was really important about ten thousand years ago, when our survival relied on making instant decisions about whom to trust and whom to shoot with an arrow. Today, those reflexes are less about safety than centuries of schematic conditioning. The USA has a particularly big perception gap when it comes to safety. While FBI data shows that everything from violent crimes to burglary rates have plummeted sharply since the 1990s, annual Gallup surveys consistently find that at least six in ten Americans believe there to be more crime than the year before.[7] These faulty perceptions have bred a climate of fearful prejudice. Strangers who 'look like us' are more likely to register as neighbours, Ahmed argues: someone who belongs there in that space, a stranger simply because you haven't met them yet. Meanwhile, anyone with any kind of physical difference becomes an 'alien stranger', somebody 'marked by strangeness', 'the one that is different from "us"'.*

* It's tempting to assume that in areas where white people are in the minority, a white pedestrian would be viewed in precisely the same way: but actually, straight middle-class white men especially have always utilised their power to travel through spaces not built for them in ways that might see them watched, but not necessarily marked out as deviant or dangerously disruptive. Consider the nineteenth-century *flâneur*, drifting around urban wastelands without having to think about his physical safety (or at least not as urgently and all-consumingly as women and men of colour have always needed to).

This phenomenon caused a lot of consternation for Nextdoor's vice president of policy, Steve Wymer, who estimated in an article for *The Atlantic* that around 10 per cent of all Nextdoor conversations relate to crime and safety.[8] A man with long hair whose vehicle sports an Iron Maiden sticker. A gang of teenagers drinking bubble tea and loitering menacingly. Skateboarders; those listening audibly to music; people in scruffy T-shirts. And of course, the never-ending stream of reports about 'people of color in predominantly white areas', as *The Atlantic* put it: people who, despite doing nothing out of the ordinary other than existing, seem to continually register as suspicious to neighbourhood spies. This led Alexandria Ocasio-Cortez, Democratic representative of the United States Congress, to call on the company in summer 2020 to 'publicly deal with their Karen problem' (Karen being a disparaging name often given to the kind of meddling white woman who tends to resolve conflicts by demanding to speak to the manager). In a bid to revamp their 'snitch app' image, Nextdoor began to 'discourage posts that use appearance as a proxy for criminality by prompting users to add more detail and blocking some posts that mention race'.[9]

Consider what bell hooks said about how the act of seeking danger and exoticism in marginalised spaces has long been a source of white middle-class pleasure, whilst Black families have been blocked from similarly crossing over into so-called 'respectable' neighbourhoods unless temporarily offering service. (See e.g. 'Eating the Other: Desire and Resistance' [1992], available at: https://genius.com/Bell-hooks-eating-the-other-desire-and-resistance-annotated; 'Choosing the Margin as a Space of Radical Openness', *Framework: The Journal of Cinema and Media* 36 [1989]: pp. 15–23, etc.)

As well as a tide of agreement, Nextdoor's decision unleashed a tirade of lofty responses – the gist of which was this: actually, the narcs of Nextdoor aren't prejudiced. In fact, they're being reasonable: because their suspicions are based not on knee-jerk bias, but on a rational assessment of who's more likely to be dangerous.

This reminded me of a scene in the 2004 film *Crash*, where Sandra Bullock is talking to Brendan Fraser about the carjacking they'd both just experienced. Bullock's character yells at her husband that the carjacking was her fault because she knew it was going to happen the second she saw two Black men walking towards them. She says that if, as a white woman, she had jumped out of the car at that point and run away, people would call her a racist. Well, she shouts, she saw them coming and felt scared, but she didn't say anything – then suddenly, just as she'd feared, she found herself staring down the barrel of a gun.

Sandra Bullock's character is a classic example of what Jody David Armour calls the Reasonable Racist. After all, the Reasonable Racist claims, they can't be prejudiced if their viewpoints are simply based on facts. In their mind, Armour says, 'their racial fears are born of a sober analysis, or at least of rough intuition, of crime statistics' that supposedly suggest Black people are prone to violence.[10] Armour tells a story about Michael Levin, a social philosopher, who argued that it's totally reasonable for someone – of any ethnicity! – to feel afraid when finding themselves alone with a Black stranger, given that '[a]pproximately one Black male in four is incarcerated at some time for the commission of a felony, while the incarceration rate for White males is between 2 and 3.5%'. Levin's premise is based, Armour says, on the 'vulgar logic' of Bayesian mathematics – a field of statistics which believes that probability can be measured on the basis of 'reasonable expectation' based on pure statistical likelihood. Levin gives a practical example to demonstrate his coldly 'objective' lack of bigotry:

> Suppose, jogging alone after dark, you see a young Black male ahead of you on the running track, not attired in a jogging outfit and displaying no other information-bearing trait. Based on the statistics cited earlier, you must set the likelihood of his being a felon at 25 . . . On the other hand it would be rational to trust a White male under identical circumstances, since the probability of his being a felon is less than .05. Since whatever factors affect the probability of the Black attacking you – the isolation, your vulnerability – presumably affect the probability of a White attacking you as well, it remains more rational to be more fearful of the Black than of the White.[11]

Armour dismantles the Reasonable Racist's faulty argument brick by brick. First of all, Armour points out, most Black people in prison are actually there for *non-violent* offences related to the War on Drugs – a policy launched by the Nixon presidency to halt the distribution of illegal substances, which has been disproportionately wielded against Black and Latino/a people. Second, with crime rates being inextricably linked to poverty and unemployment, 'explanations of crime statistics founder on the fact that crime and delinquency rates of the African American middle class are virtually identical to those of Whites similarly situated'. And finally, Armour argues, because those who *are* arrested for violent crimes make up only a tiny percentage – less than 1.9 per cent – of the Black male population, from a purely Bayesian perspective it would therefore be much more rational to trust a Black man than it is to *dis*trust him.[12] Boom. Mic drop.

Armour's argument painstakingly exposes the failure of logic that leads people to assert that their racist assumptions are reasonable because they can be rationalised. '"I merely seek to give race its correct incremental value in my calculations," the Reasonable Racist assures us', then goes on to tally up all the '"objective" indices of criminality' – like 'youth, gender, dress, posture, body movement, and apparent educational level – before deciding how to respond'. Except that's not how humans work at all. As we've seen, our supra-conscious mechanisms are just as strong as our facility for logic. Through centuries of schematic conditioning, social stereotypes can become embedded in children's belief systems before their mind is even capable of making conscious judgments. Indeed, as Armour points out, numerous studies have proven that once an individual internalises a schemata they're then likely to spend their life interpreting every experience they have in light of those biases and stereotypes, by selectively assimilating facts that validate their beliefs and disregarding those that do not.[13] This is, of course, unless we do the work to confront and then dismantle those biases.

This is work that the Reasonable Racist uses their supposed rationality to avoid. Just like the judges and juries in Chapter Three, Nextdoor users might *think* their decision-making processes are purely logical and objective. But in Ahmed's words, their instinct to separate the at-home from the out-of-place is often just 'a mechanism *for allowing us to face that which we have already designated as the beyond*', by reflecting and reinforcing internalised prejudice.[14]

When neighbours start talking, good people get harmed. That's why we need to take a long hard look at that impulse to look at other people.

The Body in the Box

At a famous London university there is a big glass box. Inside that box there is a chair, and on that chair sits a corpse. Welcome to University College London, home to the skeletal remains of a famous eighteenth-century philosopher and social reformer called Jeremy Bentham, the father of utilitarianism. Upon his death, Bentham made an unusual request: for his body to be permanently preserved within the university so that it could be used for the benefit of science, and occasionally get wheeled out for parties. Today, Bentham's terrifying mummified skull has been shoved in a drawer after a botched embalming, but his body, complete with new wax head, sits enrobed in his own clothes staring solemnly out through the glass walls in perpetuity at those who roam the halls. This is a fitting end for the man who basically invented the concept of total 24/7, 360-degree social surveillance.

From the French for 'watching over', surveillance has historically been a political imperative. If knowledge is power then powerful governing bodies have always had a vested interest in knowing as much as possible about those they're governing: a phenomenon which is now more all-encompassing than ever before. This is at least partly thanks to Jeremy Bentham.

Bentham is probably best known for coming up with a vision for a totalitarian surveillance mechanism, in the form of his new design of prison. This he called 'the panopticon', which in his 1798 pamphlet 'Proposal for a New and Less Expensive Mode of Employing and Reforming Convicts' he described like this:

> The prisoners, in their cells, occupying the circumference – The officers, (Governor, Chaplain, Surgeon. &c.) the center. By blinds, and other contrivances, the inspectors concealed [. . .] from the observation of the prisoners: hence the sentiment of invisible omnipresence. – The whole circuit reviewable with little, or, if necessary, without any, change of place. One station in the inspection-part affording the most perfect view of every cell.[15]

The idea was that every prisoner should be visible at all times, constantly vulnerable to the guards' gaze, who would themselves stay hidden from view. Bentham's dream was to extend the panopticon design from prisons out to other kinds of institutions like factories and schools. The theory was that this would create a sense of paranoiac uncertainty, which would control the behaviour of the observed more effectively than any top-down enforcement possibly could. Within the panopticon, discipline would no longer need to be meted out by authoritative individuals, but would now be enacted through *self-discipline* prompted by internalised authority. Because you'd never know if someone was watching you – only that at any moment in time they *could* be watching – you'd be forced constantly to scrutinise your own behaviour and to discipline yourself, just like the protagonists in George Orwell's 1948 landmark surveillance novel *1984*.

In the 1970s, the French philosopher Michel Foucault came across Bentham's design and had a light-bulb moment. Just like Orwell's telescreens, the panopticon, Foucault believed, wasn't simply a physical object. It was a metaphor for society itself: a vision of a world that was becoming mired within an inextricable system of surveillance, where social control operates both at the macro level of governmental spying all the way down to the micro level capillary action of interpersonal human relationships. In this model, Foucault warned, power has never solely been wielded from the top down, 'exerted over things' by an overarching authority; it is also decentralised, ever-present, and flows fluidly between people via the mundane interactions and behavioural norms of everyday life.[16]

Those Best of Nextdoor posts might be funny, but they're also a chilling reminder that the panopticon has at every level arrived. While state surveillance is obviously nothing new, politicians are increasingly benefiting from technological capital enabling them to assess, monitor, and track citizens' activities, both on and offline.* At the same time, corporations are sneaking into our homes through 'the internet

* Since the birth of the new millennium we've seen a domino effect, with nation after nation allowing their governments to seize unprecedented powers to spy on citizens in the name of security and order – installing security cameras in every conceivable nook and cranny of public space, tracking phone calls and email accounts without need for a judicial warrant, and even using data from personal home-security systems like Ring, whose small print allows them to sell private footage to the police.

of things'. Washing machines, personal assistants, fridges, music players, sex toys: these are just a few of the devices that now come already Wi-Fi-enabled and interconnected, pinging a swarm of data back and forth then funnelling findings back towards their makers. This surveillance goes both ways, with the smartphone in every pocket also enabling a surge in scrutiny of the powerful: a trend which has been termed 'sousveillance', from the French for 'watching from below'. This phenomenon has become a common feature of urban crises like protests, where the recording of human-rights violations by ordinary civilians has been the only thing standing between the state and its ability to get away with freewheeling abuses of power. We'll come back to the citizen journalist in the next chapter.

What interests me here, though, is those times when ordinary people start surveilling ordinary people. That's what my own etiquette research studied – those moments when regular arts-lovers found themselves incensed by the unruliness of their fellow audience members and decided to take matters into their own hands. When I looked, I found a term for this too: 'lateral surveillance'. This is precisely the kind of peer-to-peer monitoring we can see writ large on social media platforms like Nextdoor or a new app, Citizen, where users are specifically invited to submit reports of illegal activity.

It is this feeling of constant all-pervasive surveillance, where everyone is simultaneously watching others and being watched by others all the time, which is the ultimate realisation of Bentham's 1700s vision – and Foucault's nightmare. If the past few years have proven anything, it's that some people are constantly, *constantly* watching other people,* surveilling other people, shaming other people for bad behaviour: even, in the case of infamous internet villains like BBQ Becky and Permit Patty, trying to set the cops on people they've decided are out of order or out of place. With the release of each new 'Karen video' capturing white people harassing their Black neighbours for things like having cookouts in the park, we've seen how fervently some people seem to believe in their own right to act as the managers of everyone else, questioning and policing other people's presence.

As we've also seen, one person's 'reasonable assumption' is to another simply bigoted bias in action. Our perspectives may be embedded in problematic schemata and wrongheaded beliefs in ways we might not always understand. At the same time, these Nextdoor posts also demonstrate the danger of imposing one's own ideas about unacceptably 'disruptive' behaviour on to others. What if, sometimes, rigid behavioural standards are getting in the way of neighbourliness? What if, sometimes, knowing when to mind our own business is the most considerate thing we can do?

Mind Your Beeswax

Just like queuing, you might assume that this busybody obsession with proper behaviour is a peculiarly British thing. We

* For example, remember the launch of that famous Homeland Security campaign, 'If You See Something, Say Something'. No wonder racial profiling is rife; as well as the ever-present reports of people of colour being stopped and searched by police, they are also constantly under siege by a fellow citizenry primed to see racialisation as threat.

are, after all, the home of the ASBO – an acronym for Anti-Social Behaviour Order, a fixed-penalty notice introduced by Prime Minister Tony Blair in the late 1990s to smack down so-called 'youths' and 'yobbos' for a whole range of antisocial offences, everything from littering to loitering (or, as we used to call it when I was a kid, 'standing whilst poor'). England is also the originator of the phrase 'mind your beeswax' – which according to a popular story comes from the eighteenth century, when women would use beeswax to smooth out their smallpox scars – meaning stop staring at my face and look after your own.* But you'd be wrong. Other languages have the same expression, differently expressed:

- Bulgarian: Всека жаба да си знае гьола (Every frog should know its puddle)
- Spanish: *Zapatero a tus zapatos* (Shoemaker, to your shoes!)
- Swahili: *Pilipili usiyoila yakuwashiani* (Why does the chilli that you're not eating burn you?)
- Chinese: 河水不犯井水 (River water does not interfere with well water)
- Lithuanian: *Ne tavo kiaulės, ne tavo pupos* (Not your pigs, not your beans)
- Arabic: نزل الحمولة عن جحشك (Unload your own donkey)
- Hindi: अपना उल्लू सीधा करना (Make your own owl straight)
- French: *Occupe-toi de tes oignons* (Tend your own onions)

* Actually, the first record of this phrase seems to come from a 1929 children's book, where its usage is just a softening of the word 'business'. But that's not such a good story.

These seem like quite a reasonable reply to some of Nextdoor's most egregious demands. One of the platform's recurring themes sees neighbours going to war over unsightly blemishes, like too-long lawns and shedding trees and unswept leaves and bins put out too early or taken in too late. (After one especially heated exchange, one person posted a message: 'New trash policy SOLVED. When the new bins arrive, put yourself in them.') Another common dispute kicks off when somebody feels the sanctity of their private space has been breached by external influences, like noises or smells or other environmental 'immissions'. Just to illustrate the sheer absurdity of this mode of thinking in extremis: here's my very final Nextdoor example, a letter which went viral after being shared by its disgruntled recipient:

> Dear 'Neighbor',
> You just moved into this neighborhood a year ago, and I wanted to give you the time to correct this problem on your own, but you are apparently too inconsiderate to do so. Every day this week, when weather has been nice and windows are open, you proceed to let your small child run free in your backyard and laugh and giggle and carry on without end.
>
> This is very disruptive for my two dogs and my bird who sits next to the window and like to look into your yard. Perhaps you could ask him to tone it down a bit, or at least limit his outside time to 15 – 20 mins a day so my dogs can be outside without seeing him running around. If this kind of behavior persists, I WILL CALL THE POLICE!

As one of the newspapers that reported on this story commented wryly: 'Seems reasonable.'[17] Or as the Italians might say: *Fa i cazzi tuoi* ('Do your own dicks').

This surveillance-driven battle of spatial entitlement is playing out today throughout the English-speaking world and beyond. *Huffington Post* columnist Natalie Hopkinson wrote about how 'the warm, porch-sitting culture of our D.C. neighborhood, which was shaped by generations of black families' has slowly been replaced with a culture of incomers who 'enter and exit through fortified garages, avoid eye contact and emerge only in odd hours', preferring to complain on the internet rather than actually talking directly to the neighbours who annoy them.[18] An elementary school in the Netherlands was forced to close its playground because children were playing too noisily – just one of many such complaints by people who move in next to play parks then get angry at the families who play in them. And in 2016, the Nigerian government in Abuja shut down ninety churches and mosques due to loud congregations, part of their promise to make Lagos a 'noise-free city' by 2020. In all these examples we can see a bigger social anxiety playing out. This is a tension between concerns about selfish inconsiderate disruptions, and the human desire for fun, play, and experiences of collective joy.

Take the Japanese website DQN Today. Offering a way to crowdsource noise complaints by plotting them on an interactive map of Tokyo, the website saw a huge increase in traffic during the COVID-19 pandemic. In heavily built-up urban areas, noise nuisance is a real problem – it can cause a spree of physiological and psychological conditions. However, there's a world of difference between thumping stereos all night long and the merry gurgle of laughter and chatter from, say, a surprise meeting on the street. But on DQN Today, users can place anonymous pins on the map to report the presence of *any dorozoku* ('road tribe', a word used to describe people who block pathways or otherwise cause a public nuisance), covering everything from couples arguing in homes to people gossiping on the pavements to 'excessive swearing'. The site has particularly been criticised by parents, who 'find its approach troubling and fear a growing divide between families with children and neighbors who cannot stand them'. This fear is clearly warranted, given the developer's statement that the website was originally built to warn prospective home-buyers away from living next to 'stupid parents who let their children play on roads and parking lots'.[19]

These neighbourly disputes can partly be explained by generational differences, with older demographics commonly railing at selfish millennial parents: or Generation Me-Me-Me, as we are often called. Millennials, meanwhile, tend to retort that the selfish generation is actually Boomers, for championing policies that benefited them at the expense of everyone thereafter, and then trying to impose their own out-of-touch ideas on everyone else.* In Japan, for instance, nearly a third of its 125 million

* Again, this is nothing new. There's a famous quote, often attributed to Socrates, which complained that 'children now love luxury; they have bad manners, contempt for authority; they show disrespect for elders and love chatter in place of exercise. Children are now tyrants, not the servants of their households.' Sadly, this quotation was almost certainly just a summary of general complaints about youth by the ancient Greeks, written by a Cambridge University student in 1907. A key source was probably the play *The Clouds*, in which Aristophanes scolded Athenian youth for needing to relearn how 'to be ashamed of what is

citizens are aged over sixty-five. This plus a well-below-replacement birth rate (averaging 1.38 children per woman) means that Japan is a nation with an ageing population – a fact which experts say has created a vicious cycle. Complaints about kids are 'now happening daily', says Masako Maeda, a specialist in childcare policies at Japan's Kōnan University. 'As society has fewer and fewer children, people get less used to hearing them.' In turn, 'fewer children makes people less accustomed to hearing the noise they naturally make, which spawns complaints about them and contributes to the growing feeling among younger parents that they don't want to have more children'.[20]

Japan is now committed to reversing the value system branding children as a noisy nuisance by introducing policies allowing kids to be kids: a policy which seems to be working in countries like Germany, which also has a low birth rate (around 1.6 children per woman), and which in 2011 took a stand, legislating that 'noise from playing children is an expression of child development and blossoming and therefore has to be tolerated'.[21] Tell that to people like the former Concorde pilot – the only passenger plane to produce a sonic boom! – who raised a noise lawsuit against his neighbourhood play park.[22] Parents: get your kids outside! Tackle the scourge of video-game addiction! Let the children play! But never subject anyone else to the sight nor sound of their existence: it's inconsiderate and rude.

---

disgraceful, and [. . .] to rise up from seats before your seniors when they approach, and not to behave ill toward your parents, and to do nothing else that is base, because you are to form in your mind an image of Modesty'. Still, the point stands – intergenerational conflict has been going on for a very long time.

Again, though, that pushback against youth is just a symptom of a much bigger malaise. It speaks to a wider suppression of community pleasure in public space. I'm obviously not talking here about people who blast their music at 3 a.m., or who let their kids scream around the garden at 6 a.m., or who drop litter and destroy beauty without consequence. I'm talking about grassy areas covered in 'do not walk' signs; about cul-de-sacs where children aren't allowed to kick around a ball; about concrete spaces where even the authorised purr-and-grind of skateboards sparks fury – basically, about any kind of physical or sensory intrusion which isn't destructive, illegal, or overly disruptive, yet which still gets branded unreasonable by some people because it has the potential to waft across ~~enemy~~ property lines.

I'm thinking about how, every week or so, a white couple takes to the internet to complain about the predominantly Black and Latino/a communities who populate the neighbourhood they've just moved into, because they are continuing to hold block parties and play dominoes in the street like they've done for generations. I'm thinking about the gradual diminishment of working-class neighbourhoods, with their vanishing parks and libraries and other social spaces which don't require an entry fee; about the corporatisation of carnivals and other festivals; about a generalised shift away from collective life peppered with the delicious waft of home-cooked food and the sounds of chatter and laughter and music, so that walking down the pavement is like being immersed in a tapestry of individual lives all stitched together. About how the relentless encroachment of an individualistic logic of privatisation is eroding playful congregation. About the difficulty of balancing one person's reasonable need for peace and quiet against others' reasonable need to live out loud, and about figuring out when to mind our own business so long as nobody is hurting anybody else. In short, I'm talking about community.

What happened?

Anxious About Anarchy

Throughout most of western history, public life was generally a much livelier affair than it is today. Just look at the history of leisure, which up until the 1800s usually meant getting together to take part in some kind of live event. Prior to this, public spaces for congregation like theatres were generally designed for community intermingling, with people from all social backgrounds gathering together into the same venues (albeit confined to their carefully segregated tiers). Labourers shared experiences with nobility, sombre tragedy and bawdy farce consumed as one.* Outside the regulated walls of the royal court and rich private residences, exuberant unruliness rather than reverent silence was the norm. All around Europe and North America, art was consumed at the same time as other more bodily kinds of consumption, as people ate and drank and smoked and talked and cheered and booed, and those with lots of money preened on the side of the stage, and everyone else threw fruit at performers they didn't like.

But then came the Industrial Revolution and the rise of 'mass society', when people from all over suddenly began flocking

* I examine the implications of the changing 'audience contract' in much more depth in my academic book *The Reasonable Audience: Theatre Etiquette, Behaviour Policing, and the Live Performance Experience* (Palgrave, 2018).

to urban centres of industry. As cities grew larger and more densely packed, those carefully maintained societal hierarchies started to break down. Across the western world, the upper-class white 'elite' began to panic.*

One of the most influential thinkers of the time was an English critic called Matthew Arnold, whose 1869 treatise *Culture and Anarchy* had an extraordinary influence on the anglophone world. Through a kind of megastar cross-Atlantic lecture tour of its day, Arnold warned listeners that these new 'masses' were causing society to dissolve into chaos. But not to worry: Arnold had the answer. Cult*ure* – which he famously defined as 'the best which has been thought or said in the world' – could be used to cult*ivate* people, producing 'a national glow of life and thought' that would spread out from the individuals who experienced it and permeate social life as a whole.[23] By creating cultivated citizens capable of refined restraint, art could prevent the imminent dissolution of civilised life.

Quick sidebar: this was also when that division between cultural forms into 'highbrow' art and 'lowbrow' entertainment was formed. Have you ever wondered where those terms come from? It blew my mind when I discovered that these words originated in phrenology, the racist, classist, pseudoscientific belief that measuring skull dimensions could be used to determine

* I use the term 'elite' in its original sense, here – not to convey some kind of advanced moral fortitude, but rather to describe the tiny group of people who positioned themselves right at the very top of the social hierarchy by hoarding all the wealth and power. I'm not using it in its contemporary 'metropolitan elite' sense, which apparently applies to anyone who occasionally treats themselves to a latte or enjoys a slice of avocado toast.

moral character. Phrenologists believed that the 'high brows' of weak-chinned inbred nobles indicated a more evolved breed of human than many 'low-browed' members of the British and Irish underclass,[24] who at the turn of the nineteenth century were imagined to have closer similarities to African people than to their fellow Europeans.[25] Because they were considered incapable of responding in the right way, those low-browed masses were systematically excluded from the arts through the institution and policing of new behavioural rules. Sit quietly. Clap politely but only in these specific places. Receive the blessings of perfection and be bettered by it, rather than have a fun and sociable time. In order for that moral cultivation to work, Arnold and his contemporaries – like the German composer Richard Wagner – believed that culture must become a space for silent reverie, home to a sea of individuals sat alone in atomised stillness, bathed in the total absorption of art.

This wasn't the first time someone had tried to make shhhhh happen. As public places of leisure, theatres have always been a battlefield for the soul of civic life. All the way back to the ancient Greeks, Plato could be found bemoaning the 'vicious theatocracy' of the populace. Suddenly, people of poor taste had began to 'use their tongues', Plato wrote, to share their likes and dislikes, evidenced by 'the catcalls and uncouth yelling of the audience'. He compared this behaviour unfavourably with a time when '[p]eople of taste and education made it a rule to listen to the performance with silent attention right through to the end; children and their attendants and the general public could always be disciplined and controlled by a stick'.[26] Throughout the following two millennia, influential cultural figures debated back and forth about the dangers of unruly behaviour within public space and how to curtail it – but it wasn't until Matthew Arnold that this vision became a reality. Once indelibly woven into the fabric of social life, a culture of exuberant celebration was replaced by individualising norms demanding respectability, silence and control.

This is why I study audiences: because they're a window into a much bigger societal question. What does it mean to be together? Whether it's online or IRL, understanding what happens when people congregate is a way to take the temperature of shifting social concerns. Throughout history, public acts of engagement have always been a place for anxieties to ferment and eventually erupt into public consciousness. So it was in the 1800s – as Norbert Elias' *Civilising Process* sets out,[27] this was a time when acute societal anxieties were coming to a head; the division of Europe into sovereign states and the increased economic interconnectedness between people were producing unprecedented pressures to become attuned to others over greater distances than ever before. Instead of resulting in an international trade model built on mutual cooperation, Europe's imperial engine was geared towards the global stratification of power and wealth in the hands of a tiny few. In order for this to work, though, the many needed to be convinced that the few were uniquely deserving of that power and that wealth. This is where the civilising process came in.

After all, the theory went, if civilisation was something which came from the cultivation of total self-discipline, and if this trait was unique to rich white European elites, then they were therefore justified in taking dominion over all the other peoples of the world.

Racial Etiquette

When Europe's explorers began landing in earnest on the ancient shores of what they called 'the new world', along with plundered resources they also brought back plentiful stories of what they'd witnessed overseas. 'Everywhere they went – among the hunter-gatherers of Australia, the horticulturalists of Polynesia, the village peoples of India – white men and occasionally women' witnessed 'electrifying rites' of dancing, singing, chanting, waving arms and stamping feet, joyful vignettes of bodies illuminated by '[t]he smoke, the blazing torches, the shower of sparks falling in all directions' – all coming together, as one pair of explorers breathlessly exclaimed, to form 'a genuinely wild and savage scene of which it is impossible to convey any adequate idea in words'.

The colonisers were not impressed by such vibrant scenes. In fact, they were horrified. These accounts and more are collected within Barbara Ehrenreich's history of collective joy, *Dancing in the Streets*,[28] in which she explains how, on the whole, 'white observers regarded the ecstatic rituals of darker-skinned peoples with horror and revulsion. *Grotesque* is one word that appears again and again in European accounts of such events; *hideous* is another.' Charles Darwin, witnessing the corroboree rite of Western Australia, was prompted to call these rituals 'a most rude, barbarous scene', featuring men and especially women – this time in the words of Captain Cook on visiting Tahiti – 'singing the most indecent songs and using most indecent actions', permeated throughout by what nineteenth-century Swiss missionary Henri-Alexandre Junod in southern

Mozambique called the 'frightful din' and 'infernal racket' of traditional drumming and chanting and song.[29]

To European eyes, Ehrenreich explains, there was only one possible conclusion. 'Since these strange behaviors could be found in "primitive" cultures almost everywhere, and since they were never indulged in by the "civilised", it follows that they must result from some fundamental defect of the "savage mind"' – a mind that colonial elites believed to be malleable like plastic, childlike, and incapable of logic. After all, social and political theorists of the time gravely agreed, any body which allowed itself to be brought to ecstasy (or *ecstasis*, literally meaning 'outside the self') by loud, energetic, communal acts of public joy must be led by a brain that was similarly uncontrolled, 'lacking the discipline and restraint that Europeans of the seventeenth century and beyond came to see as their own defining characteristics'.[30]

And that's how the imagined 'reasonable person' became the stick Europe used to beat the rest of the world into submission. Their colonising ideology rested on the belief that being truly civilised meant achieving total mental and physical discipline: the rational mind subduing the animal body. That meant that all the people around the world – both abroad and those at home – who engaged in irrational and undisciplined cultural practices could be labelled 'primitive savages' in comparison.

Percolating throughout the white imagination, we can see how that constructed figure of the uncivilised native provided exactly the rallying cry that powerful elites needed to legitimise their imperial project. With the bogeyman of ecstatic dancing bodies firmly in mind, Europe began to unleash earth-shattering brutality on a scale never before imagined whilst paradoxically claiming their own imperial savagery as a civilised moral imperative. This is what the most-beloved children's author Rudyard Kipling, in an 1899 poem, solemnly called 'The White Man's Burden'. In breathtakingly racist doggerel, Kipling urged the USA to take up the duty of empire just like Europe before them, and selflessly use the Philippine–American War to seize colonial control from the Filipino people. All around the world, the moralising agenda of colonialism was intertwined with the missionary zeal of Christianity, with its malevolent rhetoric of benevolent self-improvement.

This is why Norbert Elias called his model the *civilising* process. Entering into French and English usage in the 1760s as a noun, 'civilisation' was seen as being synonymous with Europe, and crystallised the idea within the ruling class that they personally just happened to be naturally superior to everyone else in the world.[31] Previously seen as a way to cultivate moral emotions through the polishing of behaviour, manners were now becoming all about appearances: a way to legitimise rather than resist immoral actions. In India, for example, the British imperialists set up a range of associations, like debating clubs, in which local people's 'appearance and behaviour, from modes of dress to rituals of conversation and dining, were regulated by informal but tangible protocols'.[32] In Taiwan, the Japanese subjugation of local tribes was spurred on by a 'constellation of images of deficiency, nakedness, and infantilism' used to justify the need to retrain Taiwanese people in formalised Japanese behavioural customs: a colonial discourse called *dōka*, or 'living as Japanese', that emerged in the 1920s advocating equality and fraternity through assimilation.[33] And in African nations like Zimbabwe, 'manners' for Black residents now meant being forced to enact performances of diminished status: things like stepping aside in the street, doffing hats, and sitting on the floor of officials' offices. Around the globe, the aim of this kind of 'racial etiquette' was to humiliate colonised people into becoming the deferential subjects of their oppressors.[34]

Racial etiquette* was also an important tool for regulating the behaviour of Black people within North America and Europe. Looking at Southern USA plantation society, Clarence R. Talley and Theresa Rajack-Talley describe the emergence of an elaborate set of rules 'developed to regulate race relations during slavery'.[35] In 1936, Bertram W. Doyle called this period '[t]he Golden Age of etiquette in race relations'. The extreme politeness of enslaved people was 'remarked by more than one traveller and generally attributed to innate disposition,' Doyle writes,[36] before going on to give an incredibly detailed account of the violently enforced rules of behaviour (in the street, at church, on buses) that produced this behaviour – to the extent that 'it would seem accurate to state that [. . .] [t]here was a code of etiquette in slavery that covered practically the whole of relations existing between persons of the white and Negro groups'.[37] This code was then carried forwards after emancipation into the laws of Jim Crow: Black people were '(i) never to assert or even intimate that a white person may be lying; (ii) never impute dishonorable

* In the book *Jim Crow's Legacy: The Lasting Impact of Segregation* (Rowman & Littlefield, 2014) by Joe Feagin, Leslie Houts Picca, and Ruth Thompson-Miller, the authors argue for using the term 'racial social control' instead of 'racial etiquette' – because '[t]he word etiquette is too tame and implies that there is an interactive agreement, even some equal status' when the reality was that these rule systems were always about constructing and maintaining extreme hierarchies between first- and second-class citizens (p. 8).

intentions to a white person; (iii) never suggest that the white is of an inferior class; (iv) never lay claim to, or overly demonstrate, superior knowledge or intelligence', and so on.[38] In his 1937 autobiography of living under Jim Crow, Richard Wright describes the psychological impact of these 'hidden transcripts' on the people who suffered under them:

> There were many times when I had to exercise a great deal of ingenuity to keep out of trouble. It is a southern custom that all men must take off their hats when they enter an elevator. And especially did this apply to us blacks with rigid force. One day I stepped into an elevator with my arms full of packages. I was forced to ride with my hat on. Two white men stared at me coldly. Then one of them very kindly lifted my hat and placed it upon my armful of packages. Now the most accepted response for a Negro to make under such circumstances is to look at the white man out of the corner of his eye and grin. To have said: 'Thank you!' would have made the white man think that you thought you were receiving from him a personal service. For such an act I have seen Negroes take a blow in the mouth. Finding the first alternative distasteful, and the second dangerous, I hit upon an acceptable course of action which fell safely between these two poles. I immediately – no sooner than my hat was lifted – pretended that my packages were about to spill, and appeared deeply distressed with keeping them in my arms. In this fashion I evaded having to acknowledge his service, and, in spite of adverse circumstances, salvaged a slender shred of personal pride.[39]

All around the world, the rhetoric of manners and propriety became a way for the oppressing social class to weaponise their power over everyone else.* The 'undeserving poor' at home were also hit by these moralising agendas. '[W]hen we have so many people sunk in the lowest depths of barbarism round about our very homes,' one Victorian journalist wrote of London's street-selling communities in the 1840s, 'our many [efforts] for the civilization of savages on the other side of the globe appear like a "delusion, a mockery, and a snare"'.[40]

As one way to fix this, the ecstatic abandon of European carnivals faced the ire of a determined pamphlet campaign. One 'converted Hindu' confided that the German Fastnacht celebrations reminded him of 'the idolatrous feasts and dances of my fellow-countrymen'; a visitor to rural Burgundy remarked that he 'didn't need to go [abroad] to see savages'; and an imaginary 'Hottentot' had an imaginary conversation

* Wright's moving testimony shows how grossly hypocritical this was, given that the people being colonised often had deep cultural traditions of dignity and collective respect which the imperialists refused to recognise as civility. 'Precisely because whites taught deference and etiquette as a foundation of civilization,' historian Allison Kim Shutt explains, oppressed communities 'could attack racial etiquette as out of step with whites' ostensible efforts to civilize [them] – there was a yawning gap between what whites said they believed and what they did' (*Manners Make a Nation: Racial Etiquette in Southern Rhodesia, 1910–1963* [Boydell & Brewer, 2015]: p. 2). This hypocrisy became the cornerstone of a number of anti-colonial campaigns: like in the Federation of Rhodesia and Nyasaland (1953–63), where – as educated young nationalists began to take over from their respectable middle-class parents – '[t]he wide divide between the rhetoric of a polite society and the reality of rude, disagreeable, ill-tempered, and violent whites infused the politics' of their movement (p. 13).

with an imaginary Christian about the barbarity of white heathens' rituals.[41] Reformers pushed for the peasantry to be offered educational fairs and classical music concerts – at least until the traditional festivals could be heavily policed, and turned into a way to safely amuse and thereby politically neutralise the poor.[42] In 1906, a New York physician founded the Society for the Suppression of Unnecessary Noise to bring quiet to Mahattan's streets, with attempts to ban street vendors' bells evolving into harsh crackdowns on boom-boxes as the twentieth century unfolded. Another mechanism for social control was civic prizes, which were introduced across the twentieth century to shame poverty-stricken communities into maintaining neat, clean, well-kept homes and gardens.[43] From dressing suitably to scrubbing doorsteps to obliterating 'untidy' wildflower lawns in favour of sterile grass that could be measured with a ruler: regulating outward appearances was widely believed to produce good moral character.

The ultimate aim of this 'civilisation offensive' was, paradoxically, to destroy civilisation in its oldest and truest form – by which I mean, the civic impulse to look after our fellow citizens. The 'abundant street life' of working-class communities 'where neighbouring mothers had coffee in front of their homes and a great number of children played in the street' was all but destroyed.[44] No more of that 'it takes a village' nonsense! Instead of watching out for each other, the new norm was to watch in order to judge. Neighbourhood associations popped up to standardise the colour of everyone's front doors, while neighbourhood watches began roaming the streets distrustfully looking for strangers to police – but all this left less and less room for genuinely neighbourly behaviours like mutual aid and communal childcare. Instead, families were simply told to stop letting their kids play in the 'gutter',[45] and were generally chastened into living their lives inside alone. This is what I mean when I call it 'malevolent benevolence'. Even those social reformers driven by a genuinely earnest desire to help the working poor have often risked doing more harm than good overall. Demonised, dehumanised, and often legally deemed by the state to hold the same status as children, people everywhere from Indonesia to Ireland were considered incapable of looking after themselves, and therefore in need of the guiding hand of the civilised elite.

And who was this magical civilising figure? Mr Reasonable, of course – our man on the Clapham Omnibus, with his business suit and his newspaper and his stiff upper lip, the very model of moderate restraint. Sent overseas from the 1800s in droves of civil servants, his rationally superior mind, refined masculine body, and love of genteel pursuits – like cricket, or murdering fluffy and feathered animals in cold blood – were all seen to exemplify the 'moral fibre' of a quintessential gentleman, uniquely endowing him with the fitness to rule.[46]

Private Bubbles of Reserve

Today, the frenzy of overt imperial expansion may have abated. But in the Nextdoor commentary I see deafening echoes of that same old fitness to rule.

A reasonable person is one who believes fervently in their own innate ability to contain their natural urges through a rigid performance of respectability. Their mind is always rational, never inflamed by passions.* Their body is refined, honed, and kept firmly in check. Because they are singularly able to resist the State of Nature within every aspect of life (bring out the leaf blowers!), they alone are fit to set the rules of mutual coexistence, and to ensure that *their* community – for it is always theirs to command – remains neatly ordered and tightly controlled. Working-class people, disabled people, people of colour, women, fat people, pregnant people, queer people, children, and every combination thereof – these are just some of the people who have historically been seen as undisciplined, possessed of hysterical minds and unstable emotions and unruly bodies. These are the people who have been systematically assimilated, excluded, or else violently eliminated from the newly civilised and 'respectable' public sphere.

As Chapter Five explains, public space has always been right at the heart of the struggle for power. Anyone who's ever pushed a pram will have experienced a new depth of understanding about what disabled people have been saying for decades, which is that the lived environment is systemically hostile to

* The exception to this, of course, is that most manly of emotions: rage. In his 1615 work *Mikrokosmographia*, Helkiah Crooke wrote: 'Anger and Wrath are two distinct things. Anger is a disease of a weake mind which cannot moderate it selfe but is easily inflamed, such are women, childeren, and weake and cowardly men.' However, 'Wrath which is *ira permanens* ("permanent anger") belongs to stout heartes.' Watching Brett Kavanaugh's epic meltdown during the Christine Blasey Ford hearings, as he shouted and ranted and cried and was then approved to the Supreme Court anyway, I understood once and for all that the biggest trick the devil ever played was to rebrand in the popular imagination the hissy fits of powerful white men as a display of righteous masculine strength.

people who rely on wheels to get around. Anyone who appears in public as a woman may have found themselves playing the occasional game of Patriarchy Chicken,[47] which is when you walk down the pavement and refuse to demurely swerve out of the way of – then inevitably collide with – men coming in the opposite direction. See also: Racism Chicken, which is the same kind of thing, but when people of colour stand firm as white people barrel into them. Any kid who wears a hoodie then commits the crime of standing still in public risks being hit with a fine for loitering (or something much worse, if they don't happen to be white), while when the middle-class parents outside schools do it, it's called socialising.

These things are all connected, like the branches of a blasted rotting tree, and at its root is the vast global system that was spread around the world through colonialism: what we might – following the foundational Black feminist writer bell hooks – call something like imperial white-supremacist, cis-heteronormative, ableist, classist, fatphobic, capitalist patriarchy. In a revealing book called *Sidewalks*, Anastasia Loukaitou-Sideris and Renia Ehrenfeucht explain how, by the nineteenth century, the Reasonable Man had succeeded in spreading his polite-society imperative to the world's streets. Isolating themselves from the 'sidewalk culture' of working-class pedlars, the white middle class – but especially white middle-class women – were expected to uphold rigid separations. When they did need to travel, they needed to always keep themselves apart from the masses by 'mov[ing] within a private bubble of reserve'.[48]

Private bubbles of reserve is a fantastic description for what we're seeing today. Nextdoor is emblematic of that kind of white-picket-fence mentality: one that was solidified by the White Flight of the 1950s into new suburban housing, and which is perpetuated today by the relentless gentrification of working-class communities, by the replacement of public transport with Ubers, by the loss of third places in which to congregate and play, and by the general diminishment of neighbourly conversations in favour of anonymous rants on social media.

This process is harming some of us more than others, of course, by exacerbating existing social divides, but make no mistake: this *is* harming all of us. Researchers have long studied the detrimental effects on community cohesion of the destruction of social rituals. In fact, when Europeans in the twentieth century began to take a closer look at those rites of firelight and dancing that had so horrified their forefathers, they found more to praise than to shame. These experiences of joyous physical abandonment, and the sense of 'collective effervescence' they produce, are, in fact, an essential social glue, bringing people of varying status and generational backgrounds together and strengthening mutual bonds.

Collective effervescence has always found a way of bubbling up through the cracks of white elite supremacy. Reclaiming public space for exuberant congregation has historically been a powerful act of resistance. In African nations like Zimbabwe (then Rhodesia), for example, the colonisers found public space extremely frustrating to police. 'Having suppressed Africans with their military might, whites believed Africans would act the part of the deferential subjects and withdraw into the background of the colony except when their labor was necessary to whites' survival and prosperity,' writes the historian Allison Kim Schutt. But '[m]uch to their dismay, Africans remained visible and, to whites, noisy and dangerous. In particular, whites in the urban areas complained endlessly about Africans invading spaces they considered theirs alone to use.'[49] In a very Nextdoor-esque letter, a commentator wrote to the *Rhodesian Opinion* newspaper in 1908 to complain about how, in Salisbury City Gardens, locals would 'loll and lounge about on seats which should be devoted to the exclusive use of whites; they tear through the park gates at breakneck speeds on bicycles, to the imminent danger of little children. They camp out there at night and make night hideous with their shouts and paraffin-tin music, and, in fact, it appears that the Gardens are run for the benefit and enjoyment of the Kaffirs.'[50]

Mind your beeswax, indeed. Or, as they say in Persian: *Âsh-e khodet râ ham bezan* ('Stir your own soup').

In my work observing audiences, I began to see these eruptions of collective effervescence happening a lot – along with the predictable backlash. I saw signs being thrown up at shows like *Motown: The Musical* telling audiences that it's 'dancing in the streets, not in your seats', so please 'moderate your enthusiasm'. I sat through the pomp and circumstance of countless graduations, and saw certain spectators look horrified when people celebrated their offspring too loudly – then I heard about the instances of Black graduands' families facing criminal charges in the USA for 'disrupting the peace', and the consequent trend of 'cultural graduations', a protected space in which Black and Global Majority students are invited to dance down the aisles to the vigorous sound of drumbeats and music. I watched a viral video of white working-class people celebrating happily in their own back yards, and saw white middle-class commentators sneering about the uncouthness of 'football yobs'. Back in the theatre, I heard people tell off their fellow spectators for failing to adhere to codes of silent reverence – 'this is our church!' – and then I read a foundational book by Geneva Smitherman called *Talkin and Testifyin* about Black churchgoing norms of jubilant movement and vocal call-and-response,[51] as well as writing by the award-winning African American playwright, Dominique Morisseau, who also wants theatre to be like church – by which she means a more 'buoyant' experience, where people are welcome to '[h]oot and holler or sit quietly in reverence. Worship and engage however you do.'[52] I heard about a friend's sister, who – sitting at home by herself at three in the afternoon! – had the police called on her by a neighbour for cheering too loudly while watching the Olympics. And I read endless laments about the bad manners of those bringing the joyful liveliness of street culture back to daily life.

There's a fine line between nourishing noise and dangerous nuisance, jubilant tumult and destructive mess. But with public spaces increasingly subject to the private logics of the commercial marketplace, and private spaces increasingly regulated and surveilled, that line has cracked open to reveal an aching rift at the centre of our social world. Those norms of repression, order, and restraint that were so integral to the civilising process have proven to be the perfect breeding ground for atomised isolation. Increasingly disconnected from our environment, our neighbours, even our own bodies, a whole mode of collective existence is getting lost. What we're seeing today is a culture of hermetically sealed individualism, driven by spiralling anxieties around increased heterogeneity and an imagined need to protect the fabric of society from anarchic threat.

Nowhere is this worry more evident than in the media backlash against prolific and mass protest movements, which we've seen recently re-erupting around the world.

5

Where We're Going We Don't Need Rhodes

A police car on fire throws out a surprising amount of heat.

It's March 2021, a warm weekday night just before my birthday, and I'm standing on a side street in Bristol watching flames lick through a police car's white-blue-and-yellow shell. Molten plastic drips from the open boot and puddles gold on the road just a few metres from my shoes. Its lights are already burned to stumps, but behind, through a haze of smoke and flame, I can see the blue illuminations from other emergency vehicles, flashing dreamily.

A few minutes earlier I'd been at home. I put the kids to bed, quickly checked the news, then cycled back down here: winding around the waterfront where lights dance on the harbour, nearly colliding with a couple of lads wandering down the bike lane blasting 'Linger' by The Cranberries (oh Bristol, never change). Through the city centre. Past the empty plinth where the slave trader Edward Colston's statue used to be, then turning a corner and finding myself confronted by a line of police in full riot gear – silent and watchful, barricading off the road, a throng of dancing protesters reflected in their shields. Helicopters thrum overhead: circling over the restless city, over the quiet harbour, over my small boys in their beds, over the abandoned cop car sitting empty and burning. Maybe it's my imagination but, standing this close, the fire seems so much fiercer than the big Halloween bonfires we had when I was a kid. But then when I was a kid I never dreamed I'd be involved in something like this. I was the child who got gold stars for handing in the pennies I found in the playground. I was the one who confessed every bad thought I'd had that year in my letters to Santa. I was the anxious little ginger girl whom authority figures tended to like, because I worked so hard to be liked by them. I was a nerd.

Thirty-odd years later, I'm still anxious and ginger and now a professional nerd, but what's long gone is that naive belief that breaking the rules is always a bad thing to do. I'm no longer able to take it on faith that those who set the rules are acting in the best interests of everyone else. Let's be honest: that comforting fallacy was only ever possible because I was an able-bodied white girl from a middle-class home. That's no excuse at all, given that I could have understood all this a whole lot sooner if only I'd listened properly to any of the storybooks I was obsessed with back then. Children's authors generally are pretty good at exposing the absurdities of the adult world, with its incomprehensible rules driven by greed, corruption, and incompetence. Like my childhood hero Matilda, in the face of injustice, sometimes being naughty is the only moral choice.

This is, of course, just an infantile version of the things that oppressed people have been saying forever. Where laws are unjust, preached Rev. Martin Luther King Jr., the only moral course of action is to disobey them.[1] 'Civil rights are not given,' agreed Anita Cameron, a disabled activist who took part in the Capitol Crawl in the 1990s, just one of the 139 times she had already been arrested for fighting disability discrimination. 'You must fight to get them, then fight to keep them.'[2]

'History isn't something you look back at and say it was inevitable, it happens because people make decisions,' said Marsha P. Johnson, a trans woman who was central to the 1960s US LGBTQ+ rights movement: sometimes, under certain circumstances, 'picking up the gun, starting a revolution if necessary' can be the only way to bring about equality.[3] Progress only happens when people refuse to contort and diminish themselves to fit into a world that is actively working to destroy them. In pursuit of a fairer world, sometimes it's right to be unreasonable.

But watching that police car burn, I find myself wondering . . . how do we know when we've taken things too far? Suddenly, Bristol had offered up a prime example of the riddle at the heart of this book. In a world riven with injustice, what can we reasonably do to fight it? In pursuit of a better world, when is it okay to break the rules – and who gets to decide?

To Collect in Mobs

Having dragged my family halfway across the nation for a new job, I found myself in 2016 living in England's unofficial city of protest. Right on the edge of the River Avon estuary, tucked into the crook of the elbow where England meets Wales, Bristol today is the largest city in the South West. A prosperous maritime hub built on tobacco and sugar trading, its wealth produced through centuries of enslavement, Bristol was found in 2017 to be one of the most diverse cities but also the most divided, with Black and Global Majority citizens experiencing greater levels of economic disadvantage and physical segregation than any other core city in the UK.[4] It's also a relatively small city in terms of its square mileage, which means that the superlatively wealthy bits up on the hill like posh Clifton Village are just a stone's throw away from generationally working-class areas like St Paul's and Hotwells down below.

This close proximity is one of the reasons that Bristol has always been a notorious lightning rod for public disobedience. In 1794, after the Bristol Bridge Riots the previous year ended in one of the worst public massacres that century, the populace of Bristol were said to be 'apt to collect in mobs on the slightest occasions'.[5] Since then, we've done our best to keep that reputation going. Like in 1831, when a local magistrate threatened to imprison people agitating over their lack of voting rights, then had to escape in disguise by clambering over the rooftops chased by a horde of young men. Or like in 1932, when the government cut unemployment benefits and around four thousand protesters tried to march peacefully down to the centre, but, met with heavy police resistance, started a brawl instead. Or like in the 1980s, when heavy-handed police treatment of Black residents alongside raids on local businesses led to a string of uprisings in St Paul's. Historically speaking, as a city, we haven't responded well to authorities (whether metaphorically or literally) hitting us in the face then telling us not to fight back. In just the past few years alone Bristol has marched in support of the Black Lives Matter movement, to seek meaningful government action on climate breakdown, for the liberation of trans people, against the gross mismanagement of Britain's universities – and now we're here again, on a warm spring evening surrounded by placards and banners, except this time it's slightly different. This is more of a meta-protest, really. Because what we're protesting is for the right to protest itself.

A couple of weeks before, on the evening of 3 March 2021, a thirty-three-year-old woman called Sarah Everard went missing from London's Brixton Hill. Around 9 p.m. that evening she left her friend's house and walked either around or across Clapham Common, talking to her boyfriend on her mobile. At 21.28 she was seen on doorbell camera footage; at 21.32, she was captured on the dashcam of a passing police car; then again, at 21.35, on CCTV footage from a passing bus. Then she disappeared. The next day, when Everard didn't meet him as planned, her boyfriend called the police. On 9 March, the nation was horrified to hear that a Metropolitan police officer called Wayne Couzens had been arrested for her kidnapping. One day later, a week after she went missing, her remains were found in a wood in another part of the country; two days after that, the charge against Couzens was amended to add rape and murder; and then the very next day, at Clapham Common, a night-time vigil for Everard ended with police trampling the flowers left by mourning bystanders and manhandling peaceful individuals into the mud. The photos were splashed across the papers: more young women being arrested by Metropolitan officers, held down and handcuffed staring defiantly into the camera, all for the supposed crime of grieving together publicly in the time of COVID. These photos were featured next to haunting images of Everard wearing a smile of heartbreaking innocence, her life soon to be ended by a man on that very same force.

But that's not where this story begins. A year earlier, in May 2020, just a couple of months into the pandemic, a forty-six-year-old Black man called George Floyd was murdered in broad daylight in Minneapolis by a white police officer. Derek

Chauvin was later sentenced to twenty-two and a half years for murder, after kneeling on Floyd's neck for nine minutes and twenty-nine seconds in front of pleading bystanders during a stop-and-search. Protests seeking urgent police reform began in the USA the next day, soon followed by demonstrations in more than sixty other countries on all seven continents. Bristol was no exception. On Saturday 7 June, a large crowd of citizens gathered on College Green before spilling out across the city and marching through the city centre, famously stopping along the way to drag the bronze statue of Edward Colston off his pedestal and to throw him into the harbour.

This act was a long time coming, inspired by similar calls around the world to de-memorialise enslavers and other historic white supremacists: from the Rhodes Must Fall movement that began in 2015 at the University of Cape Town to the dismounting of Confederate generals in the USA. A year after its fall, in a decision that caused international controversy, Colston's statue was placed within a local museum for public viewing. Featured disgraced and defaced, the statue lay on its back, marble plinth replaced with an undignified plywood pillow, peering dolefully up at the ceiling through a crimson glaze of paint.

What happened in the ten months between Colston's watery burial and that police car being set on fire? Over that uneasy year, all around the world, governments galvanised by the encroaching threat of mass resistance found a new weapon in their anti-protest arsenal. They began using emergency pandemic restrictions to crack down on the right of oppressed people to fight their oppression. Pro-democracy protests in Eswatini (previously Swaziland) led to the king calling protesters 'satanic' and enforcing a ban on marches,[6] while in Thailand a student-led movement saw citizens defying Prime Minister Prayuth Chan-ocha's similar prohibition by taking to the streets of Bangkok to protest hyper-royalism and the nation's massive monarchist military.[7] In Hong Kong, determined to stamp down once and for all on the uprisings that began back in 2019, seven thousand police officers were brought in to enforce a ban on the annual vigil that usually takes place on the anniversary of the Tiananmen Square massacre.[8] And within the USA, it was the widespread demonstrations that erupted following George Floyd's murder which sparked fresh attempts to silence public dissent.

As calls to 'defund the police' echoed across the globe, the news filled night after night with images of an old world order under attack: stores getting raided, glass being smashed, police stations either barricaded in or set on fire, Confederate statues cut up or torn down, all surrounded by violent clashes between protesters and police. The newspapers reported that President Trump had to be talked out of his plan to invoke the Insurrection Act and deploy the full might of the military against his own civilians. 'When the looting starts, the shooting starts,' his Twitter account blared, in a tweet swiftly deleted but never forgotten.[9] Just 'beat the fuck' out of protesters, he reportedly told his advisors, 'crack their skulls'.[10]

Meanwhile, in the UK, the government's response was to back a suite of new laws that would permanently change how acts of protest are policed. Since Colston fell the year before, generational tensions had come to a head – both within the city and beyond. When his bronze shape splashed into Bristol harbour it sent ripple effects around the nation, exposing fundamental divisions between those who believed that bringing him down was democracy in its purest form, and those who saw it as an undemocratic assault by a mob of hooligans who needed to be brought under control. Under the 2022 Police, Crime, Sentencing and Courts (PCSC) Act any kind of peaceful assembly could potentially be deemed a 'public nuisance', with participants at risk of arrest whether or not they knowingly breach police-imposed conditions, and with protesters who damage monuments or topple statues facing punishment of up to ten years in prison.[11] The goal, said Home Secretary Priti Patel, was to allow police to crack down on the small minority who gleefully use protests as cover for theft and property destruction. If you're protesting peacefully, you've nothing to fear!

Which sounds reasonable enough on the face of it. But scratch the surface just a little and the proposals were deeply troubling. After all, police have always been able to step in to stop any activities as soon as they become illegal – property damage, trespassing, violence. What this Bill actually seemed intended to do was to change the meaning of peaceful protest itself: by giving police legal justification to shut down protests whenever *they* decide a demonstration has gone too far. One passer-by complains that a peaceful gathering is making an unreasonable level of noise? Shut the whole thing down. Oil exec wants the people outside to stop telling everyone his company has just set the ocean on fire? Protesters get arrested. And even worse: with this Bill, the government gave itself the power to change the meaning of the law unilaterally at any time by redefining 'disruption' and 'distress' to suit themselves. Astonishingly, when the Bill was debated in parliament, one of the people who spoke up against it was the Conservative ex-prime minister Theresa May. It's tempting to think that 'giving powers to the Home Secretary is very reasonable because we all think we're reasonable,' said May, 'but actually future Home Secretaries may not be so reasonable.'[12]

This brings us back to that warm Bristol evening, where 'Kill the Bill' protests are aiming to draw global attention to the danger of giving governments unlimited powers to shut down any demonstrations they don't like. It all started peacefully enough: protesters have spent Saturday afternoon on College Green, a grassy puddle in front of Bristol's famous cathedral, before marching through the city to the central police station. The mood throughout has been pretty relaxed. Some people have been drawn here in horror at the institutional cruelty shown by the London Met officers who shut down Sarah Everard's vigil – I hear plenty of people saying things like 'When police trampled those flowers, something inside me broke.' For others, this violent overreaction just reaffirmed what historically marginalised communities have been saying all along, which is that the police exist to protect the interests of the powerful, not the people, and if you weren't broken long ago by watching officers trampling on *actual human beings* then you haven't been paying attention. Either way, what unites the crowd today is a shared understanding that civic protest is the bedrock of democracy, not an attack on it: an inalienable right that must never be chipped away.

Night changes everything. With the mood getting rowdier, and seemingly realising that protesters aren't planning on dispersing any time soon, the police change tactics, abruptly deploying riot officers, a police drone unit, dogs, and horses; while on the protesters' side, fireworks and paint get thrown, the windows of the police station end up shattered, and not one but two police vehicles are set aflame.* By the time I get back to the action from tucking in my kids, the damage has been done.

The following morning, in the sickly light of day, the entire gathering will be condemned by the mayor of Bristol, the government, the majority of both the right-wing and liberal press, and of course the police themselves, who will claim (incorrectly) that their officers sustained broken bones and a punctured lung. This, the Conservatives say, is precisely why a new set of laws is needed in the first place. Meanwhile, protesters say that this is precisely why those laws are so dangerous – because when you cut off options for peaceful protest, violence becomes the only recourse.

Crossing a Line

It's not protest itself that's the problem but *how* you're protesting.

What if I were to, say, break into the offices of a billion-dollar conglomerate engaged in immoral business practices in order to expose them to the world? Then you'd be a criminal who

* For anyone who may be wondering, my phrasing here is deliberate. It's the exact inverse of the way these things are commonly reported. Protesters injure police officer. Protesters injured by bullet. Active voice for civilians, who fight and destroy and attack; passive voice for the police, whose weaponry is seemingly capable of breaking loose from its holder and wreaking havoc all by itself.

deserves to go to jail. How about if I barricade the road and hold up traffic? That would inconvenience innocent bystanders and damage your cause. How about if I simply withdraw my labour? A strike would inconvenience people and damage your cause. Okay, I'll just quietly chain myself to a railing then. That's empty virtue-signalling – it won't change anything.

Is there any legitimate way to protest at all?

In 2016, in a blistering interview, *The Daily Show* host Trevor Noah asks Republican commentator Tomi Lahren that very question. Talking about Colin Kaepernick famously taking a knee during American football games, Lahren expresses the opinion that the players who refused to stand for the National Anthem went about expressing grievances in the wrong way. Noah interrupts. What is the right way to protest, he asks? He walks Lahren through an example. Imagine you're a Black man in the USA, whose community has been proven to be disproportionately at risk of extreme state violence, but who can't work out a legitimate way to make people care. If you march in the streets, then people call you a thug. If you join a protest, then people call it a riot. If you bend down quietly on one knee, people tell you that's the wrong way to get attention. So what would the 'right way' look like?

Over an excruciating few minutes, they go back and forth – Lahren repeating her talking points that to disrespect the anthem, the flag, and the nation's servicemen by kneeling down is the wrong way to address injustice, while Noah asks her again and again, what's the right way? *How* should people protest? How would *you* protest? – until Lahren finally snaps and replies that she doesn't protest, because she is not a victim.[13]

For some people, apparently, it's not *how* you protest that's the problem. It's the act of pointing out any kind of societal disadvantage at all.

In 2020, more than half of Americans polled said they thought that kneeling during the national anthem was never an appropriate thing to do.[14] 'It's just gesture politics!' some pundits said. By that logic, other actions have merely been gesture politics, too: like when French revolutionaries stormed the Bastille in 1789. As a symbol of royal tyranny, its fall was the flashpoint of the revolution, but by that point the prison only housed seven inmates and officials had recently announced the decision to pull it down. Pure protest theatre.

'I don't oppose statements of anti-oppression,' others complained, 'but I don't support taking a knee. That gesture is too divisive. If we could all get the chance to vote on a more palatable symbol, it would be easier for us to sympathise!' In 1961, a Gallup poll found that 61 per cent of Americans disapproved of the Freedom Riders, an activist movement seeking to test an earlier Supreme Court ruling that segregation of transport facilities was unconstitutional. Fifty-seven per cent thought diner sit-ins and 'other demonstrations' were hurting the cause.[15]

The point is that no expression against oppression has ever been seen as universally acceptable. 'We Will Not Go Back!' declared pro-choice picket signs in 2022, when the historic abortion ruling *Roe v. Wade* began to fall. 'People Will Die Because of This Decision'. But while right-wingers threw tantrums about 'bullying' and 'incivility', and while President Biden equivocatingly asked for 'people's privacy to be respected', protesters pointed out the irony. The really appalling invasion of privacy wasn't standing noisily on a public street. It was the attempt to overturn citizens' constitutional right to privacy that had guaranteed access to abortion for fifty years.[16] Similarly, whether it's throwing soup over paintings, interrupting cricket matches and flower shows, draping a politician's empty home in fabric, or infiltrating the stage during *Les Misérables*, climate activists have got people calling for the death penalty in response to the most harmless of acts. Obsessing over *how* people protest is just another way of refusing to deal with *what* is being protested, by endlessly moving the goalposts and postponing actual change.

Civil disobedience is where the language of boundary-drawing is at its most powerful. Things have *gone too far*. I support their right to fight societal problems, *but not like that*. They have *crossed a line*. What separates a march from a riot? A concerned citizen from a careless thug? A democratic collective from a mob of yobs? An acceptable level of civic disruption from an intolerable inconvenience? Yet again, the answer depends both on who is doing the looking and whom they are looking at.

After the police car incident, I do what I always do. I examine how people are talking about it. What I find is a predictable chain reaction – the same discursive manoeuvres we've seen time and time again. First of all, an act of gross injustice takes place. This exposes the broken system that allowed it to happen. A group of concerned citizens respond by organising in pursuit of structural change – if the entire edifice of justice is rotting from the ground up, surely the only reasonable thing to do is to tear it down and start again? Instead of meaningful systemic reform, though, protesters are offered small gestures and empty words: a police officer arrested here, a governor resigning there.

Knowing this won't fix the underlying rot, generations' worth of righteous anger bubbles up, froths over, and spills into action – over the annals of history, guillotines have been sharpened, monuments destroyed, buildings burned to the ground. No justice! No peace! But power rallies to protect power: so the final move in this vicious cycle is for police officials and government figures and prominent media commentators to come together to mount a concerted propaganda campaign. Look at all these people refusing to act peacefully! Why can't they seek justice through the proper channels? They're beyond reason, a baying mob, with no respect for the law. The system doesn't need to be reformed – in fact, the system is working to protect *you* from *them*!

But what about when the proper channels have been blocked for generations? If the law has generally been used to harm you, not help you? If you've asked nicely and made petitions and done everything right for decades, and still nothing's changed? If the world is literally burning, the ice caps melting, loved ones dying, and the people responsible for it all are sitting in an office right over our heads, breaking much more catastrophic laws and getting away with it with impunity? What's the reasonable thing to do in circumstances like these?

Obedience to the Law

On some level I can't believe we're still having this debate. Especially given the very large number of very smart people who've explained why – throughout history – direct action has often been a necessary weapon in the fight for justice, how are we still going back and forth about the merits of breaking broken rules? Yet on the other hand it's unsurprising. After all, the connection between justice and the law has been a perennial problem plaguing moral philosophers, going back at least as far as Socrates – who even disagreed with himself.

Remember when Socrates was visited in prison by a student who wanted him to escape? Socrates used an early version of social contract theory to argue that the right thing for him to do was to abide by the laws of the city, even if that meant dying a horrible (and horribly unfair) death. Well, in Plato's other writings Socrates argued that it's actually *good* to disobey the law if the law is getting in the way of justice.

Philosophers since have spent a long time untangling this contradiction – and the answer seems to be that Socrates wasn't really fussed about being the victim of harm himself. The 'suffering of injustice,' he said, 'while certainly not an occasion for rejoicing, need not be a great tragedy either. The good man cannot really be harmed by it.' That vial of hemlock you're about to drink might prove you wrong, Socrates, but I see what you mean. If the only one being harmed by injustice is you, the right thing for that citizen to do is to 'abide by his just agreements' and martyr himself obediently. But wait! – far worse, Socrates argues, is causing injustice to another. If the case is one in which obedience leads to the *doing* of injustice to other people (rather than simply the *suffering* of it yourself), a different judgment would become necessary, and it would then be right to refuse to obey.[17]

Two thousand years later, in his 1963 'Letter from Birmingham Jail', Martin Luther King Jr. agreed. 'An individual who breaks a law that conscience tells him is unjust,' he wrote about the US Civil Rights movement, 'and who willingly accepts the penalty of imprisonment in order to arouse the conscience of the community over its injustice, is in reality expressing the highest respect for the law.'[18] A couple of decades after that, in apartheid South Africa in the 1980s, Archbishop Desmond Tutu made a similar argument about the immorality of watching oppression unfolding in front of you without taking action. Being neutral in situations of injustice, he said, is to choose the side of the oppressor.[19] These are neither new nor radical ideas.

And yet, how can breaking the law ever *not* be a radical thing to do? In a powerful 1970 speech that could have been written today, the historian Howard Zinn called this the 'topsy-turvy' problem. When wrestling with the ethics of dissent, Zinn said, we are essentially examining the ideal of 'obedience to law'. But what if the rule of law is actually 'the darling of the leaders and the plague of the people'? What if the primary purpose of the law has been to allow powerful people to embed existing inequalities more firmly into society, rather than to ensure societal justice for the disenfranchised? Instead of uncritical obedience, Zinn said, perhaps we need to take a more 'realistic' look at the law – examining how it *is* working, rather than how we'd *like* it to work.[20] This is especially important in the case of civil protest:

> In every city in this country, when demonstrations take place, the protesters, whether they have demonstrated or not, whatever they have done, are assaulted and clubbed by police, and then they are arrested for assaulting a police officer. [. . .] If you don't think, if you just listen to TV and read scholarly things, you actually begin to think that things are not so bad, or that just little things are wrong. But you have to get a little

> detached, and then come back and look at the world, and you are horrified. So we have to start from that supposition – that things are really topsy-turvy. And our topic is topsy-turvy: civil disobedience.[21]

This topic is topsy-turvy, Zinn argued, because as soon as we start talking about civil disobedience, we assume that civil disobedience is the problem. In 2022, when *Roe v. Wade* came under attack, pro-choice demonstrators instigated a peaceful rally outside the homes of the US Supreme Court Justices responsible. These six unelected individuals unilaterally decided to overthrow a fifty-year precedent, activists explained, and to take away our fundamental right to privacy. So why should they get to keep theirs? In response, conservative senators started calling for protesters to face criminal prosecution. 'The rule of law demands no less,' Senator Josh Hawley, Republican of Missouri, wrote in a letter to the Justice Department.[22] But as Zinn pointed out, back in 1970, in cases where the law is deliberately being weaponised for violent ends, it's not civil disobedience that's the problem. The real problem is civil *obedience*:

> Our problem is the numbers of people all over the world who have obeyed the dictates of the leaders of their government and have gone to war, and millions have been killed because of this obedience. [. . .] Our problem is that people are obedient all over the world, in the face of poverty and starvation and stupidity, and war and cruelty. Our problem is that people are obedient while the jails are full of petty thieves, and all the while the grand thieves are running the country. That's our problem.[23]

After all, things can be legal yet deeply evil. Lots of things that were once illegal are, with the benefit of hindsight, now societally understood to be ethical acts. Harriet Tubman led a military operation that destroyed millions of dollars' worth of Confederate property and freed nearly eight hundred enslaved people. Emily Davison threw herself under the king's horse fighting for the right to vote. While resisting South African apartheid, Nelson Mandela was sentenced to life in prison for his activism as leader of the Defiance Campaign. Miep Gies hid Anne Frank's family from the Nazis. Rosa Parks refused to move from her seat on the bus. In the twenty-first century, the Standing Rock Sioux Tribe of the Lakota and Dakota nations has been fighting alongside thousands of other Indigenous American supporters to block oil pipelines from scarring sacred lands and adding unfathomable pollution to the climate crisis. Justice can't be reduced to a matter of obedience to the law, because all too often the law has been designed specifically to inculcate injustice. The rule of law is topsy-turvy. This is a feature, not a bug.

A few years ago I found myself arguing on national radio with a self-styled comedian who built his career by sneering at so-called 'woke culture'.* His argument was that protesters today need to relearn to employ rational rather than emotional means of persuasion. You know, he said, like LGBTQ+ people did: they stood up and argued their case calmly, they didn't yell about it and smash things and make a scene. Are you kidding? No, he

* 'Woke' as a term was originally coined within African American Vernacular English (AAVE) to describe the process of awakening to the complex violent realities of systemic oppression. It has since been coopted by the right as a new synonym for that old bogeyman 'political correctness'.

wasn't kidding. Nor, it seems, was he familiar with the events of 1969, when the police raided a gay bar in New York's Greenwich Village and set off the Stonewall Riots – often called the very first Pride. The Latina-American trans lesbian activist Sylvia Lee Rivera described how patrons were led out of the bar when police 'cattled us all up against the police vans. The cops pushed us up against the grates and the fences. People started throwing pennies, nickels, and quarters at the cops. And then the bottles started. [. . .] We were not taking any more of this shit.'[24] Within weeks, residents of the Village had organised into activist groups, borrowing tactics from the Black Panthers to demand the right to live their lives without fear of state interference.

Equal rights aren't like pudding – something you only get if you behave yourself and look proper and ask nicely. That's why they're called 'rights'. The right to marry and start a family. The right to a life free from torture, enforced labour, and inhuman or degrading treatment. The right to protection from discrimination. If somebody's fundamental human rights are being denied, the problem isn't the palatability of their response. Martin Luther King Jr. famously expressed his despair at people who talk the language of justice whilst getting in the way of any attempt to realise it. In a passage that also could be written today, King singled out for special criticism 'the white moderate'. This is the person who

> is more devoted to 'order' than to justice; who prefers a negative peace which is the absence of tension to a positive peace which is the presence of justice; who constantly says 'I agree with you in the goal you seek, but I can't agree with your methods of direct action'; who paternalistically feels he can set

> the timetable for another man's freedom; who lives by the myth of time and who constantly advises the Negro to wait until a 'more convenient season.' Shallow understanding from people of goodwill is more frustrating than absolute misunderstanding from people of ill will.[25]

In 1964, a student activist called Mario Savio stood on the steps of the University of Berkeley in California and exclaimed: 'There's a time when the operation of the machine becomes so odious, makes you so sick at heart, that you can't take part! [. . .] And you've got to put your bodies upon the gears and upon the wheels [. . .], upon the levers, upon all the apparatus, and you've got to make it stop!'[26] Instead, many of today's centrist commentators are acting just like King's moderates have always done: asking the machine nicely if it could please stop grinding us into dust, and seeking a calm and rational solution to a violently irrational problem.* Some people have always

* In a 2018 piece for *The Atlantic* called 'King's Message of Nonviolence Has Been Distorted', Dara T. Mathis writes about how contemporary white liberals and conservatives alike have been busily invoking Martin Luther King's rhetoric to justify their criticism of the Black Lives Matter movement: using his writings as 'convenient fodder for warm-and-fuzzy quotes', twisting his words, and flattening the complexity of his legacy. King 'was adamant that his nonviolence did not constitute passivity or mollification', Mathis explains, 'but a militant commitment to change'. In King's own words, riots are simply the language of the unheard. 'And what is it America has failed to hear? It has failed to hear that the promises of freedom and justice have not been met. And it has failed to hear that large segments of white society are more concerned about tranquility and the status quo than about justice and humanity' (www.theatlantic.com/politics/archive/2018/04/kings-message-of-nonviolence-has-been-distorted/557021).

been more worried about seeming reasonable than making things right.

Flipping the Script

My husband Tom snores. Not a light breathy snore, either; this is the real deal. If I were to try to describe the noise I might say that, when he really gets going, he sounds a bit like a blender chewing thoughtfully on a spanner. Like two donkeys making love in a dustbin lorry. Like a man who's recently had his voice box replaced with a trombone, and is repeatedly yodelling the word *DIVOOOOOOOORCE*.

One night, after two hours of rolling him over and kneeing him in the back, I'd had enough. I leaned out of bed to grab the hairdryer from the floor where I'd left it plugged in, slowly brought it level with Tom's sleeping face, and pulled the trigger.

The hairdryer screamed. Tom screamed. Tom fell out of the bed.

In retrospect, that was probably not the best way to handle it. But in my defence, I was very, very tired. I hadn't had a proper night's sleep in weeks. I snapped. When judging my reprehensible behaviour, should the long nights of sleep deprivation leading up to that moment matter at all? Or should we only judge the act itself?

As ever, the language of reason is designed to make things seem simple. Peaceful protest is fine, but as soon as one protester raises their fist – either in anger or self-defence – that line has irrevocably been crossed. It doesn't matter what happened beforehand, or what the other side did to provoke them. The protesters are now in the wrong, and the whole cause is irrevocably tainted. This sets off a chain reaction. Panicking, other supporters of the movement rush to denounce the bad actors, too. Don't blame us all for the behaviour of a criminal minority! The intention of this denunciation might be good, but the impact is harmful. The movement is immediately divided, that faulty narrative of virtuous protesters versus bad rioters solidified. Instead, if the narrative itself is topsy-turvy, how can we flip it back on its head?

First of all, the rise in sousveillance I talked about in Chapter Four has helped to complicate the story. Smartphone technology has enabled teams of citizen journalists to uncover deliberate provocateurs behind some of the more extreme acts of violence. Minneapolis, 27 May 2020: a white man in a gas mask carrying an open umbrella is spotted smashing up AutoZone with a hammer then committing arson. His grainy image swiftly spreads across the internet under the hashtag #Umbrellaman. Oakland, 30 May: a masked figure commandeers a digger, careening it around the streets while a crowd of others break windows with skateboards, feet, and fists. Los Angeles, 31 May: a Black woman tweets a video she's just taken of two white women graffitiing a Starbucks with the letters BLM. 'Don't spray stuff on here,' we can hear her saying. 'Y'all doing that for us, and we didn't ask you to do that. They gonna blame that on us.'

While some of these agitators are simply opportunists and some are even rumoured to be plants organised by the police, others are known to the FBI as 'accelerationists': members of hardcore libertarian extremist groups whose aim is to infiltrate protests, aggravate officers, and escalate conflict into chaos. The goal of these accelerationists is to foment a full-scale uprising against the government.

At the same time, there's the police themselves. Emboldened behind riot shields and loaded up with army-issue weaponry, they often don't seem to need much provoking. Every day during those first few weeks, a fresh spray of videos showed peaceful protesters smacked down by sudden waves of police brutality – officers using horses to charge into bodies and trample them to the ground; officers hauling journalists from their bystander vantage points or shooting them in the face with rubber bullets; officers detaining 'legal observers', the term for individuals with the state-sanctioned right to observe and document how protests are policed without being implicated. Even the mainstream press has begun gradually to acknowledge the possibility that police might sometimes deploy escalating tactics to provoke retaliation,[27] so they can then use demonstrators' reactions as a reason for their own 'reasonable use of force'. Sure as anything – in Bristol, after having been reported dutifully by the media, officers' broken bones disappeared overnight. Afterwards, with dozens of protesters seriously injured, a report found that police 'failed to distinguish between those protesting peacefully and those engaging in acts of violence', which resulted in 'excessive force' being used.[28] Overall, that enduring schema of aggressive anarchists forced into submission by a virtuous police protectorate is beginning to break apart.

But what if this counter-narrative, too, sometimes risks hurting rather than helping? What if, instead, we stopped arguing that rioting and looting and property destruction are just the actions of an unreasonable minority? What if, rather than seeing these things as an undesired failure of democratic protest, we hammered home the message that direct action can itself be *a legitimate part of the fabric of democracy itself* – a reasonable way of responding to unreasonable circumstances when other tactics have failed? After all, protest *has* to be disruptive to someone, in some way, in order to be a protest. Sometimes that means disrupting the comfort of the comfortable through preying on their conscience (in the case of hunger strikes); sometimes it means disrupting the smooth operation of society by withdrawing one's labour, thereby demonstrating the value of one's labour to society (in the case of employment strikes); other times it means physically disrupting something tangible (like traffic, or bulldozers, or the ability of corporations to operate unhindered). Either way, protests have to do *something* to halt the gears and the workings of an unjust machine – or else they're not protests at all, but just a meaningless charade. In a world that's gone topsy-turvy, what if we could learn to collectively embrace disruption as a necessary way to put everything the right way up again: to see civil disobedience as a net good, and civil obedience as the real social evil?

'But violence is never the answer!' Like many people, I think it depends on the question. As someone who has never needed to break the law because the law has generally been built to protect and serve me, I understand how tempting it can be to see windows getting smashed and stores being looted, and to rush to condemn those actions as an unjustifiable act of immoral destruction. But when in the UK police launched their brutal response to the Sarah Everard vigil, and when in the USA they started physically attacking women demonstrating desperately for their right to essential healthcare, we saw an awful lot of comfortable middle-class white commentators suddenly realise that the promise of protection can be withdrawn at any time.

Sometimes violence itself is the question: one that can't reasonably be answered any other way. The woman who fights off an attacker isn't wrong for trying to wound him. The civilians forced to ward off an invasion aren't just as morally compromised as the army that invades. Similarly: look at Black Lives Matter protests through the lens of centuries of enslavement followed by segregation and discrimination, of unjust lending practices designed to keep Black families in poverty, of pay gaps and life-expectancy gaps and infant-mortality gaps and Black women being up to six times more likely to die in childbirth than white women, of callous violence rationalised away for generations as the result of 'reasonable fears', of public outcries against police brutality in Charlotte in 2016, Baltimore in 2015, Ferguson in 2014, Cincinnati in 2001, LA in 1992, Miami in 1980, Tennessee, Newark, Detroit in the 1960s, and on and on and on, with nothing ever changing . . . and suddenly, these uprisings start to look less like the irrational breakdown of civil society, and more like a 'tactically reasonable response to the crisis of policing', as *Slate* put it.[29]

In an essay for *The Nation* called 'In Defense of Destroying Property',[30] R. H. Lossin, an academic at the Brooklyn Institute for Social Research, argues that the tide is finally turning. 'There seems to be an understanding that too many lines have been crossed, too many innocent people murdered, too many communities over-policed and otherwise neglected to expect anyone to react "reasonably",' she says. Rather than a 'frustrated, emotional reaction', the result of an 'understandable lapse of judgment and loss of control', what if we reimagined property damage as 'reasoned, calculated acts with their own perfectly legitimate political logics'? Via this perspective, smashing the windows of a police station is just as rational and revolutionary an act as tearing down the Bastille was during the French Revolution. In the face of unendurable state brutality, a powerful political spectacle can be the only reasonable way to counteract the tremendous power of the status quo.

At the same time, Lossin also reminds us that we need collectively to get a better handle on what 'violence' in the context of protest actually means. There's a major flaw in the idea that violence is like a big pile of building blocks, and that protesters are just counterproductively chucking yet more violence up on top of the violence pile, making it increasingly unsteady as they add to an imagined sum total of awfulness. But the violence that has generationally been aimed at minoritised communities, and the tactics that those communities have historically used to resist that violence, *are fundamentally not the same kind of violence at all.* The goal of civic disobedience is to chip away at, and ultimately topple, the overwhelming tower of aggression that is constructed and maintained by the state. In terms of severity of suffering, these things are rarely equivalent at all. 'People are not objects,' Lossin writes. '[B]roken windows and burnt cars are simply not commensurate with the violence of state-sanctioned murder or the structural violence of poverty that has placed people of color at a disproportionate risk of dying of Covid-19. Plateglass windows don't bleed. [. . .] They just break, and then, at some point, they are replaced by identical sheets of glass.' It's seeming increasingly difficult to keep up the pretence that violence on both sides is equally condemnable, or that giant chain stores and luxury-goods outlets are worth defending in the face of abject suffering, or that buildings are more sympathetic victims than actual human beings.

Defund the Police

'Defund the police.' If you plug that term into Google's 'Trends' tool, the graph it returns is a completely flat line up until 24 May 2020. On that date the global popularity of this search term suddenly spikes, peaking during the week of 7 June 2020 before falling again just as rapidly the following week. Online searches for 'defund the police' have remained relatively low but consistent ever since. How did this slogan leap from the placards of a protest movement and become the bedrock of a political campaign?

Calls to 'defund' or 'abolish' the police are just the latest iteration in decades of activism intending to dismantle the 'carceral state', which refers to the sectors of government associated with the institutions of police, prosecution, prisons, and parole. This system, as social work scholar Mimi E. Kim points out, is in opposition to the 'welfare state', whose aim is to facilitate the redistribution of resources to the most vulnerable parts of the population rather than doling out punishment.[31] The carceral state was built on the Benthamian principle of social reform through surveillance and incarceration: activities that have always focused on criminalising those vulnerable communities who are most likely to be recipients of welfare. Alongside a team of researchers, Kim examined the long history of collaboration in the west between social work and the police. They call this 'carceral social work': a system in which vast amounts of money are spent every year on 'coercive and punitive practices [. . .] used to manage Black, Indigenous, other people of color, and poor communities', rather than on overhauling the economic factors designed to keep these communities mired in poverty.[32]

But imagine you're being robbed and nobody is coming to save you. Well, the one time I called the police my student house had just been broken into. It was summer, so all my housemates were back home or on holiday – meanwhile, I was working three jobs so I was staying there by myself. I called a couple of friends who were still in town, and they came and sat with me on the pavement. The afternoon ticked over into evening, twilight fell, and still we waited for the police to arrive. Finally an officer showed up, sighed loudly, took a statement, and left. I never saw my belongings again. That very same evening, all around the country, homes were being burgled and women assaulted and purses snatched, yet only a fraction of these crimes are ever solved.

When people talk about defunding the police, they're usually not advocating for a free-for-all society which has abandoned any attempt to deter or investigate criminal offences of any kind. Hardcore libertarians aside, even those who want to see the police abolished entirely are unlikely to be hungering for lawlessness. What abolitionist activists often mean is that the carceral state simply isn't fit for purpose. Firstly, as an institution, the police are expected to deal with a vast array of societal problems, yet US officers on average are expected to complete only 672 hours of basic training before joining the force. In comparison, barbers usually need around 1,300 hours of training just to be licensed to cut people's hair.[33] It's like if the entire healthcare system of your city were run from one centralised department – so if you needed your gall bladder taken out, you might get someone whose training had loosely covered that procedure, but whose day thus far had also included a spot of heart surgery and tooth extraction. Secondly, 'defunding' only seems to be a radical leftist position when it's about the police or military – other social programmes like education and social housing and the arts get their subsidies reduced all the time. Meanwhile, at more than $100 billion, the money spent annually on police in the USA outstrips the military budget of almost every other country in the world. And thirdly, there are so many methods for reducing crime that don't involve the carceral state at all. In fact, there's plenty of evidence to suggest that investing just some of the bloated budget that currently goes towards the policing of communities back into those communities instead would deter crime much more effectively.

The statistics are compelling. A 2016 report from the Obama White House's Council of Economic Advisers found that increasing wages for non-college-educated men by just 10 per cent can reduce crime rates by at least the same figure or even up to 20 per cent.[34] In 2013, a randomised controlled trial in Vancouver found that providing apartments around the city to unhoused mentally ill people reduced crime rates,[35] while in 2018 a team of researchers compared three sources of homicide data to find that funding treatment facilities for substance abuse can reduce both violent and financially motivated crimes in those areas, with particularly pronounced effects on serious crime.[36]

And that's just crime *prevention*. In terms of crime *detection*: under the current system, in the USA only around 11 per cent of all serious crimes result in an arrest and 2 per cent in a conviction.[37] As for the area of sexual violence, as many as two hundred thousand rape kits are sitting unopened in police storage,[38] while the Rape, Abuse & Incest National Network (RAINN) estimates that only twenty-five out of every thousand perpetrators will end up in prison.[39] By 2017, the Murder Accountability Project found that while nationally the rate of solved murders had fallen to a low of 61 per cent (down dramatically from around 90 per cent in the 1960s), this figure concealed a massive racial disparity: for white victims, the rate of solved cases was 76.9 per cent, while for Black victims it was only 59.8 per cent.[40] Police, it seems, are neither protecting equally nor serving adequately.

This may partly be because they're so busy dealing with issues that used to be the responsibility of the welfare state, which is something that *has* been steadily defunded – decimated by round after round of spending cuts. Police are now doing things like spending up to a quarter of their time transporting people with mental illnesses, for example;[41] or being dispatched to deal with homeless people and, instead of helping them, incarcerating them at horrifying rates; or conducting hundreds of thousands of stop-and-searches every year in hope of finding small amounts of cannabis – a drug that is now legally being advertised by smiling white entrepreneurs on YouTube.

Luckily, plentiful alternatives to policing exist. These involve diverting focus (and funding!) away from carceral punishment back into welfare activities like youth programmes and low-income housing initiatives. Emergencies could be dealt with by trained teams of healthcare workers and domestic-violence specialists, for example; social workers could offer rapid-response emergency housing; conflict-management advocates trained in restorative justice could be sent in to mediate interpersonal conflicts where physical safety is not at risk. Abolitionist thinkers have offered detailed pathways for achieving these goals.* There are no longer any justifiable excuses for dismissing police defunding out of hand as an illogical or ill-considered proposition. In fact, without manpower devoted to arresting people on the streets for petty offences, those post-abolition personnel responsible for investigating things like sexual violence and murder will be better able – not less – to fight and solve serious crimes, experts say.

Given all this information, defunding the police is not a radical idea at all. It's simply a way to bring both crime prevention and detection into the twenty-first century. In fact, from this perspective, the system of policing that we have at present seems itself to be radically illogical. So why has there been such resistance to change? Is 'defunding the police' just a case of 'right message but wrong slogan', perhaps? No – because that question leads us right back into the trap of squabbling over semantics. Whether it's ACAB or abolition, the branding

* For further reading see e.g. Mariame Kaba's book *We Do This 'Til We Free Us* (Haymarket Books, 2021), or Derecka Purnell's *Becoming Abolitionists* (Verso Books, 2021), or Philip V. McHarris and Thenjiwe McHarris's viral *New York Times* article 'No More Money for the Police' (www.nytimes.com/2020/05/30/opinion/george-floyd-police-funding.html), which all explain in detail what carceral abolition means and what a post-police society would actually look like.

shouldn't matter. With so many lives at stake, we can't afford to waste even one more second trying to find the exact right combination of words to convince people who clearly do not want to be convinced. Instead, let's start working on the solution.

It turns out that this particular solution is so reasonable, in fact, that even police themselves have become accidental advocates! Speaking in 2016 after a civilian in Texas shot five officers to death and injured nine more, officers complained that they're now 'expected to do everything for everybody'. 'We're just asking us to do too much,' said the Dallas police chief David Brown. 'Every societal failure, we put it off for the cops to solve. [. . .] That's too much to ask. Policing was never meant to solve all those problems.'[42] Which raises the question: what *was* policing meant to do? This brings us back around to the problem of public space.

Cultivate and Destroy

In the last chapter, I explained how the civilising process was legitimised via the rhetoric of cultivation. Morality came from the individual act of cultivating oneself. Cultivate your mind to repress emotion in favour of pure rationality. Cultivate your body by making it better, fitter, stronger, more productive. Cultivate passions like cricket and classical music, avoiding impure diversions. Cultivate your mode of dress, of speech, of gesture, so that every ounce of natural human exuberance is restrained. And once you've cultivated yourself, then you can cultivate *the world*.

All around the globe, imperial invasion imposed an alien value system on top of public space. From Australia to North

America, colonisers called these vast fertile spaces *terra nullius* – territory without a master, nobody's land, ripe for the taking. But of course the terra wasn't nullius at all. The problem they were facing is that they wanted to mine those natural riches and to farm that fertile ground. All that was standing in the way were the people who already lived there. This prompted a series of mental gymnastics. Ownership of land, they decided, could only be granted to those who *cultivated* the land.

In many Indigenous worldviews, to quote Tewa professor Gregory Cajete, 'everything is related, that is, connected in dynamic, interactive, and mutually reciprocal relationships'.[43] Rather than the masters of the universe, people are seen as just one part of a finely balanced ecosystem – bound up in a web of relations with land, water, animals, and spirit beings, so that caring for the natural world is like caring for a family member who then nurtures and supports your human family in turn. As philosopher and member of the Jicarilla Apache tribe Viola Faye Cordova explains:

> It is commonly known that the Native American found the concept of holding ownership of parts of the Earth quite alien. They did not think of their homelands as something they owned but instead as something that they belonged to. [. . .] Contrast this idea of place and boundaries to that of the Europeans who come equipped with a conceptual notion of themselves as the rightful owners, not of a specific place, but of a world that their mythology encourages them to 'subdue and dominate'.[44]

Through the colonisers' gaze, this philosophy provided a convenient rationale for land theft. Ownership of the land, they decided, could be granted only to those working to dominate the land (that State of Nature again!) through brute force and reasoned intellect. That domination meant importing a European model of property ownership: parcelling the land up into individually owned segments, atomising its communities into nuclear families, then submitting it to the form of intensive farming practices that would eventually exhaust it. Horrified by this way of thinking, the Paiute leader Wovoka in 1890 exclaimed: 'You ask me to plow the ground. Shall I take a knife and tear my mother's bosom? Then when I die she will not take me to her bosom to rest. You ask me to dig for stones! Shall I dig under her skin for bones? Then when I die I cannot enter her body to be born again.'[45]

The earth, the trees, and every other living creature – all were reimagined as resources to be owned, managed, and exploited. The rhetoric was cultivation. The logic was extraction. The result: ecological destruction.

What does all this have to do with the police? As soon as you have a system of individualised ownership, you need people to protect it. This is why, in 1762, Jean-Jacques Rousseau's *The Social Contract* posited private property as the root of the world's biggest evils: envy, rivalry, greed, all congealing to form awful inequalities that separate man from man. And this brings us back to protest itself – because in the USA, as with other colonies around the world, the very first police force was specifically designed to protect the property of the powerful, by crushing people who were rising up against an unjust system. I am talking, of course, about slavery. In his book *Black Police in America*, W. Marvin Dulaney explains that in the seventeenth century 'Africans enslaved in America' had become 'a troublesome presence' for their enslavers:

> Belying their captors' claims that they were made for slavery, Africans rebelled against the institution in a variety of ways. They resisted on a daily basis by refusing to work, destroying crops and farm implements, and killing livestock. They poisoned their owners, destroyed property through arson, and fought with their owners and other whites. Some ran away from slavery; others cooperated with native Americans or white indentured servants to resist through physical force. This resort to violence created the greatest problem in American history. They lived in constant fear of slave rebellions, and as a result passed many laws to deter, control, and suppress such insurrections.[46]

By the beginning of the eighteenth century, lawmakers had created a series of 'slave codes' to regulate the behaviour of enslaved people, prohibiting them from assembling in groups, leaving plantations, and resisting punishment. These codes also established a system to enforce them. This was the 'patteroller', or slave patrol – usually filled with poor white men, though in some places all white people were expected to be on the rota – which Dulaney calls 'the first distinctly American police system'. At the same time, America's cities were expanding rapidly, filling up with 'a diverse group of people':

> absentee planters from the rural areas, middle-class artisans, merchants, immigrants from Europe, sailors, vagabonds,

> runaway indentured servants, free African Americans, and fugitive slaves. As crime and disorder, licentious behaviour, and arson became more prevalent by the late seventeenth century, many cities developed watches, city guards, or constabulary forces to control the 'dangerous classes' that they attracted.[47]

This paralleled what was happening across the Atlantic, in Europe, where watch patrols and city guards were providing the blueprint for today's system of policing. In the 1700s, the primary imperative of city watchmen began to shift from catching thieves and murderers to the end goal of stamping out any form of public unrest at all. Starting in England and then adopted elsewhere, a spray of new legislation began to clamp down on people's behaviour in both private and public space. These were 'pre-emptive laws' which effectively criminalised things that hadn't previously been crimes at all, but which were believed to be a kind of gateway drug to civil disobedience: things like vagrancy and idleness. The 1771 London Streets Act, for example, gave watchmen the power to arrest 'disorderly persons loitering, wandering, or misbehaving themselves'.[48]

More than just a response to public dismay over petty-crime waves, this change was designed to secure the moral stability of the nation itself.[49] Newspapers at the time were full of public dissent: turnpike riots against toll roads in Bristol, strikes by keelmen (men who transported coal by boat) in Newcastle, unruly revels at London fairs . . . With poverty-stricken communities becoming increasingly angry at rising taxes and massive disparities between the very wealthy and the very poor, a magistrate at London's Bow

Street Public Office called Henry Fielding complained that 'the common people' nowadays are so 'audacious, insolent and ungovernable'.[50]

From 1780 on, around the western world, the law changed from being a collective way to assert citizens' rights and responsibilities to a system designed to maintain order specifically for the purpose of providing protection and reassurance to elite propertied groups.[51] In this way, as Gaye Theresa Johnson writes: 'The arrangement of space has been one of the most important ways to distribute and hinder opportunity.'[52] Cracking down on what the public can and cannot do in public has always been a way to shut down space for dissent. The most effective way to defuse unrest is to separate social groups into silos, where the struggles of white middle-class women, of working-class communities, of LGBTQ+ people, of disabled people, and of people of colour are seen as isolated pockets of rebellion rather than constituent parts of a collective fight. Looked at the other way around, this means that one of the most effective ways to resist is to reclaim the right to congregate in public space.

By the 1950s, in the USA especially, the arrangement of space seemed rock solid. This was a time when appearance was everything. Think about the American Dream of the picture-perfect suburban home, everything homogenised and everyone assimilated, women particularly expected to keep up appearances by keeping up their own appearance. In research on this time the metaphor of concealment comes up a lot: descriptive imagery full of smiling masks and glossy facades covering up the roiling dissatisfaction underneath. Meanwhile, within deliberately disadvantaged urban areas, that long struggle for social justice was starting to erupt into view.

The Civil Rights campaigns of the 1960s took strength and unity from the collective organisation fostered by street culture, and in turn provided strength and unity to other fights. When Stonewall began, rioters 'representing a cross section of the city's radical groups, including the Black Panthers, Yippies, and members of street gangs from as far away as New Jersey' came to help.[53] In 1970, Huey P. Newton issued a manifesto in the Black Panther Party newspaper encouraging an alliance with the Women's Liberation and Gay Liberation movements. In 1977, the 504 Occupation began. For twenty-five days, dozens of disabled people from diverse racial and social backgrounds occupied San Francisco's Office of Health, Education, and Welfare in protest against the endless delays to Section 504 of the 1973 Rehabilitation Act, which was supposed to ensure that every service involving the US government should be fully accessible to disabled people: everything from schools to public offices, and from public transit to hospitals. This wasn't the only disability group to take over a federal building, but it was the only one that lasted: most of the others were quickly starved out. The San Francisco protest, however, was able to hold out for almost a month because of its dedicated coalition of supporters, including the Black Panthers, the gay community's Butterfly Brigade, and the help of labour unions.[54]

Martin Luther King Jr. famously said that riots are the language of the unheard. They're also the language of the unseen, the deliberately misrepresented and unrecognised: those who have been pushed out of the centre and forced into the margins, denied opportunities to participate on equal social terms. And for those people who have been deliberately gatekept out of outlets like mainstream media, the major arena for unrestricted expression has historically been public space. Coalitions of solidarity are forged in public, out there on the streets. As Sylvia Lee Rivera reflected, many of the Stonewall participants were part of multiple movements: the women's movement, the peace protests, the fight for civil rights. After all, 'we were all fighting the same thing: oppression'.[55]

In comparison, at the end of the nineteenth century, the suffrage movement was busy leveraging anti-Black rhetoric to divisive effect, with leading figures agitating for the right to vote only for 'respectable' temperate white women like themselves, and not their fellow women of colour. The American suffragist Frances E. Willard exclaimed in horror at seeing Black people collecting in taverns, which she called their 'center of power. Better whisky and more of it is the rallying cry of great, dark-faced mobs. [. . .] The safety of woman, of childhood, the home, is menaced in a thousand localities at this moment.'[56] Later, in 1913, the woman who is often heralded as the 'heroine' of English suffragettes, Emmeline Pankhurst, on a visit to the USA, pitted women's suffrage against Black people's emancipation. But of course, justice can never be a zero-sum game.

In 1977, a collective of Black lesbian women famously published 'The Combahee River Collective Statement', a powerful distillation of their Black feminist, socialist, queer, political movement, which was 'actively committed to struggling against racial, sexual, heterosexual, and class oppression, and [. . .] the fact that the major systems of oppression are interlocking'.* Their challenge, they wrote, was 'to use our position at the bottom [. . .] to make a clear leap into revolutionary action. If Black women were free, it would mean that everyone else would have to be free since our freedom would necessitate the destruction of all the systems of oppression.'[57] Instead of divide and conquer, we need to unite, and fight, and rise.

Activists have long recognised the power of congregation – of a vibrant street culture for community formation, of uncensored noticeboards for organising, of free access to open spaces for political rallies and other forms of democratic engagement. Whether it's displays of kink at Pride as a way for LGBTQ+ people to refute the palatability politics of cis-heteronormativity, or Take Back the Night marches asserting the need of women to exist in public without fear of verbal street harassment and physical assault: demanding the right to be visible and audible en masse, in public, on your own authentic terms, is itself a form of collective resistance. No wonder governments everywhere are so eager to shut it down! Controlling what's allowed to happen in our shared social world, and by whom and when and where and in what ways, has always been a way to ward off revolution.

But we have power, too, to fight back. There is radical potential in reclaiming the streets, occupying the streets, taking to the streets. Protest movements split into weaker factions when these public opportunities for solidarity formation

* These interlocking layers of multiple oppressions have more recently been interrogated via scholarship on 'intersectionality' – a term popularised by the legal scholar Kimberlé Crenshaw.

are destroyed. We have to push back against those seductive topsy-turvy narratives – the ones in which the people trying desperately to prevent ecocide are branded disruptive villains while those who physically assault them get heralded as heroes, and where the fury of motorists inconvenienced by a roadblock somehow trumps the much greater inconvenience of having one's home washed away in a flood, and where the moderate sensible position is to let the earth burn around us while the radical position is to do literally anything to stop it. The crackdowns on protests are the end result of that dangerous atomisation we've been talking about, which pits respectable individuals against the unreasonable mob. If we can't learn to act collectively then we're going to 'let's be reasonable!' ourselves out of a liveable world.

6

Whatever Happened to Public Reason?

'Monty, don't hit your brother on the head. No, don't kick him either. Stop pinching. Montgomery Sedgman, headbutting is completely forbidden!'

'Sorry, Mum.'

'What should we do instead?'

(*Sighs deeply.*) 'Use our words.'

When I told my husband I was ending this book with a chapter on why reasonable discourse isn't always the answer, he blinked a few times and said: 'But Kirsty . . . you *love* talking.' He's not wrong.

Earlier in this book I wrote about living with invisible disabilities. Over the years, one of the things I've needed to learn to navigate is a history of chronic depression. Ever since I was a teenager, when I was taken to hospital following an overdose and ended up in years of therapy, I've believed in the power of communication to foster mutual understanding. In the almost two decades we've been together, Tom has grown amusedly resigned to my need to talk through every tiny instance of household conflict, working the whole thing over and over for hours as though it's a stubborn crease I'm trying to iron out of our marriage. I love talking so much that I made studying talk my entire life's work.

But because of this, I also know that there are times when words aren't enough to solve the problem. In fact, sometimes words are what's getting in the way.

The Colston Conundrum

When Colston's statue fell, a common complaint was that protesters were acting undemocratically. Why didn't they just ask for it to be removed? This is a civilised country – you can't form a mob and wildly pull down statues on a whim! If you don't like seeing a slave trader memorialised forever in the middle of your city, find someone who agrees with you and campaign to get them elected. If that doesn't work, create a petition – and when that gets ignored, make another one, and another. Talk about the problem calmly and politely. Eventually you'll reach a compromise that's acceptable to all.

The problem is, in Bristol, they tried all those things. Campaigners had lobbied for decades for the statue to be removed, a new petition emerging every few years – beginning to gather steam at the new millennium with plans for the opening of a new slavery museum, then again in 2007 during the 200th anniversary of the abolition of the slave trade, and once more in 2016 when the group 'Countering Colston' arranged a demonstration outside Bristol's largest concert building, then called Colston Hall.

Across 2016 and into the following year, concert-goers grew used to walking over pavements chalked with Colston's crimes. Kidnap, human trafficking, torture, murder. Venue officials responded by saying they might one day be open to changing the name – yet the big letters outside the building remained, and so did the statue. The only visible things that changed were that a local pub quietly became the Bristol Yard, and Colston Primary School turned into Cotham Gardens. Meanwhile, Bristol Council showed no signs of opening even a consultation on the future of the monument itself. In fact, throughout twenty years of opinion polls and local radio phone-ins, whenever the question was asked it seemed the majority of respondents wanted the statue to stay. It was a listed monument, taking it down would be erasing history, how else will people learn about the past if not by looking at a lump of metal? In return, campaigners argued that the descendants of people who had actually been enslaved by Colston should have more input than those with no personal stake in the matter, and perhaps those who wanted to learn about history could read a history book instead – because nobody *was* learning the truth about Colston's slave trading from his monument, anyway, given that its original 1895 plaque read only: 'Erected by citizens of Bristol as a memorial of one of the most virtuous and wise sons of their city'.

Finally, in 2018, a compromise was reached – a new plaque would be commissioned. An initial draft was reportedly more informative:

> As a high official of the Royal African Company from 1680 to 1692, Edward Colston played an active role in the enslavement of over 84,000 Africans (including 12,000 children) of whom over 19,000 died en route to the Caribbean and America. Colston also invested in the Spanish slave trade and in slave-produced sugar. As Tory MP for Bristol (1710–1713), he defended the city's 'right' to trade in enslaved Africans.

> Bristolians who did not subscribe to his religious and political beliefs were not permitted to benefit from his charities.[1]

Bear in mind that the Conservative (Tory) government's own policy is now to 'retain and explain', not remove, evidence of Britain's problematic heritage. Surely this new plaque was doing precisely that?

Wrong. The proposed text caused an uproar. One local Conservative councillor even went on the record to say that if the plaque were to be approved in that form then stealing or vandalising it 'may be justified'.[2] The committee spent the rest of the year wrangling over the wording with the help of a local historian. And this is important – the historian was a member of the Society of Merchant Venturers, an organisation founded in 1552 to represent the interests of Bristol's wealthiest families.* Draft by draft, the proposed phrasing of the plaque gradually got watered down: references to Colston being a 'Tory' were removed and references to his 'philanthropy' reinstated, trafficking was changed to 'transportation', and the horrifying statistic of twelve thousand children disappeared entirely. Eventually the team reached a compromise, and even went so far as to commission the plaque to be made. But in March 2019 – a full year after the solution was first announced, and with just days to go before the official unveiling – the whole

* In the eighteenth century, one quarter of the Society's members were directly involved in the slave trade; today, its membership list is still full of some of the most powerful and influential people in the city. In a macabre twist, with Colston being one of the Society's most famous alumni, they even kept his fingernails and hair on display at their headquarters up until 2016, according to Bristol247.com reporter Martin Booth.

thing screamed to a halt again. Bristol's mayor, Marvin Rees, saw the final wording and objected. 'It was extremely naive of the Merchant Venturers to believe they should have the final say on the words for a new plaque for the statue of Edward Colston without reference to the communities of descendants of those Africans who were enslaved and treated as commodities by merchants like Colston,' a spokesperson said. 'It's an oversight to put it mildly not to even have had a conversation with Mayor Marvin Rees, Europe's first mayor of African heritage and the mayor of a city whose wealth has been inseparable from slavery and plantations and who is himself the descendant of enslaved Africans. The proposed words are unacceptable.'[3]

At the last minute, they had to scrap the whole thing and start again.

Unfortunately, the story of Colston's statue demonstrates the absurdity of believing that civil discourse is the only reasonable way to get things done. For months, the Merchant Venturers seemingly used their considerable influence to dilute the wording of a plaque that campaigners didn't even want in the first place. For years, the campaign to get Colston's statue taken down democratically was ignored. For decades, Bristol forced Black citizens to explain over and over that actually Colston's statue wasn't even erected via a democratic mandate but was put there relatively recently by wealthy white people as an act of nostalgic propaganda – and anyway, memorialisation isn't meant to be a history lesson but rather an act of collective celebration, because the people we choose to put on pedestals are supposed to change with the times as communities continually re-evaluate whom they want to honour, and expecting residents to walk every day past the statue of the man who caused such tremendous pain is inhumane and we can't do much to right *that* injustice but we can fix *this* – and on and on and on, with nothing ever happening and nothing ever changing aside from the spilling of thousands upon thousands of *words*.

Then, suddenly, in June 2020, Colston was pulled down and thrown in the harbour. A few weeks later, Colston Hall announced that it was definitely changing its name this time. In September the big letters on the building were taken down and the name Bristol Beacon went up. By the following June, an array of other institutions had followed suit: Colston's Girls' School, Colston Lodge, Colston House, Colston Street, Colston Weir, Colston Avenue, Colston Window in Bristol Cathedral, gone gone gone gone gone gone gone. In January 2022, following a high-profile trial, the four defendants charged with criminal damage for bringing the statue down were acquitted by a jury of their peers. Dubbed by newspapers the 'Colston Four', they argued that they'd actually used reasonable force to prevent a crime, because the ongoing presence of the statue had been contravening a 1981 law prohibiting displays of 'indecent matter'.[4] With all that backstory in mind – knowing that words had so totally and completely failed, and witnessing the sudden leap into action following Colston's dethroning – can we honestly say that toppling him was wrong?

Remember what Martin Luther King Jr. said about the 'white moderate' who 'lives by the myth of time', and who constantly advises oppressed people to wait until a 'more convenient season' for their liberation. Remember the American professor and Black Panther member Angela Davis, who pointed out how

Black people are forever told to be patient, 'advised that as long as we remain faithful to the existing democratic order, the glorious moment will eventually arrive when we will come into our own as full-fledged human beings'.[5] Remember James Baldwin, answering with palpable frustration a white interviewer's challenge in 1989. 'You always told me that it's going to take time,' Baldwin says. 'It's taken my father's time, my mother's time, my uncle's time, my brother's and my sister's time, my niece's and my nephew's time. How much time do you want, for *your* progress?'[6] Remember the disabled people who've been told for decades that public amenities will be made accessible in a future that rarely seems to arrive. Remember the suffragists movement, which began with belief in the power of polite democratic argument, then morphed slowly over decades of inaction into the suffra*gettes*, whose slogan 'Deeds not Words' advocated a reign of righteous terror: a campaign of mail bombs, and stones thrown through windows, and hospitals targeted with arson. Remember the endless delays to legalising same-sex marriage, with politicians and media figures advising that progress doesn't happen overnight. 'I forever nagged gay-rights advocates to be patient and go slow,' one American pundit recalled in *Time* magazine in 2015. 'They retorted that I was underestimating the country's movability. It took a few more years, but starting in 2012, when the tide turned, they proved right.'[7]

Always soon. Never now. Trust the process. Wait your turn. But as the story of Colston shows, the process tends to favour the status quo. Progress *can* happen overnight. The right thing can be done immediately if enough pressure is applied. All too often, that pressure means deeds – not words.

But why do words fail?

Change My Mind

In 2018 a photograph went viral of a white man sitting at a table on a college campus somewhere in middle America behind a sign reading: 'Male Privilege is a Myth. Change My Mind'. The meme immediately began to spawn new variants. 'Pineapple Goes on Pizza'. 'Hemingway is Overrated'. 'Pop Tarts Are Ravioli'. Change My Mind! For many of the people making and sharing images, the intention was to mock this particular brand of human known colloquially as 'Debate Me Guy'. Lots of us, it seems, have come face to face at some point in our lives with one of these people. The kind who stands around at parties loudly insisting that the gender pay gap doesn't exist, or that white people are the real victims of racism, then demanding that anybody in earshot waste precious drinking time teaching him things he could easily read in books. Usually, this ends either in a pointless argument in which he gets more and more smugly wrong yet refuses to be persuaded, or else his would-be antagonist declines to engage, in which case he declares an ipso facto win. In this case, the primary result of all that outrage was to bring Change-My-Mind Man the international fame he was clearly gasping for, boosting his YouTube channel by millions of subscribers.

Online, this kind of 'Debate Me' argument usually goes as follows. Somebody says something that is both actively harmful and provably ridiculous. Instead of earnestly debating, other people respond by ridiculing them. 'Help, I'm being arrested for thought crimes!' they cry, conveniently ignoring the fact that these are things they actually said, out loud, with their mouths.

'Why are snowflakes so afraid of healthy disagreement? Surely they should want to persuade me. See if they can refute my argument in the marketplace of ideas.'

That phrase comes from a Supreme Court Justice called William O. Douglas. In deciding the 1953 case *United States v. Rumely*, Douglas argued that anyone who shares an opinion publicly 'bids for the minds of men in the market place of ideas'.[8] A saying – and an ideology – was born.*

Meanwhile, all across 1950s post-war America, the Manifest Destiny promise of virtuous industrial progress had reached its boom period. From cars to fridges to big new houses full of plastic-covered furniture, the fruits of prosperity were being made available to more people (specifically, more white middle- and working-class people) than ever before. Families overall were getting happier and healthier and more prosperous. On the surface, at least, from the economy to the suburbs to quality of life, everything was on the up! This was the Golden Age

* In his 1644 *Areopagitica*, the English poet John Milton had written that it's not necessary for governments or publishing bodies to place restrictions on speech, because 'in a free and open encounter' the truth will necessarily prevail (Reproduced: https://genius.com/John-milton-areopagitica-annotated). Likewise, in his First Inaugural Address in 1801, the US president Thomas Jefferson argued that 'error of opinion' should be tolerated 'where reason is left free to combat it' (Reproduced: https://genius.com/Thomas-jefferson-first-inaugural-address-annotated). Freedom of expression only began to be likened to free-market economics in the early 1900s, when Justice Oliver Wendell Holmes Jr. famously posed the idea that a 'free trade in ideas' should be governed by 'the competition of the market' (Quoted by Vincent Blasi. 'Holmes and the Marketplace of Ideas', *The Supreme Court Review* (2004), pp. 1–46: p. 3.

of Capitalism, where ad agencies' Mad Men began using new techniques and technologies to bid for customers' wallets in the marketplace of consumer needs.

By the 1970s, though, this promise had begun to fracture. Rather than continuing to grow, the economy was faltering. The term 'stagflation' was established, social divisions became more visible, and that impossible ideal of infinite progress was starting to collapse. This is why historians call the 1970s the 'pivot of change'.[9]

It's here we can see the seeds of our particular contemporary disconnect, which is structured around two interwoven moral value systems. On the one hand we have the ideal of 'personal responsibility', which is most commonly upheld as a whole by those who call themselves conservatives. Looking at the world through the utopian lens of hard work and gumption, it seems reasonable to believe that the pursuit of happiness is an individual task, with the good life there for the taking for anyone willing to work at it. On the other hand there's the ideal of 'collective responsibility', which is a broadly liberal concept. This is based on the idea that while all people may be born equal, in that nobody has the divine right to rule over others, we are all caught up in a system that renders us unequal, with some given certain advantages that others are denied. From this position, it's equally reasonable to believe that the moral goal of a good life for all can only be achieved through economic policies designed to redistribute the unequal distribution of resources via government intervention. Politicians have long debated which precise balance of personal and collective responsibility the state should encourage.

As the 1970s began, the rise of the New Right saw the 'silent majority' become more and more vocal about the perils of any state intervention at all. In fact, these welfare policies – previously understood as a way to make society more just – became widely seen as the true injustice: a fundamental denial of civil freedoms, namely the freedom to sink or swim on one's own merits, without being made responsible for throwing a life jacket to anybody else. This was the start of that vast shift towards modern social conservatism with which we're still continuing to reckon today.[10] At the end of the 1960s, a tide of support swept Nixon into power to begin dismantling the welfare state; a decade later, in Britain, Margaret Thatcher began to do the same. Governments worldwide began to move towards the enticing scent of Reaganism and Thatcherism: an orthodoxy in which the excesses of corporate profit could never effectively be curtailed by the state but should be regulated purely by the need to compete for both consumers and labour. By the mid-1970s, free-market ideology had completely taken over.

Writing in *New York Magazine* in 1976, the novelist Tom Wolfe called it 'The "Me" Decade', pointing towards a growing attitude of atomised individualism in the west.[11] The Age of Aquarius, with its penchant for collective consciousness and communal liberation, had inadvertently given birth to its opposite – the cult of the self and the nuclear family over all. This was a belief system which disrupted that personal/collective balance entirely, by shifting the burden of moral responsibility for failing to prosper away from society and on to the individual. Suffering inequality? It's not a structural problem, it's *your* problem (or, at best, your community's problem) – you could always just work harder, speak nicer, say no to drugs and violence, transform your weak body into a strong one, transform your savings into a business, transform your bad neighbourhood into a good place to live, or simply move somewhere else. The system is rigged against you? Don't be a victim! Learn to take responsibility for the choices you made to get yourself into that mess, or make your parents take responsibility for miring you there. Want the American Dream for your own family? Just pull yourself up by your bootstraps.* Fail to achieve it? It's your own damn fault.

Enter the philosophers. Stricken by this deepening rift in our most fundamental of societal value systems, an American thinker called John Rawls made a suggestion. He proposed that differing ideals about the good life and how to achieve it could only be reconciled via that free market of ideas. Rawls called this process 'public reason'. A frank and open exchange of views, he argued, would offer a way to solve the puzzle of justice within modern liberal democracies, which are built on contested ideals of freedom. After all, if we're all freely equal and equally free, and therefore not subject to the moral or political authority of anyone else, Rawls asked – and in light

* This is my second favourite commonly misused phrase. Coined in the late 1800s in a physics booklet, via the question 'Why can not a man lift himself by pulling up on his bootstraps?', it was originally used sarcastically, to point out the absurd impossibility of trying to lift oneself out of poverty without the necessary socio-economic support to do so. It's like when I'm riding up a hill on my bike, and my four-year-old Sully sits in the child seat behind me going 'I help you, Mummy!' and pushing me in the back. A cute idea in theory, but in practice: nonsense. My very favourite misused phrase, though, is 'blood is thicker than water'. The full phrase is 'the blood of the covenant is thicker than the water of the womb' – so it literally means the opposite of its modern usage of putting family first.

of the fact that there has *always* been deep and intractable disagreement between citizens on matters like morality, religion, and the good life – how then can certain moral or political rules ever rightly be imposed on everyone?[12]

Rawls' solution was simple. All we need is a way for people to clearly and rationally propose the 'norms they view as reasonable for everyone to accept and therefore as justifiable to them', he said, and then in return be 'ready to discuss the fair terms that others propose'.[13] The problem is that we tend to come to discussions from differing epistemic positions: different ways of knowing and making sense of the world. By working collectively towards a common point of fundamental moral agreement, Rawls suggested, we won't help but be able to gain a deeper understanding of others' knowledge and value systems, and those divides will inexorably be bridged. Not to be outdone, the German thinker Jürgen Habermas suggested a model based on rational discourse within the public sphere, which he called 'procedural reason' – a mature and healthy exchange of views in which all participants are situated equally, in which everybody appeals to rational judgments, and where each is given the necessary time and space to discuss everybody's proposed norms without coercion or incivility.[14]

It's such an alluring idea, isn't it? The problem, though, is that on the level of society as a whole *it hasn't worked*. The arguments we're having today – abortion, gun control, austerity vs welfare, capitalism vs socialism – are the exact same arguments we've been having for decades. If rational debate were the answer, we'd have reached mutual agreements by now. Why haven't we?

John Milton, William O. Douglas, Thomas Jefferson, John Rawls . . . What do all these names have in common? They were all white gentlemen, whose public reasoning was more than likely to take place amongst a homogenous group of white gentlemen at a time where those were the dominant voices. Diversity of opinion can perhaps be bridged through debate when each side has a similar amount of power, are working at a similar level of knowledge, and where the topic on the table is something that affects them all relatively equally. Not, however, when the subject is whether one side believes the other side deserves basic human dignity, and also holds the power to deny it. In modern partisan democracies, public reason is all too often 'an excessively idealized' process:[15] one which *can* work, and which *does* work, but only under ideal circumstances. Participants have to enter on equal footing, have to be arguing in good faith, and need to share a genuine commitment to achieving common moral aims.

In simpler terms: just like the free market itself, the marketplace of ideas requires meritocratic foundations. But 'meritocracy' was famously coined in 1958 by the sociologist Michael Dunlop Young as a satirical attack on those who believe in it.* As we'll see in the next section, debate is all well and good in theory, but in practice what *seems* like civil discourse is often just a wolf in sheep's clothing. Engage and it'll bite your face right off.

* Imagine an unequal race. One person has a clear running track, a decent head start, and the benefits of a life of excellent nutrition and training. Meanwhile, their opponent is undernourished and poorly shod and expected to leap over barbed wire just to get started. In an unmeritocratic world, individual aptitude is rarely enough to win, and success will never be meted out fairly.

Truthiness, Grievance Studies, and Vādavidyā Debates

When I say that public reason hasn't yet fixed society's deep and enduring problems, I don't mean that words have never changed anything. On the contrary: as the famous linguist J. L. Austin once said, speech is 'performative' because it performs real-world actions. A priest pronounces you husband and wife and the legal status between you changes. A government official calls for a minoritised ethnic group to be exterminated like 'cockroaches', and the genocide that follows suddenly feels less like murder and more like swatting a bug. An activist proclaims that he has a dream, and the movement gains a reverberating message of hope. Words have extreme power. That's why debates can be such a rousing and dangerous social tool. When performed in the spirit of seeking common ground and reaching consensus, like in the post-reconciliatory German political system, cross-party discussions can bring huge socially beneficial changes into being overnight.[16] In systems like the British Parliament, though, with its divided parties jeering at each other from opposing benches, acts of public reason often harness the power of words for bad, widening divisions rather than collapsing them.

The idea that there are good and bad ways to engage in debate has a long history within philosophies around the world. Take the *vādavidyā*, an Indian system designed to seek understanding and thereby reach 'truth', described in a range of ancient manuals:

> Of these manuals, the one found in the Nyāyasūtras of Akṣapāda Gautama (circa AD 150) is comparatively more

> systematic than others. [. . .] Debates, in Akṣapāda's view, can be of three types: (i) an honest debate (called vāda) where both sides, proponent and opponent, are seeking the truth, that is, wanting to establish the right view; (ii) a tricky-debate (called jalpa) where the goal is to win by fair means or foul; and (iii) a destructive debate (called vitaṇḍā) where the goal is to defeat or demolish the opponent, no matter how. This almost corresponds to the cliché in English: the good, the bad and the ugly.[17]

In the good kind of debate, *vāda*, participants rely solely on logical arguments based on full and thoughtful use of evidence. In *jalpa*, the bad, participants can use tricks and false moves to demonstrate that their own position is the truth. But in the ugly form of debate, *vitaṇḍā*, the winner is not supposed to establish their own position – in fact, they may not *have* a position, or even believe in truth at all. The goal is just to win at any cost. Those engaging in *vitaṇḍā* are free to use *chala* (underhanded tricks) like quibbling over tiny details, equivocating around the topic, and pretending to confuse metaphorical language for literal points, until their opponent's argument has been dragged so far from its original position that the entire debate has fallen apart. Believing this to be a deliberately and 'explicitly destructive and negative' mode of discussion, philosophers like Vātsyāyana (the *Kama Sutra* writer!) circa AD 350 unambiguously denounced this form of debate as detrimental to social functioning.[18] In his *Republic*, Plato also drew a distinction between the 'dialectic' mode of argumentation, which collectively seeks out truth via logical reason, and the 'eristic' method, whose goal is to win arguments by persuasion without caring about the truth at all.

That word 'truth' has become rather a sticky one in recent years. Parents in America have been storming school-board meetings in a moral panic about the imagined influx of 'critical race theory' into the educational system, a term which they seem to apply to any attempt to teach students about diversity at all. Meanwhile, in the UK, the heritage sector has recently seen a fresh interest in unveiling a side of history that hasn't historically been told: like how certain owners of stately homes lived happily in lifelong same-sex relationships, for example, or how posh museums were often built on the wealth of slavery. In return, some government ministers have responded with angry demands to quit all this cancel culture 'wokeness'.[19] The official guidance might be 'retain and explain' – but in practice, the threat is often that if these places want to keep their funding they should celebrate rather than criticise the nation's past. Oddly enough, those members of our professional commentariat who are usually most concerned about protecting free speech have been rather silent about all these efforts to interfere in free speech. Instead, they have seemed much more concerned that the effort of trying to understand injustice more deeply is itself having a 'chilling effect' on free thought.

The primary target of these complaints is, apparently . . . me. Or at least, people like me with jobs like mine. With the worst wrath reserved for people of colour, but especially women of colour, those who work in universities and colleges and schools around the world have increasingly come under fire. We are – or so our opponents constantly tell us – just a professionalised bunch of 'social justice warriors', committed to inculcating in our nation's youth a sense of liberal guilt and victimhood, through a new field of study called 'Grievance Studies' (their term, not ours). Grievance Studies, they say, is built on a philosophy of 'cultural relativism' – the idea that all truth is relative apart from the statement 'truth is relative', which is the only true truth. Cultural relativists, they say, believe that every culture has its own distinct systems of knowledge and value, and that all of those systems are equally valid. According to this worldview, they argue, there can be no such thing as absolute right or wrong at all – only things that are deemed right or wrong by the varying moral standards of each culture.

It sounds like a clever summary of a rather silly position, doesn't it? But the problem is that those claims are deliberately inaccurate – or at best, woefully incomplete. Generally speaking, scholars of 'Critical Justice' (our term, not theirs) do *not* believe that there's no such thing as right or wrong, good or bad, truth or lies. That's why we're seeking justice – because we believe in it, genius. It's just that we *also* believe that what we've previously been told is true is often based on partial information, or is only one part of a much bigger picture. As a schoolgirl in 1990s England, I can personally confirm that the unvarnished horrors of things like enslavement and colonialism were pretty much totally obscured behind simplified jingoism: like the singular truth that Britain conscientiously abolished transatlantic slavery first, or that Winston Churchill was an entirely virtuous and unproblematic leader because he won the Second World War. Today, any attempt to show a more complete picture gets denounced as 'rewriting history' and 'doing Britain down' – like the more complex truth that

Britain's conscience only awakened at the time that slavery began to seem less profitable, as the Trinidadian historian C. L. R. James wryly put it, or that after a long day of heroically fighting the Nazis, Churchill could also be found advocating for a spot of genocide himself.

Instead of attacking professional researchers, we should probably remember that the job of a historian is literally to rewrite history – by which I mean, to update and complexify the historical record as new information comes to light. Rather than spreading the idea that there's no such thing as right or wrong, what these scholars are usually doing is trying to right past wrongs – to engage in a process that Germans call *Vergangenheitsbewältigung*, to which they've been committed since the Second World War, and which means understanding the horrors of the past in order to 'work through' history collectively, rather than repeating it.

And actually, isn't it pretty clear by now that, on the whole, it's the extremists on the right of the political spectrum who are working to destroy truth? Facts don't care about your feelings; here are some feelings, which I am now going to mistake for facts. How many lies did Trump tell again? According to the *Washington Post*, he made 30,573 false statements over four years, an average of twenty-one erroneous claims a day.[20] Sorry, not lies – 'alternative facts'. In Britain's last general election, the Tories were called out hundreds of times for spreading misinformation,[21] even rebranding their own Twitter account 'FactCheck' during a debate and when criticised responding 'no one gives a toss'.[22] From nation to nation, right-wing voters have been found to be more likely to share 'fake news' featuring verifiably misleading or inaccurate information than left-wing voters.[23]

Stephen Colbert famously called this phenomenon 'truthiness' – if your gut feels like it's true then it is true, facts be damned.

This is why using debates to platform conspiracy theories and hate speech is such a dangerous thing to do. Because it doesn't seem to matter how thoroughly those claims about flat planets or 5G mind-melds are refuted, or how comprehensively the scientific evidence is weighted against them. All an argument needs to do is to appeal to deep-rooted *feelings* of truthiness, and some people will want to believe it.

A book called *Four Theories of the Press*, published in 1956, suggests that the marketplace of ideas was bound up in the rise of libertarianism as a political system. 'Let all with something to say be free to express themselves,' the authors summarise. 'The true and sound will survive. The false and unsound will be vanquished. Government should keep out of the battle and not weigh the odds in favor of one side or the other.'[24] This libertarian ideal of a self-regulating and non-state-intervening marketplace of ideas has failed for three main reasons.

Firstly, it's no coincidence that the adage 'sunlight is the best disinfectant' has been actively and enthusiastically promoted by the alt-right, who have a vested interest in seeding their heinous beliefs into the mainstream:*

* Let's put this myth to bed right now. According to the *Journal of Swine Health*, the best disinfectant is bleach. Actually, it's a mix of formalin added at 9 to 15kg per m3, 40 per cent calcium hydroxide added at 25 to 40kg per m3, and sodium hydroxide added at 8 to 12kg per m3, according to Sandra F. Amass ('Diagnosing Disinfectant Efficacy', *Journal of Swine Health and Production* 12:2 [2004]). Now we know.

Platforming a fascist – fantasy vs reality

> *What I think happens*: I logically refute all their arguments one by one and convert their audience to my side. The fascist slumps to the floor defeated, and the crowd goes wild!
>
> *What actually happens*: I lend the fascist my audience, give their illogical ideas the false legitimacy of seeming worthy of discussion, and drag the Overton window of acceptable, permissible discourse further and further to the right.

There is a supreme arrogance to rationalists' mindset here, I think. The person with a large platform who decides to take on an extremist seems to believe that they uniquely have the power to defeat xenophobes and misogynists and Holocaust deniers through sheer force of intellect. 'As soon as I face them in a battle of intellect, the weakness of their ideas will be exposed!' Like nobody has ever tried that before. 'I am conscious that I have no equal in the art of swaying the masses,' Hitler is supposed to once have said. What we do know for sure is that, in between the repeal of his speaking ban on 6 March 1927 and the Reichstag election five years later, Hitler made 455 public appearances to an estimated minimum 4.5 million people. We also know that over that same period his party went from a radical fringe, gathering less than 3 per cent of the vote, into the most popular German party, with more than 37 per cent of the national vote in July 1932.[25] When we platform a fascist, the thing that benefits most is fascism.

Secondly, what we seem to have forgotten is that free speech has *always* included reasonable limitations, with the absolute right to say anything we want stopping where harm to marginalised communities begins. This is a moral conflict that goes back at least as far as the ancient Greeks, who drew a division between *isegoria*, the equal right of citizens to voice an opinion, and *parrhesia*, the specific right to make provocative statements by speaking truth to power.[26] In the centuries since, certain intellectuals and politicians have twisted *parrhesia* into their personal ideal of free speech absolutism, while handily ignoring the equal importance the classical world placed on conditioning would-be provocateurs 'into normative modes of factuality and accountability' via social constraints.[27] In Athens, for instance, the right to *parrhesia* was carefully regulated through mechanisms like *dokimasia* (a robust character test that every nineteen-year-old man had to pass before he was allowed to speak his mind), as well as being bound by hierarchical power dynamics allowing speakers to punch *up* but not *down*. These kinds of accountability mechanism were carefully designed to ensure that 'the *parrhesiast* (1) believed in the truth of his assertions and (2) spoke with goodwill for purposes of community building',[28] and thereby to safeguard against 'dangerously and demonstrably false ideas [being allowed to] compete on equal footing with those grounded in fact'.[29*]

Thirdly, even when the marketplace of ideas *does* work as it's supposed to, free speech advocates still cry foul. What we're now calling 'cancel culture' is often just a case of

* In Germany, the government waited until 2016 before they allowed *Mein Kampf* to be republished and sold again, and only then with extreme caution. That's how thoroughly they had learned their lesson about the dangers of unconstrained *parrhesia*, allowing toxic falsitudes to spread unfettered throughout public discourse.

powerful people who are not used to being held accountable finally realising that actions have consequences. A university invites a Holocaust denier; the rest of the student body protests; security is deemed too expensive; the event is shut down. A known bigot is given a book deal; conscientious objectors call for a boycott; the publishers realise they may end up losing money; they cancel the book. That is literally the free market in action. In fact, that is the definition of the marketplace of ideas as it was originally imagined back in the 1950s. The market has listened, decided those views are false and unsound, and vanquished them before they can do further harm. The right to speech does not equal the right to reach an audience via high-profile platforms. Nor does it protect the speaker from experiencing the costs of others' disagreement. We live in a society; shared commitments to truth and community-building are part of the contract.

Once upon a time, I was a willing participant in the Reasonable Tango. I too spent hours at parties politely offering good-faith rebuttals to bad-faith arguments and backing up my points with earnest statistics – painstakingly explaining, for example, that, no, Europe didn't 'bring progress' to the world, in fact Europe's deliberate policies of economic and political destabilisation destroyed the natural social progress of entire continents, so the 'developing world' should really be called the 'recovering world' and . . . Or: yes, okay, the pay gap *is* partially a result of women being more likely than men to take time out for childcare, but this phenomenon is also the consequence of that same patriarchal culture which simultaneously devalues women's labour while placing powerful social expectations of nurture on to them so that . . . blah blah blah blah. Over and over and over. After spending my twenties having identikit discussions with identikit strangers, I pretty much gave up.

Sure, every now and again I'd get somebody engaging in good faith – someone who was willing to go away and do the baseline reading necessary to get up to speed on the complexities of the topic, rather than cherry-picking evidence and spouting half-informed views.* More often than not, though, I'd find my opponent using *vitaṇḍā* tactics – things like deliberately dragging the discussion off-course through introducing rhetorical red herrings, or doing the 'Gish Gallop',† peppering out specious arguments and half-truths so rapidly that they're impossible to refute at once. This is sometimes combined with a tactic called 'sealioning' – a discursive manoeuvre which according to Harvard University researchers:

> fuses persistent questioning – often about basic information, information easily found elsewhere, or unrelated or tangential points – with a loudly-insisted-upon commitment to

* This isn't me being an elitist snob, by the way, for gently suggesting that people might want to bolster their understanding of a topic by engaging with just some of the decades of expert peer-reviewed evidence on that topic before beginning to opine. Remember how Rawls himself said that beginning from completely uneven perspectives is anathema to the whole idea of public reason? Either the discussion will end up being entirely one-sided, as one party educates the other rather than debating on common ground, *or* they'll simply waste their time talking past each other and having two completely different conversations – one based on a commitment to truth, the other a dangerous disregard for it.

† A technique named after the creationist Duane Gish to argue with scientists against the evidenced consensus of evolution.

> reasonable debate. It disguises itself as a sincere attempt to learn and communicate. Sealioning thus works both to exhaust a target's patience, attention, and communicative effort, and to portray the target as unreasonable.[30]

Ultimately, the win-condition for a sealion is to goad their opponent into raising their voice, so they can triumphantly denounce them. Civil debate means being civil, remember? Lose your temper, lose the argument. But as we've already seen, respectability politics is a weapon: one that's always been disproportionately wielded against working-class people, women, queer people, and people of colour, but *especially* against Black women, who are frequently smeared as hostile and aggressive even when they're carefully keeping their voice as flat and level as a paving slab.[31] Meanwhile, the people with no personal stake in a societal problem – the ones who are often knowingly forcing those with lived experience of harm to persuade people of their trauma over and over again – get to be seen as reasonable, rational, and therefore right. Topsy-turvy, indeed.

I saw some of these tactics first-hand in the breastfeeding debates. If you can get your tits out in a restaurant and leak milk everywhere, men kept saying to me triumphantly, then I guess I can get my penis out? Well, first of all, breasts are not primary sex organs – the direct anatomical correlation to my nipples isn't your downstairs area, *it's your own nipples*. And secondly, if I can feed my baby in a restaurant then you too are entitled to . . . eat food . . . in a restaurant. All you've done there is invented a straw man to argue against, taken my rational point to illogical extremes, and in doing so painted me as the unreasonable one. As Audre Lorde put it, it always seems to be 'the responsibility of the oppressed to teach the oppressors their mistakes':

> Black and Third World people are expected to educate white people as to our humanity. Women are expected to educate men. Lesbians and gay men are expected to educate the heterosexual world. The oppressors maintain their position and evade their responsibility for their own actions.[32]

The end result, Lorde says, is a 'constant drain of energy which might be better used in redefining ourselves and devising realistic scenarios for altering the present and constructing the future'.[33] Play stupid games, win stupid prizes. All too often, the modus operandi of a serial debater isn't to find common ground. The goal, writes Toni Morrison, is distraction. 'It keeps you from doing your work. It keeps you explaining, over and over again, your reason for being' – endlessly forced into justifying your worth, your art, your language, your history, your humanity. 'None of this is necessary. There will always be one more thing.'[34]

There will always be one more thing to prove. The debate is never-ending. All talk, no action – that's the reasonable way. Nowhere is this truer than on the internet.

Someone is Wrong on the Internet

One of the most popular webcomics in the world is called *xkcd*, created in 2005 by American author, illustrator, and former NASA roboticist Randall Munroe. One of Munroe's most frequently shared images shows a person sitting hunched over an old-fashioned desktop computer. Trailing off the side of the page, a speech bubble asks if they are ready to come to bed. They can't, they reply. They are doing something important. Someone is *wrong* on the internet.

Every January first, I make the same New Year's resolution. Do *not* get into fights with strangers online. By the time the second rolls around, I've invariably lost the battle. Why? Because someone, somewhere, is being wrong on the internet. And I cannot let it stand. What the hell is wrong with me?

It's going to take a lot more than one book to answer that question. So instead let's ask a different question. What the hell is wrong with *us*? And how can we resist?

This question brings us back full circle – back to the disconnection economy itself. Remember when I said that there are huge profits to be made in encouraging divisions? This only works if our arguments are taking place very visibly, out there in the public domain. The internet was meant to be an amazing new forum for public reason – that utopian image of a global town square, open 24/7 for productive debates about what the world is now and what we'd like it to become. Instead, thanks to the combined efforts of political troll farms and corporate greed, what it's actually done is fortified a desire to wade into online debates, which are often deliberately intended to intensify – not to resolve – conflict. If you hover your mouse over Munroe's cartoon, a comment box pops up that reads: 'What do you want me to do? LEAVE? Then they'll keep being wrong!'

I call it the old bait-and-bitch technique. They *need* us to argue with each other. So why are we so willing to give them the satisfaction?

In a 2011 *Wired* article, Chris Colin identified a phenomenon he termed the 'Yelpification of the universe'. 'For every ocean of new data we generate each hour,' Colin said, 'an attendant ocean's worth of reviewage follows. The Internet-begotten abundance of absolutely everything has given rise to a parallel universe of stars, rankings, most-recommended lists, and other valuations.'[35] Around the same time, a study of media consumption was published by researchers at the University of California, which found that modern Americans are deluged with information – consuming on average 100,500 words per day, the equivalent of thirty-four gigabytes of data. They found that information consumption grew at an annual rate of 5.4 per cent between 1980 and 2008.[36] It has continued to increase in the decade since.

The overload of consumed information. The desire to form and share an opinion. Twined around each other like a double helix, I believe that these two things are both completely connected – and mutually reinforcing. After all, everything is so *confusing* nowadays.* With trust in public institutions

* Of course, divergent opinions and conspiracy theories have existed throughout history. In her book *Going Dark* (Bloomsbury, 2019), on the social lives of extremists, Julia Ebner describes how in AD 64, as a great fire roared around Rome leaving hundreds of thousands of citizens homeless, a rumour spread that Nero had purposefully set the city alight himself. But Ebner explains that the online sphere is not only accelerating our ability to rapidly spread hoaxes and misinformation – research has found that it's also the ideal breeding ground for conspiracy-theory logic

being eroded, and with various social crises looming (climate catastrophe, pandemics, the rocketing wealth disparities caused by late-stage capitalism), people have begun to invest in ever more extreme ideas. And as the ground we're walking on gets increasingly uncertain, this explains how we might come in turn to cling harder to those mistaken beliefs. When our internal reality is called into doubt, it can shake us to the core, threatening what sociologist Anthony Giddens calls our 'ontological security',[37] the comforting sense of certainty in an uncertain universe. Contradictory information is experienced as a threat to that security, something to be warded off at any cost. Meanwhile, loudly affirming our own position can be a way for us to combat information overwhelm, helping us clear a path through the mess we're mired in and restoring a sense of order to the chaos. Instead of asking *why* our opinions differ from others, we often find ourselves loudly doubling down on that sense of ourselves *as a reasonable person* – and of others as fundamentally unreasonable.

This further exposes the fallacy of fixing the problem by talking about the problem. The ethicist C. Thi Nguyen[38] says that changing minds through discourse only works when what we're stuck in is an 'epistemic bubble': 'an informational network from which relevant voices have been excluded by

---

and culture to flourish. Politics expert Phoenix Andrews says that post-war democracies were marked by a liberal consensus, then from the 1980s onwards we had the *neo*liberal consensus – now we're entering a political period that he terms 'digital dissensus', where 'the internet and social media become forums for noisy debate and extremist voices' ('Receipts, Radicalisation, Reactionaries, and Repentance', *Feminist Media Studies* 20:6 [2020]: pp. 902–907).

omission', whether purposeful or not. 'As social scientists tell us, we like to engage in selective exposure, seeking out information that confirms our own worldview,' he points out. 'But that omission can also be entirely inadvertent. Even if we're not actively trying to avoid disagreement, our Facebook friends tend to share our views and interests.' Just like how Rawls' framework has the best chance of working in an idealised scenario where everyone shares a common base framework and set of reference points, '[w]hen we take networks built for social reasons and start using them as our information feeds, we tend to miss out on contrary views and run into exaggerated degrees of agreement'.

The problem with public reason in the information age is that it relies on the idea that we are all floating around in bubbles, which can fairly easily be popped 'simply by exposing its members to the information and arguments that they've missed', as Nguyen puts it. It's tempting to think that all we need to do to counter the virulent spread of misinformation and fake news is to puncture that bubble through the careful introduction of reasonable doubt. Meanwhile, what we're *actually* stuck in is an echo chamber: 'a social structure from which other relevant voices have been actively discredited. Where an epistemic bubble merely omits contrary views, an echo chamber brings its members to actively distrust outsiders.'* Much like a cult, 'echo chambers aren't weakened but are

* If we think about Vint Cerf's metaphor of the internet as a mirror of society, it's increasingly looking like the painter Magritte's *The False Mirror*. In a letter to Paul Colinet, dated to 1957, Magritte wrote about the problems with viewing his paintings: 'What represents the picture are our ideas and feelings – in short, whoever is looking at the picture

actually *strengthened* by opposing views'.

Hold on. Who is this 'we' I'm talking about? You might be worrying here that I've fallen into a common trap – an affliction I call bothsides-itis. This is the assumption that we're all identically stuck in the exact same kinds of echo chambers, each side full of anti-expert cultists programmed to knee-jerk reject any evidence that opposes our own beliefs. 'Not the violent conflict between parts of the truth, but the quiet suppression of half of it, is the formidable evil,' wrote the English philosopher John Stuart Mill in his 1859 essay *On Liberty*. '[T]here is always hope when people are forced to listen to both sides; it is when they attend only to one that errors harden into prejudices, and truth itself ceases to have the effect of truth, by being exaggerated into falsehood.'[39] See? Your side is just as atomised and intolerant to alternative beliefs as ours! Again, though, this relies on an idealised system in which each party is equally situated on two sides of a divide, both appealing to their half of the truth – the half of the truth that they are able to see.

But what about when one side's version of the truth is more likely to be built on a commitment to evidenced consensus, whilst the other side is based on the truthiness of gut feeling and misinformation? What happens when one side is basically in agreement about the need to make life better for everyone, and the other side mainly just wants life to

---

is representing what he sees.' (Quoted by Richard Wolff. 'Magritte: A Painter Brushes with Overdetermination', *Rethinking Marxism* 8:1 [1995]: pp. 27–47). Stuck in echo chambers designed to refract and strengthen people's identities through appealing to their core beliefs, online communities begin to see what they want to see.

get worse for those they don't like? Is listening to each side equally such a good idea then?

Yes, I'm aware that even asking this question risks sticking me back in the box of condescending liberal elite with all its attendant stereotypical traits. And it's absolutely true that those on the left – me included – aren't by any means immune to that gleeful impulse to share false information without fact-checking it first. But, surely, at some point we have to reckon with the reality that expertise, knowledge, the search for truth isn't in itself an elitist pursuit. As the Journalism 101 adage goes: 'If one side says it's raining and the other says it's sunny, your job isn't to report them both – it's to look out of the window and find out which is true.' The scales of justice will never be rebalanced if we keep on heaping up truth on one side and lies on the other and calling them the same. It's time now to look out of that window.

In an Age of Unreason

'Ask those who are giving [the COVID vaccine]: has there been any deaths? Ask them what's in it. Get their names. Email them to me [. . .]. With a group of lawyers, we are collating all that. At the Nuremberg trials, the doctors and nurses stood trial – *and they hung*. If you are a doctor or a nurse, now is the time to get off that bus. Get off it and stand with us, the people. All around the world, they are rising!'[40]

This speech was given in London in July 2021 by a virulent anti-vaxxer and former nurse, at a national rally against the COVID vaccination programme. Struck off the Nursing and Midwifery Council register for promoting harmful conspiracy theories, she has called the pandemic itself a 'scam' promoted by an international council of politicians, media figures, bankers, and the military. The National Health Service, she has previously said, is 'the new Auschwitz'.[41] It's time for the medical profession to tell the truth.

This is not an isolated incident. It's a global phenomenon: one which may have found a new enemy to fight in the pandemic restrictions, but is really just a symptom of an ongoing problem. This is the concerted mobilisation since the early 2010s of a 'curious coalition' uniting 'far-right agitators, far-left conspiracy theorists and "concerned citizens"' against scientific, political, and media expertise.[42] Whether it's people setting fire to 5G masts, or the storming of Capitol Hill by Trump supporters certain the election had been stolen, the connecting thread is the sense that The People are being lied to by sinister forces, and that this is a deep injustice that has to be righted.

'In pursuit of justice, we need to be unreasonable!' I've argued here, blithely. 'If words are failing, sometimes we need to act!' Well, it turns out that 'become unreasonable' is also the motto of an alt-right group called the Boogaloo Boys in the USA, who are currently agitating for a new civil war. Whenever a protest is planned – whether by liberals or conservatives – there they are online, swarming in droves on to their 4Chan and Reddit discussion boards, planning to crash the party, overthrow the government, and bring about the end of democracy as we know it.

A surface reading of this book might assume that I'm telling anyone who *feels* they've been wronged to rise up and fight against the people who have wronged them. What I've *actually* said is that *sometimes*, in pursuit of a better world *for everyone*, we may need to become temporarily unreasonable – where absolutely necessary! – in order to fight back against evidenceable injustice. This doesn't mean I'm saying that those hopped up on fake news should be allowed to burn the world to the ground. Nor am I suggesting that we should let the side with an unequal amount of power do whatever they like to tip the scales further in their favour. When marginalised groups take to the streets, it's usually a political move to claw back just some of the power they've long been denied. When spoiled rich white people take to the streets, they are often seeking to augment and enforce the overwhelming power they already have. To quote Elie Wiesel's 1986 Nobel Peace Prize acceptance speech: 'We must take sides. Neutrality helps the oppressor, never the victim. Silence encourages the tormentor, never the tormented. Sometimes we must interfere.'[43] But this kind of moral interference requires us to be able to tell the difference between tormentor and tormented, oppressor and victim.

In our divisive political landscape, the pernicious demand to meet our opponents in the spirit of empathy and compromise and tolerance has become manifestly one-sided. Increasingly it seems that the right-wing reserve the right to cry 'oppression' and to break the rules when it suits them, while decrying even the most moderate opposition for being unreasonably extreme. Political scientists call this 'asymmetrical polarisation': a phenomenon in which conservatives tend to go further right than liberals go left, yet each side is still often seen as being equivalently partisan. In order to combat this asymmetry, we have to develop a better collective understanding of what injustice and oppression actually *mean*.

For example, let's start with the asymmetries of protest. On the one side, we have a group of protesters who are fighting back against centuries of coordinated state violence. This is an injustice which has been confirmed time and time again by vast swathes of peer-reviewed evidence, produced by thousands of researchers working in every kind of discipline and identified within every aspect of life: from economics to employment to education to the law. On the other side, protesters like the anti-mask brigade are using verifiable untruths to fight a made-up problem: refusing to take the most basic of measures to protect vulnerable people, while busily comparing themselves to Holocaust victims and Rosa Parks.[44] One side is battling actual oppression, the other side is advocating an every-man-for-himself approach to global health, and confusing inconvenience with persecution. *We are not the same.*

Now look at what happens when politicians are accused of wrongdoing. The *Washington Post* called this 'asymmetrical accountability'. When the Democratic politician Andrew Cuomo was accused of sexually harassing his subordinates, he was rightfully vilified by both the left-leaning media and by his own party. 'How often, by contrast, do you see the right uncovering misconduct among Republicans or demanding accountability?' the *Post* asked. 'Almost never.' In fact, 'right-wing media and politicians act as apologists for far worse miscreants – such as former president Donald Trump'.[45] *We are not the same.*

Finally, think about the asymmetries of empathy. Think about all those heartfelt spreads of heartland voters justifying away white rage as economic anxiety. Think about the sympathetic profiles of high-earning businessmen who voted for Brexit because they didn't like the idea of having foreigners for a neighbour, and are now watching their produce rotting amid all that new red tape. Think about the tendency in the liberal press to reason away insurrectionists' anger as an understandable reaction to a society that is changing too fast. They feel left behind and disenfranchised; they've been told that democracy itself is under attack; they just wandered into the Capitol peacefully and stuck to the rope-lined routes of the guided tour, it's no big deal! Luckily, social media – and the FBI – told another story. A man stealing a White House podium to (possibly) sell on eBay.[46] A crowd baying spit and fury in the faces of security staff. People who travelled to the rally by private jet. Men breaking windows with a riot shield tussled away from a police officer or roaming the halls shouting for women representatives to 'come out and play', in tones so reminiscent of a horror movie it chills the blood.[47] Many of these people weren't the poor or the left-behind at all; a lot of them were realtors and college students and politicians' kids, furious at the possibility that just a little bit of their massive power and influence might be slipping out of their grasp, and determined to keep the systems in place designed to advantage them. Think about Trump's eventual message 'go home, we love you' to the insurgents;[48] think about Fox News host Tucker Carlson calling BLM protesters 'poison' one minute, then the Capitol perpetrators 'solid Americans' who were just 'deeply frustrated' the next.[49] *We are not the same.*

And what about when, squeezed down and suppressed for decades, the frustration felt by progressive social groups finally does erupt? At that point, the right-wing press swoops in, screeching gleefully: just look at that rabble, no respect for due process, they're animals. See for example the response to the pro-choice uprisings following the rapid destruction of *Roe v. Wade*. Conveniently, there seemed to be a Republican bubble of amnesia surrounding all those abortion clinics that for decades had been bombarded by threatening blockades, bomb threats, and arson; a collective forgetting of all the healthcare providers who'd been murdered over the years just for doing their jobs. Instead, lots of conservative commentators suddenly seemed overwhelmed with concern about the dangers of passionate disagreement.[50] 'When we lost in 1973, we accepted it with sadness and grace – we didn't throw our toys out of the pram!' No, you threw Molotov cocktails instead.[51] This is what media scholars call 'the protest paradigm'.[52] No matter which methods progressives use to signal their dissent, they will inevitably get smeared as anti-democratic and unpatriotic to an extent that conservatives do not. Whether it's John Carlos and Tommie Smith making their famous Black Power salute at the 1968 Olympics, or Colin Kaepernick taking a knee today: when it comes to the left, the media has always preferred to foreground endless debates over method instead of paying attention to the actual message. This has produced such a skewed vision of acceptability that, throughout history, even the most sedately liberal campaign has been dismissed as divisive and disrespectful. Meanwhile, the radical right consistently deploys violent tactics and demands understanding for their side, while refusing to offer it in return.[53] *We. Are. Not. The. Same.*

Just before the 2020 US election, the *New York Times* cited academic evidence of this 'liberal suckerdom' in action.

Democrats' obsession with fairness and bipartisanship, they said, has been leading them to make many more compromises than Republicans.[54] They cited a paper called 'Sunsets Are for Suckers' by Kristen Underhill and Ian Ayres,[55] professors at the universities of Columbia and Yale respectively, which sought to understand legislative compromise by studying 'sunsets': 'agreements to make a law lapse after a certain number of years. Agreeing to something you don't like, so long as it is time-limited is a way to be open-minded and allow a law that one might personally disagree with to be tried out for a while.' The researchers found that self-identified liberals were much more willing to allow conservative priorities to be enacted so long as that time-limited get-out clause is safely in place, while conservatives 'tend to simply reject liberal proposals, no matter what'.[56]

For anyone who studies politics, this shouldn't be a surprise. Certain factions of the right have *always* been given licence to spit and scream: branding judges 'Enemies of the People' for doing their job,[57] bellowing, 'COMMUNISM!' and 'THE DEATH OF FREEDOM!' at any little hint of liberal reform, then steaming ahead with their own agenda. In the USA, the Republican Party as a whole has an acknowledged culture of aggressive gerrymandering, manipulating the boundaries of electoral constituencies to the benefit of its candidates.[58] They have developed a consistent policy of denigrating and seeking to discredit their opposition, with Republicans more likely to air negative advertisements compared to Democrats,[59] as well as being found to show stronger out-group negativity and hostility towards fact-checkers.[60] They ignored both Trump's robber-baron grift and the left's pleas to impeach him, instead supporting the 'alternate view of reality promoted by Fox News, Breitbart, Newsmax, and other right wing media outlets, in which only fraud could defeat' such a beloved candidate.[61] And in Obama's final year as president, Republicans famously argued that it would be unconstitutional for his government to nominate the Democratic candidate Merrick Garland as Supreme Court Justice so close to the election,[62] then immediately swore in Amy Coney Barrett just days before Trump was voted out.

On the whole, liberal politicians are often happy with a win-win, when everyone gets what they want and the world is made a little better for everyone – including those who traditionally vote right. This is because, for many centrist progressives, it's the sanctity of democratic institutions that must be protected above all else. Meanwhile, for many on the right, these institutions are increasingly being treated as a means to an end, bending and twisting the democratic process to the point of rupture so long as it gives them what they want. This means that a win-win is often anathema. In fact, to some right-wing politicians, a lose-lose outcome seems to be preferable: because the only win they'll accept is if the other side fails. While liberals tend genuinely to believe in norms of fairness and decency, reactionaries are more likely to know when to wield and when to break them.

Let's return to Rawls' 'public reason' doctrine. Rawls says that rules can be imposed on people as long as those rules can be *reasoned*, and are therefore justifiable to both sides. In order to mount a justification, though, the reasonable citizen needs to commit to appealing to underlying shared principles: a moral system which everyone over whom those rules have authority can accept.* The problem with trying to both-sides everything through civil debate is that it only works when both sides are operating within a shared moral system. What happens, though, when each side is working from a different 'conceptual universe'?

I found this phrase in a book called *Moral Politics: How Liberals and Conservatives Think* by the American linguist George Lakoff – and suddenly I understood the problem of public reason so much better. Remember how, earlier, I said that the 1970s exacerbated the divide between two distinctly different visions of morality: collective responsibility and personal responsibility? Lakoff explains this in terms of a central metaphor. Liberals, he says, are by and large invested in a 'nurturant parent' moral system, in which equality relies on creating the fair and nourishing societal conditions needed for everyone to have equal opportunities to thrive. The conservative worldview, meanwhile, is based on the model of the 'strict father', where equality means that people either thrive

* By 'justifiable', Rawls argued, people couldn't simply appeal to controversial standards like religion, over which people are assumed to disagree and which have to be taken on faith rather than via evidence. Also, in making your justification, he said, you couldn't simply point to the rules to which people already consent, because they might be consenting to immoral rules; nor were you allowed to coerce others to agree with you, by simply appealing to the truth as you see it, because what you see as self-evidently true might for somebody else be completely wrong. Instead, public reason relied on a mutual belief in those core moral values everyone was expected to share: things like freedom and equality and justice (Jonathan Quong, 'Public Reason', *Stanford Encyclopedia of Philosophy* [2013], https://seop.illc.uva.nl/entries/public-reason).

on their own merits or are punished if they fail. When it comes to liberal vs conservative politics, Lakoff says, they are often in entirely alternate conceptual universes. This makes it impossible to reason with each other.

Lakoff breaks down the metaphorical logics that underpin the 'strict father' moral system. The idea of 'moral strength' sets up a dichotomy where ascetic self-denial is seen as a sign of virtue, while any lapse in self-control is seen as moral weakness. The notion of 'moral order' reinforces 'traditional hierarchical power relations and, together with moral strength, makes it seem reasonable to think that the rich are either morally or naturally superior to the poor'.[63] The immoral pursuit of self-interest is reimagined as a sign of morality: the strict father looks out for himself in order to look after his family. So too is the need to separate the strong from the weak: 'contact with immoral people is [seen as] dangerous because the immorality might spread in a rapid and uncontrollable way like an epidemic', Lakoff argues.[64] Finally, and most revealing of all, the 'strict father' worldview *does* believe in nurturing people (through charity, for example) – but also believes that helping people only becomes a moral virtue under specific circumstances:

> Help is never moral when it interferes with the cultivation of self-discipline and responsibility and therefore leads to moral weakness. Since reward and punishment are seen to be effective in promoting learning, the giving of nurturance as reward and withholding of nurturance in the name of discipline and punishment can serve the moral purpose of teaching self-discipline and responsibility. Nurturance is not unconditional.

> It must serve the function of authority, strength, and discipline.[65]

What do all these have in common? These are the qualities upheld and promoted by Mr Reasonable, that patriarchal-colonial construction of upright civility and disciplined order. Meanwhile, the 'nurturant parent' seems to have more in common with the way of thinking described by many colonised peoples around the world, in which self-nurture is considered part of a healthy balance with nurturing one's familial, communal, and ecological bonds. This explains why appealing to those core principles of liberty, justice, and equality usually fails to have the hoped-for effect. For the strict father, these core principles are bound up with an individualising ideal of 'moral accounting', in which helping someone means imposing a weighty moral debt on to them. For the nurturant parent, helping people is just the moral debt we owe to each other: a mutually beneficial necessity for strengthening social bonds and building a better, more liveable world.

So: what now? Should liberals today 'be sick of being reasonable', as that 'liberal suckerdom' article asked? Led by principled progressive politicians like Alexandria Ocasio-Cortez, the electorate may finally be reaching a critical sense of 'exhaustion with playing the decent human being; weariness from unilaterally sticking up for the genteel norms of the Enlightenment and getting steamrollered in the process.'[66] No wonder bothsides-itis isn't working: only one side is doing it! Given the urgency of problems like the climate catastrophe, the exponential wealth-hoarding of billionaires, and the resurgence of far-right populism, should liberals abandon their game of sensible centrism and begin supporting candidates who are willing to play hardball?

By now you probably know how I would answer that question. Yes. Absolutely. In fact, I think it is long past time. You can only treat others reasonably when you can expect them to be reasonable to you in return. When they go low, we go high – and lose. No more. It's time to pick a side.

Conclusion

Respect, Reciprocity, Renewal: An Anti-Reasonable Manifesto

This book has grown out of a series of questions I began asking a few years ago. If we reimagined the rules of public togetherness, what would get better? What would change for the worse? And for whom?

What surprised me was how *angry* people often got whenever I tried asking these questions. The way their shoulders would go up, the 'yes, but' that leapt into their throats, propelled by that unbearable urge to wade in. But it *is* simple! If you're taking your baby on a plane then just do your best to keep him quiet. Just hire a car instead and if you can't do that then stay at home. Just go back in time and don't have kids, so you won't have to deal with the consequences. Just buy a bunch of earplugs and candy, and put together a little goodie bag for everyone nearby to thank them for tolerating you. Tolerance. *Ugh.* Is there any more perniciously patronising word?

Whenever a bigwig is faced with the realities of bigotry and cries out 'but ours is such a tolerant country!', I think about what that word implies. It's the belief that *we* have a greater claim over this space than *you* do. That our kindly willingness to tolerate your presence in this space is conditional on you behaving exactly the way we want. But as equal citizens with an equal right to be together in public, surely we all have equal right to chime in on what we want that to mean?

Sara Ahmed says that when you expose a problem you become the problem. When you try to fix that problem, the problem stops being the thing that actually needs fixing, and becomes *you.*[1] We see this every time somebody names their oppression or calls out a gross abuse of power and gets told to watch their tone. Women are branded hysterical or strident. Disabled people are forced to choose between accepting an unacceptable compromise and disappearing quietly from view, or pushing for equitable access and becoming 'the ungrateful cripple'.* Queer people are permitted to be out and proud in the public eye so long as they render themselves palatable to the cis-heteronormative gaze, embracing the trappings of nuclear families, cosy jumpers, and chaste glances – sexuality stripped of sex – in order to be 'an acceptable, respectable, unthreatening, loveable gay'.[2] Malcolm X argued that any time Black people 'are not able to be controlled by the man, the press immediately begins to label those Black people as irresponsible or as extremists'.[3] The status quo is designed to destroy resistance – to impede, halt, exhaust, grind down, making the process as mentally and emotionally gruelling as possible, and painting the resister as unreasonable.

Becoming unreasonable doesn't mean everyone for themselves. Quite the contrary. As the Chicana activist Elizabeth Martínez argued in 1998, instead of 'Oppression Olympics' the goal of social justice movements should be to embrace the potentials of coalitional resistance, understanding that our

* 'The ungrateful cripple' is a term used by disability activists and scholars to describe the hostile way disabled people are labelled when advocating for reasonable accommodations to be made on their terms, not those of the institution.

own struggle is part of a common struggle against the complex system of domination formed by white-supremacy, patriarchy, homophobia, and global capitalist exploitation.[4] I believe in the power of Martínez's collective to build a better world. I believe that, by and large, we are social animals, who act selfishly not because we can't help ourselves. We become selfish when that is made to seem the acceptable (even desirable) thing to do, the tectonic plates of normative behaviour beginning inexorably to shift when we're made to feel like other people are pushing the boundaries and benefiting. I believe that developing a shared system of both formal rules and informal guidelines for mutual cooperation can be a powerful tool to prevent this, backed up by social censure from the body politic, where necessary, when somebody acts in their own interests at the expense of everyone else. If there's no cost to behaving badly, and when selfishness is met only with tolerance, people are more likely to look out just for themselves. We're living in a society. I believe in society.

But I also believe that parts of the social contract have been designed by those right at the very top, in response to acute status anxieties, to keep the rest of us in our neatly ordered boxes below. I know that *some* of the rules we think are common sense have never been held in common, while others may no longer be fit for purpose. I understand that the ideal of civilised propriety was designed to regulate increasingly unwieldy and diverse societies: keeping power and wealth located in the hands of the few while pushing the rest of us to be ever more productive, then spending the rest of our time at each other's throats fighting for scraps. I think the requirement to discipline every inch of our lives and our bodies to repressed perfection is harming more of us than it's helping.

What I'm *not* saying, of course, is that people from marginalised communities are unable to enact self-discipline or show consideration of others or act politely. Absolutely not. In fact, as Brittney C. Cooper's book *Beyond Respectability* explains, the careful construction of a respectable persona has always been one of the strategies necessary for marginalised people to survive a hostile public sphere.[5] The problem is that 1) the public sphere should never have been hostile to parts of the public in the first place, and 2) it's those members of the public who are visibly and/or audibly non-normative – like being poor, or young, or a person of colour – who tend to be most vulnerable to accusations of disrespect, at risk of being surveilled and suspected and policed, *even if their behaviour is exactly the same as the rich older white person next to them*. Fundamentally, I believe that kindness, civility, and empathy are more essential today than ever. But I also understand that telling oppressed people to #BeKind, speak civilly, and empathise with their oppressors makes me complicit in their oppression.

In researching this book I came across a lovely adjective: 'Minnesota Nice'. Often used as a backhanded compliment, it refers to the kind of passive-aggressive people who smile politely to your face then talk behind your back. Minnesota Nice is a bit like Norway's *Janteloven*, the law of Jante, that idea that nobody should try to place themselves over another, which it's been suggested might feed a Norwegian tendency towards conflict-avoidance in the face of unfairness.* Courtesy and

* In his radio show *A Prairie Home Companion*, Garrison Keillor coined the term 'Wobegonics' to describe the language system of this kind of person, who usually avoids using any 'confrontational verbs or statements of strong personal preference' – which means that the uncle

solicitude are good qualities to have, of course (that willingness to pull together regularly shoots Minnesota to the top of the list of the most generous states in the US, while Norway is famously egalitarian-minded). But those qualities cannot only be surface-deep. Style is no use without substance.

For some people it has always been more important to maintain Martin Luther King's 'negative peace which is the absence of tension' than it is to endure the societal discomfort needed to bring about 'a positive peace which is the presence of justice'.[6] Well, I for one would prefer radical kindness over a wishy-washy pretence of niceness any day. Radical kindness doesn't mean speaking nicely to those who maintain oppressive systems, but instead being kind to those they're oppressing – by swiftly and firmly deplatforming bigots, cancelling abusers, and shutting hate-speech down. Instead of unthinkingly imposing out-of-date ideals on to everyone and calling it simple common sense, we need to decide collectively which bits of the social contract are truly designed for the common good. Which norms are making society better and safer and fairer and kinder for all of us, and which are only uplifting some while keeping others down?

The trick, of course, is figuring out how to ask these questions in a world that is fundamentally divided. How can we possibly

---

making homophobic jokes is diplomatically ignored while the niece who calls him out is seen as the rude one (Quoted in: www.prairiehome.org/story/1997/04/19/wobegonics.html). 'People who have grown up with it know that Minnesota Nice doesn't have all that much to do with being nice,' says the playwright Syl Jones. 'It's more about keeping up appearances, about keeping the social order, about keeping people in their place' (Quoted in: www.mprnews.org/story/2009/12/14/syljones).

work these things through as a collective when productive discourse has become impossible? Good-faith conversations are fragmenting. Civil debate is being weaponised to stall progress. Public reason has broken down. There is a solution – and it's to *stop weighing both sides equally*. In order for public reason to work, we need to get much more comfortable with acknowledging the uneven operations of power, and making reasonable accommodations to rebalance it.

The problem with the 'fitness to rule' doctrine is that it relied on people like Mr Reasonable handing down his terms of respectable engagement from on high. At least as far back as ancient China, when the Qin Kingdom defeated its last rival and began bringing together feuding states into an empire, powerful bodies have reacted to worries about cultural pluralism by systematising codes of behaviour. Like Norbert Elias explained, rigid deference norms like etiquette have tended to be imposed as a kind of symbolic tax on the masses whenever elites feel their authority being threatened. As society has become increasingly heterogeneous, we're seeing a renewed urge to assimilate the competing lineages, visions, and values of disparate groups by reasserting the tax of reasonableness from the top down. Instead, what if we started thinking bottom up?

It sounds like a drastic proposal, I know, but in a healthy society, this kind of evolution would be accepted as a natural process. It doesn't mean throwing the baby out with the bath water. When they hear me calling *some* norms into question, some people seem to believe that I am ipso facto threatening the existence of *all* norms. But there's a lot of good in our current social contract, too: values like think before you judge, fair play, live and let live . . . At the same time, we can't just gaze wistfully at 'other' cultures around the world like they're a buffet full of mystical wisdom we can pick and choose from at will: this too risks falling into the coloniser's trap of orientalising extraction. However, it *is* worth taking a careful look at the alternative systems of knowledge and value that the system of imperial white-supremacist capitalist patriarchy worked so hard to suppress. To get back to those reasonable moral principles of compassion, integrity, and human dignity for everyone, we need to reject the appearance of respectability in favour of building a genuinely respectful world in which everyone has equitable chance to thrive.

In *This is Not a Peace Pipe*, politics professor and Temagami First Nation scholar Dale Turner explains how Haudenosaunee norms of togetherness are built on three fundamental principles – respect, reciprocity, and renewal.[7] From western nations to Indigenous philosophies elsewhere, these have long been the core principles of successful social contracts around the world. In lieu of reasonableness, I propose these as three pillars we might adopt again today.

Respect

The 'respect' principle begins from the understanding that all life on earth has intrinsic value. Acknowledging this means recognising that each person has 'the right to speak their mind and to choose for themselves how to act in the world', Turner writes. 'It follows that in principle, one cannot tell another what to do or how to behave.' He tells the story of when the Haudenosaunee people were first invaded by European nations. The Haudenosaunee produced treaties of peace and friendship symbolised by the Gus-Wen-Teh, or Two Row Wampum, in the form of a belt made of shell beads. Those two rows symbolise 'two paths or vessels travelling down the same rivers together'. The first row, a birchbark canoe, 'will be for the Indian people, their laws, their customs and their ways'. The second row, a ship, 'will be for the white people and their laws, their customs and their ways'. These visualise how the two parties 'should each travel the river together, side-by-side, but in our own boat. Neither of us will try to steer the other's vessel.'[8] As Viola Faye Cordova explains, though, this ideology didn't stick. For colonial Europeans:

> there is always the enemy other who exists as a competitor in a barren land with scarce resources (the Earth, outside the garden of Eden, as depicted in the Old Testament). The other represents an enemy also in the sense that he would challenge the 'truths' held by one group over the truth as held by another. Competing paradigms, in other words, are not allowed within the European conceptual framework: 'One World, One People' signals more than just a vision of peaceful existence of diverse peoples – it signals the eventuality of no diversity at all. Monoculturalism is seen as a naturally occurring event in the teleological progressivism that rules the views of the European.[9]

As human beings, Cordova reminds us, we are not solitary creatures held reluctantly together by the power of authority. We are bound together in a system of mutual dependence: with each other, and with the earth. In almost all the Bantu languages of South Africa, there is that concept called

Ubuntu, which is summed up in the lovely phrase 'a person is a person through other people'. As Eric Yamamoto, professor of law and social justice, puts it: Ubuntu is 'the idea that no one can be healthy when the community is sick. Ubuntu says I am human only because you are human. If I undermine your humanity, I dehumanise myself.'[10] Similar ideas can be found across the globe. In humility consider others as more important than yourselves, the Christian Bible says. Allah enjoins justice, and the doing of good to others, and giving like kindred, says the Qur'an. Do not separate from the community, Judaism teaches; do not judge your fellow humans until you reach their place. Rather than assuming one singular correct method of living on the planet and trying to steer everybody's vessels for them, we need to work towards a communal respect for pluralistic ways of knowing and being.

But respect can't flow one way. A healthy social contract also requires reciprocity.

Reciprocity

Live and let live. The ethic of reciprocity is also a moral principle found in virtually all religions and cultures. Do unto others as you would have them do unto you (that's Jesus). Never impose on others what you would not choose for yourself (that's Confucius). One should never do that to another which one regards as injurious to one's own self (Brihaspati, from the *Mahābhārata*). *Egbe bere, ugo bere* ('let the eagle perch, let the hawk perch': an Igbo proverb). It's called the Golden Rule for a reason.

But that right to speak our minds and to choose for ourselves how to live in the world can never be absolute. Rights go hand in hand with responsibilities. From 'don't murder' to 'wear a seatbelt' to 'no smoking in bars', societies have always introduced limitations for the social good, along with consequences when those limits are breached. Virtually every culture recognises that the need to respect others' beliefs and behaviour stops when their individual actions cause harm to the collective. In her research into peacemaking in the Káínai tribe, for example, Annabel Crop Eared Wolf explains that peace relies on individuals working collaboratively to maintain a system of mutual balance. Any person who throws off that balance by acting in accordance with their own selfish interests must be brought back into the collective fold via intra-community peacekeeping practices: a series of 'prevention measures and sanctions carried out by family, clan, friends, societies, leaders, and elders', like advising, cautioning, and wise counsel. Crucially, this process recognises the value of expertise. 'When a person wishes to know something of importance' they will engage in *ákapssopowahtsi'si*: seeking out 'a knowledgeable person for purposes of making an inquiry', Crop Eared Wolf writes.[11]

We might usefully think about reciprocity in the context of western countries battling over vaccines. When it comes to those who have the means and access to be vaccinated yet who choose to disbelieve the scientific consensus, there has been a liberal tendency to call for empathy and compassion. But in this context, being kind to anti-vaxxers and respecting their beliefs is to be extremely *un*kind to the many immunocompromised people whose lives they are putting at risk.

Societal consequences, led by those with deep and fair commitment to knowledge, are part of reciprocity – because they're a way to ensure that *everyone* gains the respect they deserve. 'Seek justice, correct oppression; bring justice to the fatherless': Isaiah 1:17. 'You shall not spread a false report. You shall not join hands with a wicked man to be a malicious witness. You shall not fall in with the many to do evil': Exodus 23:1–33. Having one's worldviews respected by one's community is a privilege that must be earned through respecting one's community in return. There can be no rights without responsibilities.

But moral understandings don't remain static; they have always evolved over time. This is why we need the final principle: renewal.

Renewal

'The main idea behind the principle of renewal,' Turner explains, 'is that change is a natural part of any relationship whether that relationship is spiritual, physical, or political. This is because nature moves in cycles of renewal: life and death; the four seasons; planting cycles; migration patterns, and so on. Relationships between people go through natural changes as well.' For this reason 'it is important to periodically recognise, affirm, and renew a relationship in order to revitalise it so that peaceful coexistence can be preserved'.[12] Compare this with the following statement by Thomas Jefferson, about the US Constitution:

> I am not an advocate for frequent changes in laws and constitutions, but laws and institutions must go hand in hand

> with the progress of the human mind. As that becomes more developed, more enlightened, as new discoveries are made, new truths discovered and manners and opinions change, with the change of circumstances, institutions must advance also to keep pace with the times. We might as well require a man to wear still the coat which fitted him when a boy as civilized society to remain ever under the regimen of their barbarous ancestors.[13]

Reconsidering societal norms *is neither a new nor a radical idea.* The social contract was never meant to be a rigid doctrine: it was meant to evolve through time, through consultation with the community, in order to better suit the evolving needs of that community. In societies that follow Ubuntu, for example, norms come to be decided via what is called the Common Moral Position. This position can't just be established by one person; rather, 'the community is the source, author and custodian of moral standards', with norms set according to 'communo-centric' obligations rather than individualistic rights,[14] continually readjusted to ensure they produce benefit from the bottom up. In Haudenosaunee societies, Turner explains, the core moral principles of peace, friendship, and compassion are all pivotal to *maintaining* social relationships, not just *establishing* them. 'These principles need to be renewed if they are to function properly: healthy political relationships are dynamic [. . .] – if they are left alone they die.'[15]

Faced with the 'anarchy' of social changes like migration, community fragmentation, and shifts in generational value systems, the response of those in charge has often been to panic and forcibly impose a singular set of values on to others. This approach doesn't just go against other cultures' moral standards, *but also our own*. Live and let live, remember? Adopting the Respect, Reciprocity, Renewal model would encourage us to: a) *respect* divergent norms, alternative needs, and opinions that are different from our own; b) find a genuinely *reciprocal* way to engage in public reason, which understands that not all opinions can ethically be weighed equally and that some ideas will always need to be unwelcome in the public sphere; and c) commit to a constant process of *renewal*, in which we collectively reconsider what it means to uplift everyone rather than benefiting favoured individuals at the expense of the whole.

This manifesto comes with two big disclaimers. First, pluralism isn't about embracing harmful societal views – homophobia or misogyny, for example – just because they're held by a particular minoritised person. Second, nor is it about going full-on moral relativism and assuming there's no such thing as good or bad at all. No – this is simply about understanding that, when it comes to deciding 'good' from 'bad', 'acceptable' from 'unacceptable', there's a difference between *popular* morality and *social* morality.[16] Popular morality refers to the norms of appropriate behaviour which are generally socially accepted, but which change over time: rules like it's rude to put your elbows on the dining table, for example. Social morality refers to those core standards that are rooted in deep ethical beliefs: rules like it's rude to sneeze on food. Sometimes popular morality feeds into social morality and helps us build a more compassionate civilisation; other times, focusing on the appearance of civility has been used to distract us from truly civilised goals. We can excise the bad without losing the good.

The aim of these pillars is to strengthen not destroy civic-minded values. The last thing we need is to breed yet more selfish assholes who go around doing whatever they want without caring about anyone else. But on the other side of the coin, we also need to be exceptionally wary of the kind of 'reasonable person' whose actions seem to be driven by a very strong sense of civic-minded purpose, yet who ends up zealously weaponising their own values to cause manifold harm to everyone else. We've seen so much of this warped conviction erupting recently: from the white couple who accused a Black man of vandalising private property for chalking 'Black Lives Matter' on his own front wall, to the evangelist Christian extreme inflicting their religious ideology on the wombs of the entire USA. What leaps out of all these instances is the terrifying thrill of self-righteousness. Why? Because they see themselves as a Decent Member of Society – an upstanding moral citizen, acting reasonably by protecting a public sphere that they feel belongs to them. Yet by the consensus of wider global society, their judgments have been judged as completely unreasonable, that sense of civic purpose visibly tainted by spatial entitlement, patriarchal control, and racist bias.

Judgment and censure are all a healthy part of community formation. But the act of judging and shaming other people can also be deeply *pleasurable*. This is what moral philosophers – previously the biggest fanboys of reasonableness! – have recently begun warning about. The German philosopher Rüdiger Bittner, for instance, argued that we often judge other people not just because we have a moral imperative to do so, but also because judging 'is so nice'. Cultivating an imagined sense of distance lets us indulge in the 'childish pleasure' of judging others.[17] Like when Matthew in the Bible advises us to remove the log from our own eye before complaining about the speck in another's, or when Buddha tells us that easily seen are others' faults yet hard indeed to see are one's own, or when Islam advises that if you want to criticise someone you must first criticise yourself more than three times: passing judgment on another can never be a simple act of observation. It's also an exercise of *power*: one that casts us as standing on a moral high ground we may not deserve. This is what Bittner is warning us about – the danger of giving in to the sense of moral superiority that comes from judging others, without having beforehand questioned our motivation (and right) to judge.

And this is really all I've been talking about. I've been told more than once that my work is 'radical' or 'dangerous' or 'an assault on democracy itself', but the message really is about as old and democratic as it gets. Before you subject other people to your judgments, think carefully about what you're doing. Am I reinforcing injustice or challenging it? Solidifying power relations or subverting them? Protecting the fundamental right of people to live their lives with dignity, or destroying others' lives and rights and dignity by imposing my own beliefs? Am I pulling people up, or squashing them back down?

In law as in life, we need to draw reasonable lines. Society needs mechanisms to figure out whether someone has acted within reason or not. But the 'Reasonable Man' standard has historically been designed to take an extremely narrow social worldview as objective and neutral, while ignoring subjective biases against women, people of colour, poor people, fat people, disabled people, queer people, and every combination of the above. Meanwhile, any time anyone tries to challenge the system or defer to scientific consensus or ask for people's basic human rights to be upheld, they get critiqued for being 'woke', smug, the truly self-righteous and overzealous ones, snowflakes simultaneously strengthened by a sense of moral superiority and apt to melt at the first sign of disagreement. *We can't win.*

So perhaps we should stop trying? If the game is rigged, maybe it's time to rewrite the rules?

I want to end by proposing the existence of a similar spectrum to Donald Rumsfeld's famous 'known-unknowns'. Bear with me now. On the Sedgman Spectrum of Reasonableness, first we have the Unreasonably-Unreasonables: the deliberate contrarians and hate-speech purveyors and greed-is-good libertarian individualists, who think they can say and do whatever they want without consequences no matter the harm to anyone else. For certain progressive factions, I think we've been so determined not to be like them that we've become something just as bad. We've become Unreasonably-Reasonable, obsessed with tone-policing and respectability politics and endless toothless debate, happy to act the devil's advocate* and platform hate-speech and injustice so long as everyone appears to be doing it politely. Meanwhile, progress has always depended on the Reasonably-Unreasonable people: those who understand that civic dissent and smashing down

* I have never understood people who like to call themselves a devil's advocate. They're usually trying to imply that we need to hear out the other side of the story. But in this analogy, the other side of the story is self-evidently the evil side. The clue is *literally* in the name.

racist statues and no-platforming bigots might sometimes be the only way to make the world a better place.

Think of this book as a riposte to the sensible centrists who say we need to hear out racists, eugenicists, and misogynists, because that's what reasonable people do. It's a kick in the crotch to the professional shock-jocks who've built their fortunes aiming deliberate offences at vulnerable people, then smearing critics as offended weaklings clutching at pearls. It's a call to arms to those who'd like to live in a fairer society but would prefer to achieve it without raising their voice or hearing a swear word or making a fuss; to those who *say* they want equality, but disagree with the tactics used by 'those people' to achieve it. It's a polite request to please stop hijacking campaigns designed to change the world for the better, by complaining about 'nasty' tone and 'disrespectful' behaviour. And it's a direct challenge to the right-wing system of fighting dirty (and winning!) while bogging leftists down in compromise and *still* branding us unreasonable.

Here I find myself following in the footsteps of thinkers like Karl Popper, who in 1945 told us that the endgame of unlimited tolerance is the disappearance of tolerance itself. 'We should therefore claim, in the name of tolerance,' he said, 'the right not to tolerate the intolerant.'[18] I want us, in the name of reasonableness, to reclaim the right to be unreasonable where we need to be. And if making things better means breaking the rules once in a while? Maybe that's an acceptable price to pay.

References

Note: Any websites referred to below were correct at time of access

Introduction

1 Merriam-Webster. 'reasonable (adjective)' (www.merriam-webster.com/dictionary/reasonable).
2 Online Etymology Dictionary. 'reasonable' (www.etymonline.com/word/reasonable).
3 George Bernard Shaw. *Man and Superman* (The University Press, 1903) (Reproduced in Bartleby: www.bartleby.com/157/6.html).

1: A Stranger among Strangers

1 Jordi Quoidbach, Maxime Taquet, Martin Desseilles, Yves-Alexandre de Montjoye & James J. Gross. 'Happiness and Social Behavior', *Psychological Science* 30:8 (2019): pp. 1111–1122.
2 Paul Seabright. *The Company of Strangers: A Natural History of Economic Life – Revised Edition* (Princeton University Press, 2010): p. 4.
3 Seabright, *Strangers*: p. 3.
4 Seabright, *Strangers*: pp. 3–4.
5 Charles Stanish. *The Evolution of Human Co-operation: Ritual and Social Complexity in Stateless Societies* (Cambridge University Press, 2017).
6 Andrew Curry. 'Gobekli Tepe: The World's First Temple?', *Smithsonian Magazine*, Nov 2008 (www.smithsonianmag.com/history/gobekli-tepe-the-worlds-first-temple-83613665).

7 Seabright, *Strangers*: pp. 3–4.
8 Stanish, *Co-operation*: p. 8.
9 Harold Garfinkel. *Studies in Ethnomethodology* (Prentice-Hall, Inc., 1967): p. 69.
10 Sachiko Ide. 'On the Notion of *Wakimae*: Toward an Integrated Framework of Linguistic Politeness', *Mosaic of Language: Essays in Honour of Professor Natsuko Okuda* (Mejiro Linguistic Society, 1992): pp. 298–305, pp. 298–299.
11 Thomas Hobbes. *Leviathan*, ed. C. B. Macpherson (Pelican Classics, [1651] 1968): p. 78.
12 Chung-ying Cheng. 'On Yi as a Universal Principle of Specific Application in Confucian Morality', *Philosophy East and West* 22:3 (1972): pp. 269–80.
13 Wimbledon. 'Queuing Code of Conduct' (www.wimbledon.com/en_GB/aboutwimbledon/queuing_code_of_conduct.html).
14 Joe Moran. 'Queuing Up in Post-War Britain', *Twentieth Century British History* 16:3 (2005): pp. 283–305, p. 304.
15 Roger Scola. 'Food Markets and Shops in Manchester 1770–1870', *Journal of Historical Geography* 1:2 (1975): pp. 153–167, p. 153.
16 Joe Moran. *Queuing for Beginners: The Story of Daily Life From Breakfast to Bedtime* (Profile Books, 2007): p. 62.
17 Moran, 'Queuing Up': pp. 286–287.
18 Yomi Kazeem. 'Nigeria', in 'A Global Guide to Queuing Philosophies, from Wimbledon to São Paulo', *Quartz* (www.qz.com/quartzy/1322666/a-global-guide-to-queuing-philosophies-from-wimbledon-to-sao-paolo).
19 Edward T. Hall. *The Hidden Dimension* (Anchor Books, [1966] 1990): pp. 117–125.
20 Hall, *Dimension*: pp. 144–145.
21 Quoted by Alastair Pennycook. 'Actions Speak Louder than Words: Paralanguage, Communication, and Education', *Tesol Quarterly* 19:2 (1985): pp. 259–282, p. 265.
22 Caleb Everett, Damián E. Blasi & Seán G. Roberts. 'Language Evolution and Climate: The Case of Desiccation and Tone', *Journal of Language Evolution* 1:1 (2016): pp. 33–46.

23 Agnieszka Sorokowska, Piotr Sorokowski, Peter Hilpert, Katarzyna Cantarero, Tomasz Frackowiak, Khodabakhsh Ahmadi, Ahmad M. Alghraibeh et al. 'Preferred Interpersonal Distances: A Global Comparison', *Journal of Cross-Cultural Psychology* 48:4 (2017): pp. 577–592.
24 Tzvi Abusch. *Male and Female in the Epic of Gilgamesh: Encounters, Literary History, and Interpretation* (Penn State Press, 2014): p. 178.
25 Britannica. 'Nervous System' (www.britannica.com/science/nervous-system/Organelle-systems#ref606302).
26 Friedrich Hayek. *Studies in Philosophy, Politics, and Economics* (Routledge, 1967): p. 61.
27 Norine Dresser. *Multicultural Manners: Essential Rules of Etiquette for the 21st Century* (Wiley, 2005): p. 17.
28 Dresser, *Multicultural*: p. 27.
29 Simon Baron-Cohen, Michelle O'Riordan, Valerie Stone, Rosie Jones & Kate Plaisted. 'Recognition of Faux Pas by Normally Developing Children and Children with Asperger Syndrome or High-Functioning Autism', *Journal of Autism and Developmental Disorders* 29:5 (1999): pp. 407–418.
30 Monique Botha, Bridget Dibb & David M. Frost. '"Autism is Me": An Investigation of How Autistic Individuals Make Sense of Autism and Stigma', *Disability & Society* 37:3 (2020): pp. 427–453.
31 Rutger Bregman. *Humankind: A Hopeful History* (Bloomsbury, 2019).
32 T. M. Scanlon. *What We Owe to Each Other* (Harvard University Press, 1998).
33 Quoted by Timothy Murithi. 'Practical Peacemaking Wisdom from Africa: Reflections on Ubuntu', *The Journal of Pan African Studies* 1:4 (2006): pp. 25–34, p. 28.

2: The Disconnection Economy

1 Daniel Hoornweg & Kevin Pope. 'Population Predictions for the World's Largest Cities in the 21st Century', *Environment and Urbanization* 29:1 (2017), pp. 195–216.

2 Seth Godin. *The Icarus Deception: How High Will You Fly?* (Penguin, 2012).

3 Robert D. Putnam. 'E Pluribus Unum: Diversity and Community in the Twenty-First Century: The 2006 Johan Skytte Prize Lecture', *Scandinavian Political Studies* 30:2 (2007): pp. 137–174.

4 Quoted by Matt Bagwell. 'Sky Launches Investigation into Claims the Chop Contestant has "Nazi Tattoos" on His Face', *Huffington Post*, 21 Oct 2020 (www.huffingtonpost.co.uk/entry/sky-history-the-chop-nazi-tattoos_uk_5f8eecbec5b67da85d21baff).

5 James Surowiecki. *The Wisdom of Crowds: Why the Many are Smarter than the Few* (Anchor, 2004).

6 Aniket Kittur & Robert E. Kraut. 'Harnessing the Wisdom of Crowds in Wikipedia: Quality Through Coordination', *Proceedings of the 2008 ACM Conference on Computer Supported Cooperative Work* (2008).

7 Gustave Le Bon. *The Crowd: A Study of the Popular Mind* (Batoche Books, [1896] 2001): p. 73.

8 Stephan Lewandowsky, Ullrich K. H. Ecker & John Cook. 'Beyond Misinformation: Understanding and Coping with the "Post-Truth" Era', *Journal of Applied Research in Memory and Cognition* 6:4 (2017): pp. 353–369, p. 359.

9 Desmond Morris. *The Naked Ape* (Dell Publishing, [1967] 1983).

10 Angela Saini. 'His Arrogance has Done Untold Damage', in 'The Naked Ape at 50', *Guardian*, 24 Sep 2017 (www.theguardian.com/science/2017/sep/24/the-naked-ape-at-50-desmond-morris-four-experts-assess-impact).

11 Sarah Chohan. 'What are Tribes (and Why Should You Be Targeting Them)?', *Linkfluence* (www.linkfluence.com/blog/what-are-tribes-and-why-you-should-be-targeting-them).

12 Hannah Westley. 'Fashion Tribes', *The Times*, 18 Oct 2006 (www.thetimes.co.uk/article/fashion-tribes-fdzlwvgs0c3).

13 Lionel Tiger & Robin Fox. *The Imperial Animal* (McClelland and Stewart, 1971).

14 David Lammy. *Tribes: A Search for Belonging in a Divided Society* (Constable, 2021).

15 Seth Godin. *Tribes: We Need You to Lead Us* (Little, Brown, 2008).

16 Cory J. Clark, Brittany S. Liu, Bo M. Winegard & Peter H. Ditto. 'Tribalism is Human Nature', *Current Directions in Psychological Science* 28:6 (2019): pp. 587–592, p. 587.

17 Bregman, *Humankind.*

18 Raymond Williams & Michael Orrom. *Preface to Film* (Film Drama Limited, 1954).

19 Bjarke Skærlund Risager. 'Neoliberalism Is a Political Project: An Interview with David Harvey', *Jacobin Magazine*, 23 Jul 2016 (www.jacobinmag.com/2016/07/david-harvey-neoliberalism-capitalism-labor-crisis-resistance).

20 Mark Ward. 'What the Net Did Next', BBC, 1 Jan 2004 (http://news.bbc.co.uk/1/hi/technology/3292043.stm).

21 Kevin Munger, Mario Luca, Jonathan Nagler & Joshua Tucker. 'The (Null) Effects of Clickbait Headlines on Polarization, Trust, and Learning', *Public Opinion Quarterly* 84:1 (2020): pp. 49–73, p. 50.

22 Peter Pomerantsev. *This Is Not Propaganda: Adventures in the War Against Reality* (Faber, 2019).

23 Richard Flanagan. 'The World is Being Undone Before Us', *Guardian*, 4 Aug 2018 (www.theguardian.com/australia-news/2018/aug/05/the-world-is-being-undone-before-us-if-we-do-not-reimagine-australia-we-will-be-undone-too).

24 Barbara Pfetsch. 'Dissonant and Disconnected Public Spheres as Challenge for Political Communication Research', *Javnost – The Public* 25:1–2 (2018): pp. 59–65, p. 59.

25 Putnam, 'E Pluribus Unum': p. 137.

26 RealClearPolitics. 'Rubio: No "Reasonable Person" Cạn Say Climate Change Is A Bigger Threat Than Terrorism', 30 Nov 2015 (www.realclearpolitics.com/video/2015/11/30/rubio_no_reasonable_person_can_say_climate_change_is_a_bigger_threat_than_terrorism.html).

27 Jacob Poushter & Christine Huang. 'Climate Change Still Seen as the Top Global Threat, but Cyberattacks a Rising Concern', *Pew Research Center*, 10 Feb 2019 (www.pewresearch.org/

global/2019/02/10/climate-change-still-seen-as-the-top-global-threat-but-cyberattacks-a-rising-concern).

28 David Moadel. 'Corporate Shuffle Won't Save Luckin', *Investor Place*, 12 Aug 2020 (https://investorplace.com/2020/08/corporate-shuffle-wont-save-luckin-stock).

29 Dan Bobkoff, Anna Mazarakis, Sarah Wyman & Amy Pedulla. 'Better Call Butterball', *Insider*, 13 Aug 2020 (www.businessinsider.com/brought-to-you-by-podcast-btyb-better-call-butterball).

30 Kif Leswing. 'The iPhone Decade', CNBC, 16 Dec 2019 (www.cnbc.com/2019/12/16/apples-iphone-created-industries-and-changed-the-world-this-decade.html).

31 Quoted by Darren Kelsey. *Storytelling and Collective Psychology: Ancient Wisdom, Modern Life and the Work of Derren Brown* (Palgrave Macmillan, 2022): p. 55.

32 John Everard (transl.) & William Wynn Westcott. *The Divine Pymander of Hermes Mercurius Trismegistus* [1650] 1894 (Reproduced: https://universaltheosophy.com/je/the-divine-pymander).

33 Margrit Pernau. 'The Virtuous Individual and Social Reform: Debates among North Indian Urdu Speakers', *Civilizing Emotions: Concepts in Nineteenth-Century Asia and Europe* (Oxford University Press, 2015): pp. 169–186.

34 Bongrae Seok. 'The Four–Seven Debate of Korean Neo-Confucianism and the Moral Psychological and Theistic Turn in Korean Philosophy', *Religions* 9:11 (2018): p. 374.

35 David B. Wong. 'Early Confucian Philosophy and the Development of Compassion', *Dao* 14:2 (2015): pp. 157–194.

36 Vaughan v. Menlove. 'The Unreasonable Hay Stacker' (Reproduced: h2o.law.harvard.edu/collages/4855).

37 J. R. Lucas. 'The Philosophy of the Reasonable Man', *The Philosophical Quarterly* 13:51 (1963): pp. 97–106.

38 Quoted & translated by Olivier Corten. 'The Notion of "Reasonable" in International Law: Legal Discourse, Reason and Contradictions', *The International and Comparative Law Quarterly* 48:3 (1999): pp. 613–625, p. 615.

39 Kevin Tobia. 'The Law in India and Other Countries Rests on What "Reasonable Person" Would Do'. *Scroll.in*, 2 Feb 2019 (https://scroll.in/article/911131/the-law-in-india-and-other-countries-rests-on-what-reasonable-person-would-do-who-is-this-person).
40 Corten, 'Notion': p. 613.
41 Corten, 'Notion': p. 619.
42 Adolphe Quetelet. *Sur L'Homme et le Développement de ses Facultés* (Bechalier, 1835).
43 Mayo Moran. 'The Reasonable Person: A Conceptual Biography in Comparative Perspective', *Lewis & Clark Law Review* 14:4 (2010): pp. 1233–1283.
44 A. P. Herbert. 'The Case of the Unreasonable Woman', *Punch*, 9 Jul 1924 (Reproduced: https://jollycontrarian.com/index.php?title=Fardell_v_Potts).
45 BBC. 'Why Should You Be More Like Bill?', 18 Jan 2016 (www.bbc.co.uk/news/blogs-trending-35344300).
46 Aaron E. Carroll. 'Yes, People Are Traveling for the Holidays. Stop Shaming Them', *New York Times*, 4 Dec 2020 (www.nytimes.com/2020/12/04/opinion/covid-holiday-travel.html).
47 Michael Goodier. 'The UK has the Highest Current Covid-19 Death Rate of Any Major Country', *New Statesman*, 12 Jan 2021 (www.newstatesman.com/science-tech/coronavirus/2021/01/uk-has-highest-current-covid-19-death-rate-any-major-country).
48 Full Fact. 'What Did the Lockdown Rules Say When Dominic Cummings Travelled to Durham?', 27 May 2020 (https://fullfact.org/health/dominic-cummings-lockdown-rules).
49 Catherine Neilan. 'Dominic Cummings Says "No Regrets" for "Legal and Reasonable" Durham Trip as Boris Johnson Stands by His Man', *Telegraph*, 25 May 2020 (www.telegraph.co.uk/politics/2020/05/25/dominic-cummings-durham-boris-johnson-lockdown-barnard-castle).
50 Daisy Fancourt. 'People Started Breaking Covid Rules When They Saw Those With Privilege Ignore Them', *Guardian*, 2 Jan 2021

(www.theguardian.com/commentisfree/2021/jan/02/follow-covid-restrictions-break-rules-compliance).

3: Uncommon Sense

1 Yuko Kato. 'Japan Etiquette Video Discourages Applying Make-Up on Trains', BBC, 28 Oct 2016 (www.bbc.co.uk/news/world-asia-37796036).

2 Molly Shea. 'Please Stop Doing Your Makeup on the Subway', *New York Post*, 8 Jun 2017 (https://nypost.com/2017/06/08/please-stop-doing-your-makeup-on-the-subway).

3 Cosmetify. 'The Rise Of The Cosmuter: More Than Half of UK Women Apply Makeup on Their Commute', Jan 2019 (www.cosmetify.com/press/the-rise-of-the-cosmuter-more-than-half-of-uk-women-apply-makeup-on-their-commute).

4 Jennifer Meierhans. 'Make-Up on the Train: What's the Problem?', BBC, 4 Sep 2018 (www.bbc.co.uk/news/uk-england-45343836).

5 Quoted by Bryony Jewell. 'Singer Who Was Tutted at by a Stranger for Doing Her Make-Up on a Train is Applauded', *Daily Mail*, 21 May 2019 (www.dailymail.co.uk/femail/article-7054073/Singers-comeback-man-tutted-doing-makeup-train-applauded.html).

6 Stephen Bottoms & Matthew Goulish. *Small Acts of Repair: Performance, Ecology, and Goat Island* (Routledge, 2007).

7 Ava Neyer. 'I Read All the Baby Sleep Books', *Huffington Post*, 6 Dec 2017 (www.huffpost.com/entry/i-read-all-the-baby-sleep-advice-books_b_3143253).

8 Kirsty Sedgman. *The Reasonable Audience: Theatre Etiquette, Behaviour Policing, and the Live Performance Experience* (Palgrave, 2018).

9 Julia Carmel. 'Nothing About Us Without Us: 16 Moments in the Fight for Disability Rights', *New York Times*, 22 Jul 2020 (www.nytimes.com/2020/07/22/us/ada-disabilities-act-history.html).

10 Corten, 'Notion': p. 618.

11 David Colon. 'Disabled NYers File Class Action Lawsuit Against MTA over Inaccessible Subway Stations', *Gothamist*, 26 Apr 2017 (https://gothamist.com/news/disabled-nyers-file-class-action-lawsuit-against-mta-over-inaccessible-subway-stations).
12 Erin Durkin. 'New York Subway: Woman Dies While Carrying Baby Stroller on Stairs', *Guardian*, 29 Jan 2019 (www.theguardian.com/us-news/2019/jan/29/new-york-subway-woman-dies-baby-stroller-stairs).
13 Stephen Nessen. 'Judge Tells MTA To Find Money For More Subway Elevators', *Gothamist*, 23 May 2019 (https://gothamist.com/news/judge-tells-mta-to-find-money-for-more-subway-elevators-you-find-it-for-other-things).
14 Jen Slater. *Youth and Disability: A Challenge to Mr Reasonable* (Ashgate, 2015): p. 1.
15 Aaron O'Neill. 'Global Fertility Rate from 2009 to 2019', *Statistica* (www.statista.com/statistics/805064/fertility-rate-worldwide).
16 Unicef. *Breastfeeding: A Mother's Gift, for Every Child*, 2018 (https://tinyurl.com/unicef-breastfeeding).
17 See e.g. Gill Thomson, Katherine Ebisch-Burton & Renee Flacking. 'Shame If You Do – Shame if You Don't: Women's Experiences of Infant Feeding', *Maternal & Child Nutrition* 11:1 (2015): pp. 33–46.
18 Jess Thom. 'Wall of Sound', Touretteshero, 26 May 2011 (https://www.touretteshero.com/2011/05/26/wall-of-sound).
19 Nancy S. Ehrenreich. 'Pluralist Myths and Powerless Men: The Ideology of Reasonableness in Sexual Harassment Law', *The Yale Law Journal* 99:6 (1990): pp. 1177–1234, p. 1177.
20 Jody David Armour. *Negrophobia and Reasonable Racism: The Hidden Costs of being Black in America* (New York, 1997): p. 26.
21 See e.g. in the USA: RAINN. 'Victims of Sexual Violence: Statistics', Jun 2022 (www.rainn.org/statistics/victims-sexual-violence); in the UK: Rape Crisis. 'Statistics about Sexual Violence and Abuse', Jun 2022 (https://rapecrisis.org.uk/get-informed/statistics-sexual-violence); in France: Cairn Info. 'Rape and sexual assault in France',

2016 (www.cairn-int.info/article-E_POPSOC_538_0001--rape-and-sexual-assault-in-france.htm); etc.

22 World Health Organization. 'Devastatingly Pervasive: 1 in 3 Women Globally Experience Violence', 9 Mar 2021 (https://www.who.int/news/item/09-03-2021-devastatingly-pervasive-1-in-3-women-globally-experience-violence).

23 National Sexual Violence Resource Center. 'Sexual Violence and Transgender/Non-Binary Communities', 2019 (www.nsvrc.org/sites/default/files/publications/2019-02/Transgender_infographic_508_0.pdf).

24 Quoted by Ruth Mazo Karras. *Sexuality in Medieval Europe: Doing Unto Others* (Routledge, 2012): p. 54.

25 Eleanor Janega. 'On Masculinity and Disease', Going Medieval, 10 Aug 2020 (https://going-medieval.com/2020/10/08/on-masculinity-and-disease).

26 Quoted by Joyce E. Salisbury. 'Gendered Sexuality', *Handbook of Medieval Sexuality*, eds. Vern L. Bullough & James Brundage (Routledge, 1996): pp. 81–102, p. 90.

27 Quoted by Antonio Varone. *Erotica Pompeiana: Love Inscriptions on the Walls of Pompeii* (L'Erma di Bretschneider, 2002): p. 91.

28 Jennifer Temkin & Barbara Krahé. *Sexual Assault and the Justice Gap: A Question of Attitude* (Bloomsbury, 2008): p. 2.

29 Temkin & Krahé, *Sexual Assault.*

30 Crown Prosecution Service. 'What is Consent?' (www.cps.gov.uk/sites/default/files/documents/publications/what_is_consent_v2.pdf).

31 James Q. Whitman. *The Origins of Reasonable Doubt: Theological Roots of the Criminal Trial* (Yale University Press, 2008): p. 3.

32 Whitman, *Origins*: p. 4.

33 Whitman, *Origins*: p. 10.

34 Dhammapada 252. Quoted by Thiên Phúc. *Buddhist Dictionary*, 2007 (https://tangthuphathoc.net/chapter-321-335).

35 Garuda Purana 112. Quoted by Diane Ackerman, Nawal H. Ammar, Naim Stifan Ateek & Scott Appleby. *Liberating Faith:*

Religious Voices for Justice, Peace, and Ecological Wisdom (Rowman & Littlefield, 2003): p. 18.

36 Whitman, *Origins*: p. 3.

37 Richard Dawkins. *Science in the Soul: Selected Writings of a Passionate Rationalist* (Random House, 2018): p. 298.

38 Roszel C. Thomsen. 'Sentencing in Income Tax Cases', *Fed. Probation* 26 (1962).

39 Shari Seidman Diamond & Hans Zeisel. 'Sentencing Councils: A Study of Sentence Disparity and its Reduction', *The University of Chicago Law Review* 43:1 (1975): pp. 109–149.

40 Adi Leibovitch. 'Relative Judgments', *The Journal of Legal Studies* 45:2 (2016): pp. 281–330.

41 Jeffrey A. Segal & Harold J. Spaeth. *The Supreme Court and the Attitudinal Model Revisited* (Cambridge University Press, 2002): p. 86.

42 Christopher Zorn & Jennifer Barnes Bowie. 'Ideological Influences on Decision-Making in the Federal Judicial Hierarchy: An Empirical Assessment', *The Journal of Politics* 72:4 (2010): pp. 1212–1221, p. 31.

43 Cass R. Sunstein, David Schkade, Lisa M. Ellman & Andres Sawicki. *Are Judges Political? An Empirical Analysis of the Federal Judiciary* (Brookings Institution Press, 2007).

44 Shai Danziger, Jonathan Levav & Liora Avnaim-Pesso. 'Extraneous Factors in Judicial Decisions', *Proceedings of the National Academy of Sciences* 108:17 (2011): pp. 6889–6892, p. 6889.

45 Quoted by H. T. M. Kloosterhuis & C. E. Smith. 'The Life of the Law Has Not Been Logic: It Has Been Experience', *Ars Aequi* 69:1 (2020): p. 99.

46 Quoted by Simon Lee. 'Law's British Empire', *Oxford Journal of Legal Studies* 8 (1988): pp. 278–292.

47 Quoted by Michael D. Greathouse. 'Criminal Law – The Right to Run: Deadly Force and the Fleeing Felon - Tennessee v. Garner, 105 S. Ct. 1694 (1985)', *Southern Illinois University Law Journal* 11 (1986–1987): pp. 171–184, p. 171.

48 Patricia Hill Collins. *Black Sexual Politics: African Americans, Gender, and the New Racism* (Routledge, 2004): pp. 56–57.

49 Patricia Hill Collins. *Black Feminist Thought: Knowledge, Consciousness, and the Politics of Empowerment* (Routledge, 1990).

50 John Paul Wilson, Kurt Hugenberg & Nicholas O. Rule. 'Racial Bias in Judgments of Physical Size and Formidability: From Size to Threat', *Journal of Personality and Social Psychology* 113:1 (2017).

51 Ben Guarino. 'People See Black Men as Larger and Stronger than White Men – Even When They're Not, Study Says', *Washington Post*, 14 Mar 2017 (www.washingtonpost.com/news/morning-mix/wp/2017/03/14/psychologists-we-see-black-men-as-larger-and-stronger-than-white-men-even-when-theyre-not).

52 Samuel R. Gross, Maurice Possley & Klara Stephens. 'Race and Wrongful Convictions in the United States', National Registry of Exonerations, 2017 (https://www.law.umich.edu/special/exoneration/Documents/Race_and_Wrongful_Convictions.pdf).

53 Ben Bowling & Coretta Phillips. 'Disproportionate and Discriminatory: Reviewing the Evidence on Police Stop and Search', *The Modern Law Review* 70:6 (2007): pp. 936–961.

54 Cassia Spohn. 'Racial Disparities in Prosecution, Sentencing, and Punishment', *The Oxford Handbook of Ethnicity, Crime, and Immigration* (Oxford University Press, 2013): pp. 166–193.

55 Jennifer L. Eberhardt, Paul G. Davies, Valerie J. Purdie-Vaughns & Sheri Lynn Johnson. 'Looking Deathworthy: Perceived Stereotypicality of Black Defendants Predicts Capital-Sentencing Outcomes', *Psychological Science* 17:5 (2006): pp. 383–386.

56 Alexis Hoag. 'Valuing Black Lives: A Case for Ending the Death Penalty', *Columbia Human Rights Law Review* 51:3 (2020).

57 Phillip Atiba Goff, Matthew Christian Jackson, Brooke Allison Lewis Di Leone, Carmen Marie Culotta & Natalie Ann DiTomasso. 'The Essence of Innocence: Consequences of Dehumanizing Black Children', *Journal of Personality and Social Psychology* 106:4 (2014).

58 Amelia Cheatham & Lindsay Maizland. 'How Police Compare in Different Democracies', Council on Foreign Relations, 21 April 2021 (www.cfr.org/backgrounder/how-police-compare-different-democracies).
59 *Washington Post*. 'Fatal Force', updated 13 Jun 2022 (www.washingtonpost.com/graphics/investigations/police-shootings-database).
60 Jelani Jefferson Exum. 'Nearsighted and Colorblind: The Perspective Problems of Police Deadly Force Cases', *Cleveland State Law Review* 65 (2016).
61 Leanne Weber & Ben Bowling. *Stop and Search: Police Power in Global Context* (Routledge, 2014): p. 130.
62 Mahzarin R. Banaji & Anthony G. Greenwald. *Blindspot: Hidden Biases of Good People* (Random House, 2013): p. 138.
63 Tania Singer & Claus Lamm. 'The Social Neuroscience of Empathy', *Annals of the New York Academy of Sciences* 1156:1 (2009): pp. 81–96, p. 89.
64 Quoted in Ben-Ami Scharfstein. 'The Western Blindness to Non-Western Philosophies', *The Paideia Archive: Twentieth World Congress of Philosophy* 5 (1998): pp. 102–108.
65 Armour, *Negrophobia*: p. 117.
66 Corten, 'Notion': pp. 617–618.
67 Lindy West. *Shrill: Notes from a Loud Woman* (Hachette, 2016).
68 Diana Spalding. 'You Don't Know Me, So Please Don't Judge My Parenting Skills', Motherly, 6 November 2017 (www.mother.ly/life/you-dont-know-me-so-please-dont-judge-me).
69 Procter & Gamble. 'The Look', YouTube, 5 April 2020 (www.youtube.com/watch?v=bxZBtWGYV1c).

F*ck Civility

1 Norbert Elias. *Über den Prozeß der Zivilisation* (*The Civilizing Process*) (Haus zum Falken, 1939).
2 Elias, *Civilizing*: p. 71.

3 Peggy Post, Anna Post, Lizzie Post & Daniel Post Senning. *Emily Post's Etiquette* (*18th edition*) (Harper Collins, 2011).
4 Pernau, 'The Virtuous Individual'.

4: Neighbours Behaving Badly

1 Gaye Theresa Johnson. *Spaces of Conflict, Sounds of Solidarity* (University of California Press, 2013).
2 Gill Valentine. 'Children Should Be Seen and Not Heard: The Production and Transgression of Adults' Public Space', *Urban Geography* 17:3 (1996): pp. 205–220, p. 205.
3 Sedgman, *Reasonable Audience*: p. 145.
4 Nextdoor. 'New Nextdoor Insights Data', 17 October 2021 (https://about.nextdoor.com/press-releases/new-nextdoor-insights-data-focuses-on-localism-mental-health-and-neighborhood-connections).
5 John Herrman. 'Neighbors Are Reaching Out on Nextdoor', *New York Times*, 25 Mar 2020 (www.nytimes.com/2020/03/25/style/nextdoor-neighbors-coronavirus.html).
6 Sara Ahmed. *Strange Encounters: Embodied Others in Post-Coloniality* (Routledge, 2013).
7 The Crime Report. 'Perception Gap', Center on Media Crime and Justice, 16 Oct 2018 (thecrimereport.org/2018/10/16/perception-gap).
8 Ian Bogost. 'What Petty Nextdoor Posts Reveal About America', *The Atlantic*, Jul/Aug 2018 (www.theatlantic.com/magazine/archive/2018/07/nextdoor-american-communities/561746).
9 Makena Kelly. 'Inside Nextdoor's "Karen Problem"', *The Verge*, 8 Jun 2020 (www.theverge.com/21283993/nextdoor-app-racism-community-moderation-guidance-protests).
10 Armour, *Negrophobia*: p. 10.
11 Quoted by Armour, *Negrophobia*: p. 37.
12 Armour, *Negrophobia*: pp. 39–44.
13 Armour, *Negrophobia*: p. 39.
14 Ahmed, *Strange Encounters*: p. 5.

15 Reproduced in Transcribe Bentham, University College London (transcribe-bentham.ucl.ac.uk/td/JB/115/020/003).

16 Michel Foucault. 'The Subject and Power', *Critical Inquiry* 8.4 (1982): pp. 777–795.

17 Quoted by Sophie Gadd. 'Grumpy Neighbour Writes Letter of Complaint Because Child Laughs Too Much', *Mirror*, 24 Apr 2015 (www.mirror.co.uk/usvsth3m/grumpy-neighbour-writes-letter-complaint-5572811).

18 Natalie Hopkinson. 'How Social Media Turns Neighbors Into Vigilantes', *Huffington Post*, 22 May 2018 (www.huffpost.com/entry/opinion-hopkinson-nextdoor-gentrification-police_n_5b036b18e4b0a046186f0e27).

19 Tiffany May & Hisako Ueno. 'Squealing Children and Noisy Neighbors? There's a Map for That', *New York Times*, 25 Feb 2021 (www.nytimes.com/2021/02/25/world/asia/japan-noise-map.html).

20 Miwa Suzuki. 'Greying Japan Complains of the Noise of Children', AFP News, 30 May 2013 (https://sg.news.yahoo.com/greying-japan-complains-noise-children-044915396.html).

21 Jenny Gesley & Sayuri Umeda. 'Is the Sound of Children Actually Noise?', Library of Congress, 28 Feb 2018 (https://blogs.loc.gov/law/2018/02).

22 Mark Reynolds. 'Concorde Pilot Loses Court Fight to Silence Playground', *Express*, 26 May 2012 (www.express.co.uk/news/uk/322541/Concorde-pilot-loses-court-fight-to-silence-playground).

23 Matthew Arnold. *Culture and Anarchy: An Essay in Political and Social Criticism* (Smith, Elder & Co., 1869): p. viii.

24 See e.g. Kerry Soper. 'From Swarthy Ape to Sympathetic Everyman and Subversive Trickster: The Development of Irish Caricature in American Comic Strips between 1890 and 1920', *Journal of American Studies* 39.2 (2005): pp. 257–296, p. 263.

25 Ann Laura Stoler. *Race and the Education of Desire* (Duke University Press, 1995): p. 125.

26 Quoted by Tony Fisher. *Theatre and Governance in Britain, 1500–1900* (Cambridge University Press, 2017): p. 4.

27 Andrew Linklater and Stephen Mennell. 'Norbert Elias, The Civilising Process', *History and Theory* 49.3 (2010), pp. 384–411.
28 Barbara Ehrenreich. *Dancing in the Streets: A History of Collective Joy* (Macmillan, 2007): pp. 1–2.
29 Quoted by Ehrenreich, *Dancing*: pp. 3–4.
30 Ehrenreich, *Dancing*: p. 7.
31 Stuart Woolf. 'Europe and its Historians', *Contemporary European History* 12.3 (2003): pp. 323–337.
32 Pramod K. Nayar. 'Civil Modernity: The Management of Manners and Polite Imperial Relations in India, 1880–1930', *South Asia: Journal of South Asian Studies* 39.4 (2016): pp. 740–757, p. 744.
33 Leo T. S. Ching. *Becoming Japanese: Colonial Taiwan and the Politics of Identity Formation* (University of California Press, 2001).
34 Allison Kim Shutt. *Manners Make a Nation: Racial Etiquette in Southern Rhodesia, 1910–1963* (Boydell & Brewer, 2015).
35 Clarence R. Talley & Theresa Rajack-Talley. 'Racial Etiquette and Racial Stereotypes', *Living Racism: Through the Barrel of the Book* (Lexington Books, 2018): pp. 51–74, p. 55.
36 Bertram W. Doyle. 'The Etiquette of Race Relations – Past, Present, and Future', *Journal of Negro Education* (1936): pp. 191–208, p. 192.
37 Doyle, 'Race Relations': p. 201.
38 Quoted by Talley & Rajack-Talley, 'Racial Etiquette': p. 56.
39 Richard Wright, 'The Ethics of Living Jim Crow', 1937 (available at https://inside.sfuhs.org/dept/history/US_History_reader/Chapter7/wrightethics.htm).
40 Henry Mayhew, *London Labour and the London Poor* (1851).
41 Quoted by Ehrenreich, *Dancing*: p. 8.
42 Francis M. L. Thompson. 'Social Control in Victorian Britain', *The Economic History Review* 34:2 (1981): 189–208, p. 198.
43 Anna M. Lawrence. 'Morals and Mignonette; or, the Use of Flowers in the Moral Regulation of the Working Classes in High Victorian London', *Journal of Historical Geography* 70 (2020), pp. 24–35.
44 Lia Karsten. 'The Upgrading of the Sidewalk: From Traditional Working-Class Colonisation to the Squatting Practices of Urban

Middle-Class Families', *Urban Design International* 13:2 (2008): pp. 61–66.

45 Jane Read. 'Gutter to Garden: Historical Discourses of Risk in Interventions in Working Class Children's Street Play', *Children & Society* 25:6 (2011): pp. 421–434.

46 Satoshi Mizutani. *The Meaning of White: Race, Class, and the "Domiciled Community" in British India 1858–1930* (Oxford University Press, 2011).

47 Charlotte Riley. 'How to Play Patriarchy Chicken', *New Statesman*, 22 Feb 2019 (www.newstatesman.com/politics/2019/02/how-play-patriarchy-chicken-why-i-refuse-move-out-way-men).

48 Anastasia Loukaitou-Sideris & Renia Ehrenfeucht. *Sidewalks: Conflict and Negotiation over Public Space* (MIT Press, 2011): p. 89.

49 Shutt, *Manners*: p. 22.

50 Quoted by Shutt, *Manners*: p. 22.

51 Geneva Smitherman. *Talkin and Testifyin: The Language of Black America* (Wayne State University Press, 1977).

52 Dominique Morisseau. 'Why I Almost Slapped a Fellow Theatre Patron, and What That Says About Our Theatres', *American Theatre*, 9 Dec 2015 (www.americantheatre.org/2015/12/09/why-i-almost-slapped-a-fellow-theatre-patron-and-what-that-says-about-our-theatres).

5: Where We're Going We Don't Need Rhodes

1 Martin Luther King Jr. 'Letter from Birmingham Jail' written to fellow clergymen on 16 April 1963 (Reproduced in *UC Davis Law Review* 26 [1992]: 835).

2 Quoted by Disability Visability Project. 'People We Love: Anita Cameron', 9 Sep 2014 (https://disabilityvisibilityproject.com/2014/09/09/disability-rights-and-history).

3 Quoted by Stephanie Kirby. '30 Marsha P Johnson Quotes from the Transgender Activist', *Everyday Power*, 15 Mar 2022. (https://everydaypower.com/marsha-p-johnson-quotes).

4 Runnymede Trust. 'Bristol: A City Divided?', January 2017 (https://tinyurl.com/2ensapyp).

5 George Heath. *The New History, Survey and Description of the City and Suburbs of Bristol, or Complete Guide* (W. Matthews, 1794): p. 90.

6 Tendai Marima. 'Pro-Democracy Protests Continue In Eswatini, Africa's Last Absolute Monarchy', NPR, 16 Jul 2021 (www.npr.org/2021/07/16/1016031822/pro-democracy-protests-continue-in-eswatini-africas-last-absolute-monarchy?t=1655376104546).

7 Thiti Jamkajornkeiat. 'Down with Feudalism, Long Live the People!', *Spectre Journal*, 3 Dec 2020 (https://spectrejournal.com/down-with-feudalism-long-live-the-people).

8 Helen Davidson & Vincent Ni. 'Hong Kong Vigil Leader Arrested as 7,000 Police Enforce ban on Tiananmen Anniversary Protests', *Guardian*, 4 Jun 2021 (www.theguardian.com/world/2021/jun/04/hong-kong-7000-police-ready-to-enforce-ban-on-tiananmen-anniversary-protests).

9 Quoted by Conor Friedersdorf. 'Against the Insurrection Act', *The Atlantic*, 4 Jun 2020 (www.theatlantic.com/ideas/archive/2020/06/against-insurrection-act/612676).

10 Quoted by Martin Pengelly. 'Trump Told Top US General to "Just Shoot" Racism Protesters, Book Claims', *Guardian*, 25 Jun 2021 (www.theguardian.com/us-news/2021/jun/25/donald-trump-general-mark-milley-crack-skulls).

11 James Cox. 'Why the New Policing Bill Threatens Our Right to Protest', *Legal Cheek*, 24 Aug 2021 (www.legalcheek.com/lc-journal-posts/why-the-new-policing-bill-threatens-our-right-to-protest).

12 Quoted by Jessica Elgot & Aubrey Allegretti. 'Priti Patel Hints UK Government Could Set Up National Register of Stalkers', *Guardian*, 15 Mar 2021 (www.theguardian.com/uk-news/2021/mar/15/priti-patel-hints-uk-government-could-set-up-national-register-of-stalkers).

13 Quoted by Tracy Brown. 'Trevor Noah Grills Tomi Lahren about "the Right Way" for Black People to Protest in America', *Los Angeles*

Times, 1 Dec 2016 (www.latimes.com/entertainment/tv/la-et-st-trevor-noah-tomi-lahren-20161201-htmlstory.html).

14 Scott Clement & Emily Guskin. 'Poll: 53 Percent of Americans Say It's "Never Appropriate" to Kneel During the National Anthem', *Washington Post*, 23 May 2018 (www.washingtonpost.com/news/sports/wp/2018/05/23/poll-53-percent-of-americans-say-its-never-appropriate-to-kneel-during-the-national-anthem).

15 Elahe Izadi. 'Black Lives Matter and America's Long History of Resisting Civil Rights Protesters', *Washington Post*, 19 Apr 2016 (www.washingtonpost.com/news/the-fix/wp/2016/04/19/black-lives-matters-and-americas-long-history-of-resisting-civil-rights-protesters).

16 Zolan Kanno-Youngs. 'A Battle over How to Battle over Roe', *New York Times*, 12 May 2022 (www.nytimes.com/2022/05/12/us/politics/abortion-protests-supreme-court-justices.html).

17 Robert J. McLaughlin. 'Socrates on Political Disobedience: A Reply to Gary Young', *Phronesis* 21:3 (1976): pp. 185–197.

18 King Jr., 'Letter': p. 841.

19 Quoted by Neo Lekgotla Laga Ramoupi. '"The Black Man in the White Man's Court": Mandela at Wits University, South Africa, 1943–1949', *Ufahamu: Journal of the African Activist Association* 2 (2016): pp. 163–196. p. 164.

20 Howard Zinn, 'The Problem Is Civil Obedience', Nov 1970 (Reproduced in History is a Weapon: www.historyisaweapon.com/defcon1/zinnproblemobedience.html).

21 Zinn, 'The Problem'.

22 Kanno-Youngs, 'A Battle'.

23 Zinn, 'The Problem'.

24 Leslie Feinberg. 'Interview with Sylvia Rivera', The Queer Bible (www.queerbible.com/queerbible/2017/10/8/interview-sylvia-rivera-by-leslie-feinberg).

25 King Jr., 'Letter': p. 835.

26 Mario Savio. *An End to History*, Virginia Students' Civil Rights Committee, 1965 (Reproduced in History is a Weapon: www.historyisaweapon.com/defcon1/savioendofhistory.html).

27 German Lopez. 'The Justice Department's Incredibly Damning Report on Baltimore Police, Explained', *Vox*, 10 Aug 2016 (www.vox.com/2016/8/10/12418428/baltimore-police-investigation-justice-department-report).

28 Sky News. 'Police Breached "Fundamental Rights" at Sarah Everard and Kill the Bill Protests, Parliamentary Inquiry Finds', 1 Jul 2020 (https://news.sky.com/story/police-breached-fundamental-rights-at-sarah-everard-and-kill-the-bill-protests-parliamentary-inquiry-finds-12346006).

29 Steven W. Thrasher. 'Proportionate Response', *Slate*, 30 May 2020 (https://slate.com/news-and-politics/2020/05/george-floyd-protests-minneapolis-police-fires.html).

30 R. H. Lossin. 'In Defense of Destroying Property', *The Nation*, 10 Jun 2020 (www.thenation.com/article/activism/blm-looting-protest-vandalism).

31 Mimi E. Kim. 'From Carceral Feminism to Transformative Justice: Women-of-Color Feminism and Alternatives to Incarceration', *Journal of Ethnic & Cultural Diversity in Social Work* 27:3 (2018): pp. 219–233.

32 Leah A. Jacobs, Mimi E. Kim, Darren L. Whitfield, Rachel E. Gartner, Meg Panichelli, Shanna K. Kattari, Margaret Mary Downey, Shanté Stuart McQueen & Sarah E. Mountz. 'Defund the Police: Moving Towards an Anti-carceral Social Work', *Journal of Progressive Human Services* 32:1 (2021): pp. 37–62.

33 Holly Yan. 'States Require More Training Time to Become a Barber than a Police Officer', CNN, 28 Sep 2016 (https://edition.cnn.com/2016/09/28/us/jobs-training-police-trnd/index.html).

34 Juleyka Lantigua-Williams. 'Raise the Minimum Wage, Reduce Crime?' *The Atlantic*, 3 May 2016 (www.theatlantic.com/politics/archive/2016/05/raise-the-minimum-wage-reduce-crime/480912).

35 Julian M. Somers, Stefanie N. Rezansoff, Akm Moniruzzaman, Anita Palepu & Michelle Patterson. 'Housing First Reduces Re-offending among Formerly Homeless Adults with Mental Disorders: Results of a Randomized Controlled Trial', *PLoS One* 8:9 (2013).

36 Samuel R. Bondurant, Jason M. Lindo & Isaac D. Swensen. 'Substance Abuse Treatment Centers and Local Crime', *Journal of Urban Economics* 104 (2018): pp. 124–133.
37 Shima Baradaran Baughman. 'How Effective Are Police? The Problem of Clearance Rates and Criminal Accountability', *Alabama Law Review* 72:1 (2020): pp. 47–130.
38 Emily Jones. 'Untested and Neglected: Clarifying the Comparator Requirement in Equal Protection Claims Based on Untested Rape Kits', *Northwestern University Law Review* 115:6 (2021): pp. 1781–1828.
39 Rape, Abuse & Incest National Network (RAINN). 'Statistics' (www.rainn.org/statistics).
40 Thomas K. Hargrove. 'Black Homicide Victims Accounted for All of America's Declining Clearance Rate', Murder Accountability Project, 18 Feb 2019 (www.dropbox.com/s/66ae30q9inwcvvt/Black%20 Homicides.pdf?dl=1).
41 Treatment Advocacy Center. 'The Role and Impact of Law Enforcement in Transporting Individuals with Severe Mental Illness, A National Survey', May 2019 (www.treatmentadvocacycenter.org/ road-runners).
42 Erika Bazaldua. 'Law Enforcement Officials Say They Are Expected to Do "Everything for Everybody"', KLTV, 3 Aug 2016 (www.kltv.com/story/32603243/law-enforcement-officials-say-they-are-expected-to-do-everything-for-everybody).
43 Gregory Cajete. *Native Science: Natural Laws of Interdependence* (Clear Light Publishers, 2000).
44 Viola Faye Cordova. *How It Is: The Native American Philosophy of V. F. Cordova* (University of Arizona Press, 2007): p. 222.
45 Quoted by Gyasi Ross. 'Keystone XL and Protecting Mother Earth' *Indian Country Today*, 13 Sep 2018 (https://indiancountrytoday.com/archive/keystone-xl-and-protecting-mother-earth-a-fight-all-native-people-should-fight).
46 W. Marvin Dulaney. *Black Police in America* (Indiana University Press, 1996): p. 2.

47 Dulaney, *Black Police*: pp. 2–3.

48 David Churchill. *Crime Control and Everyday Life in the Victorian City: The Police and the Public* (Oxford University Press, 2017).

49 Paul Lawrence. 'The Vagrancy Act (1824) and the Persistence of Pre-emptive Policing in England Since 1750', *The British Journal of Criminology* 57:3 (2017): pp. 513–531.

50 Quoted by Lawrence, 'Vagrancy Act': p. 513.

51 Lawrence, 'Vagrancy Act'.

52 Johnson, *Spaces of Conflict*: p. 63.

53 Betsy Kuhn. *Gay Power!: The Stonewall Riots and the Gay Rights Movement, 1969* (Twenty-First Century Books, 2011).

54 Catherine Kudlick. 'Disabled People's Forgotten Revolution', Patient No More! (www.patientnomore.blogspot.com/2014/04/disabled-peoples-forgotten-revolution.html).

55 Quoted by Samuel Galen Ng. 'Trans Power! Sylvia Lee Rivera's STAR and the Black Panther Party', *Left History: An Interdisciplinary Journal of Historical Inquiry and Debate* 17:1 (2013): pp. 11–41, p. 11.

56 Quoted by Angela Y. Davis. *Women, Race, and Class* (Vintage, 1983): p. 231.

57 Combahee River Collective. '(1977) The Combahee River Collective Statement' (Reproduced in Black Past: www.blackpast.org/african-american-history/combahee-river-collective-statement-1977).

6: Whatever Happened to Public Reason?

1 Quoted by Roger Ball. 'The Edward Colston "Corrective" Plaque: Sanitising an Uncomfortable History', Bristol Radical History Group, 24 Mar 2019 (www.brh.org.uk/site/articles/the-edward-colston-corrective-plaque).

2 Quoted by Tristan Cork. 'Theft or Vandalism of Second Colston Statue Plaque "May be Justified" – Tory Councillor', *Bristol Post*, 23 Jul 2018 (www.bristolpost.co.uk/news/bristol-news/theft-vandalism-second-colston-statue-1815967).

3 Quoted by Tristan Cork. 'How the City Failed to Remove Edward Colston's Statue for Years', *Bristol Post*, 5 Jan 2022 (www.bristolpost.co.uk/news/bristol-news/how-city-failed-remove-edward-4211771).
4 Matrix Chambers. 'Colston Four Cleared of Criminal Damage by Jury', 7 Jan 2022 (www.matrixlaw.co.uk/news/colston-four-cleared-of-criminal-damage-by-jury).
5 Quoted by *Ebony*. 'Political Prisoners: A Righteous Reality or Ridiculous Rant?', 10 Sep 2012 (www.ebony.com/news/photos-political-prisoners-a-righteous-reality-or-ridiculous-rant).
6 Tod Perry. 'Frustrated with America's "Progress" on Race? James Baldwin Described It Perfectly over 30 Years Ago', *Upworthy*, 29 May 2020 (www.upworthy.com/frustrated-with-progress-on-race-james-baldwin-described-it-perfectly-31-years-ago).
7 Jonathan Rauch. 'Here's How 9 Predictions about Gay Marriage Turned Out', *Time*, 27 Jun 2015 (https://time.com/3939029/heres-how-9-predictions-about-gay-marriage-turned-out).
8 Reproduced by Cornell Law School, 'United States v. Rumely' (www.law.cornell.edu/supremecourt/text/345/41).
9 Daniel T. Rodgers. *Age of Fracture* (Harvard University Press, 2011).
10 Thomas Borstelmann. *The 1970s: A New Global History from Civil Rights to Economic Inequality* (Princeton University Press, 2013).
11 Tom Wolfe. 'The "Me" Decade and the Third Great Awakening', *New York Magazine* 23.8 (1976): pp. 26–40.
12 Jonathan Quong, 'Public Reason', *Stanford Encyclopedia of Philosophy*, 2013 (https://seop.illc.uva.nl/entries/public-reason).
13 John Rawls. *Political Liberalism* (Columbia University Press, 1996): p. 49.
14 Cristina Lafont. 'Procedural Justice? Implications of the Rawls-Habermas Debate for Discourse Ethics', *Philosophy & Social Criticism* 29:2 (2003): pp. 163–181.
15 Richard Bellamy. 'The Republic of Reasons: Public Reasoning, Depoliticization and Non-domination', *Legal Republicanism: National and International Perspectives* (Oxford University Press, 2009): pp. 102–120.

16 John Kampfner. *Why the Germans Do it Better: Notes from a Grown-up Country* (Atlantic Books, 2020).

17 Bimal Krishna Matilal. 'Semiotic Conceptions in the Indian Theory of Argumentation', *Indian Philosophy: A Reader* (Routledge, 2019): pp. 335–343, p. 336.

18 Matilal, 'Semiotic': p. 336.

19 Melanie Kaidan. 'National Trust BLASTED by MPs over "Woke" Review into Britain's National Heritage', *Express*, 20 Dec 2020 (www.express.co.uk/news/politics/1374727/national-trust-black-lives-matter-movement-john-hayes-churchill-statue-woke-culture-ont).

20 Glenn Kessler, Salvador Rizzo & Meg Kelly. 'Trump's False or Misleading Claims Total 30,573 over 4 Years', *Washington Post*, 24 Jan 2021 (www.washingtonpost.com/politics/2021/01/24/trumps-false-or-misleading-claims-total-30573-over-four-years)

21 Lizzie Dearden. 'Conservative Party Used Disinformation "With New Level of Impunity" During 2019 General Election, Report Finds', *Independent*, 24 Aug 2020 (www.independent.co.uk/news/uk/politics/conservative-party-disinformation-2019-general-election-a9682566.html).

22 Frances Perraudin. 'Twitter Accuses Tories of Misleading Public with "Factcheck" Foray', *Guardian*, 20 Nov 2019 (www.theguardian.com/politics/2019/nov/20/twitter-accuses-tories-of-misleading-public-in-factcheck-row).

23 Hunt Allcott & Matthew Gentzkow. 'Social Media and Fake News in the 2016 Election', *Journal of Economic Perspectives* 31:2 (2017): pp. 211–236.

24 Fred Siebert, Theodore Peterson & Wilbur Schramm. *Four Theories of the Press: The Authoritarian, Libertarian, Social Responsibility, and Soviet Communist Concepts of What the Press Should Be and Do*, Vol. 10 (University of Illinois Press, 1956): p. 45.

25 Peter Selb & Simon Munzert. 'Examining a Most Likely Case for Strong Campaign Effects: Hitler's Speeches and the Rise of the Nazi Party, 1927–1933', *American Political Science Review* 112:4 (2018): pp. 1050–1066.

26 Harrison Michael Rosenthal. 'Speech Imperialization? Situating American Parrhesia in an Isegoria World', *International Journal for the Semiotics of Law / Revue Internationale de Sémiotique Juridique* (2020): pp. 1–21.

27 Rosenthal, 'Imperialization?': p. 586.

28 Rosenthal, 'Imperialization?': p. 596.

29 Rosenthal, 'Imperialization?': p. 590.

30 Amy Johnson. 'The Multiple Harms of Sea Lions', *Perspectives on Harmful Speech Online* (Berkman Klein Center for Internet & Society, 2017): p. 13.

31 Wendy Ashley. 'The Angry Black Woman: The Impact of Pejorative Stereotypes on Psychotherapy with Black Women', *Social Work in Public Health* 29:1 (2014): pp. 27–34.

32 Audre Lorde. *Sister Outsider* (Penguin Books, 1980): pp. 114–115.

33 Lorde, *Sister*: p. 115.

34 Quoted by L. Michael Gibson. 'Interlude E: From Destiny's Child to Coachella', in *The Lemonade Reader*, eds Kinitra D. Brooks & Kameelah L. Martin (Routledge, 2019): pp. 144–154, p. 144.

35 Chris Colin. 'Rate This Article: What's Wrong with the Culture of Critique', *Wired*, 26 Jul 2011 (www.wired.com/2011/07/st-essay-rating).

36 Roger Bohn & James E. Short. 'Info Capacity| Measuring Consumer Information', *International Journal of Communication* 6 (2012): p. 21.

37 Anthony Giddens. *A Contemporary Critique of Historical Materialism* (University of California Press, 1981).

38 C. Thi Nguyen. 'Escape the Echo Chamber', *Aeon Magazine*, 12 Apr 2018 (https://medium.com/aeon-magazine/escape-the-echo-chamber-7ce91164421c).

39 John Stuart Mill. 'On Liberty' (Reproduced: www.econlib.org/library/Mill/mlLbty.html).

40 Laura Tobias. 'Ex-Nurse Who Calls COVID-19 Doctors "Nazis" Believes the Devil is Orchestrating Pandemic; Son Says She is "Beyond Help"', *Scrubs Magazine*, 27 Jul 2021 (https://scrubsmag.com/ex-nurse-who-calls-covid-19-doctors-nazis-believes-the-devil-is-orchestrating-pandemic-son-says-she-is-beyond-help).

41 Tobias, 'Ex-Nurse'.

42 Julia Ebner, *Going Dark: The Secret Social Lives of Extremists* (Bloomsbury, 2019): p. xiii.

43 Elie Wiesel. 'Nobel Prize Speech' (Reproduced in The Elie Wiesel Foundation for Humanity: https://eliewieselfoundation.org/elie-wiesel/nobelprizespeech).

44 Ben Mathis-Lilley. 'Anti-Vaxxers Only Have Two Historical Reference Points, Apparently', *Slate*, 21 Sep 2021 (https://slate.com/news-and-politics/2021/09/why-mask-and-vaccine-opponents-keep-comparing-themselves-to-holocaust-victims-and-rosa-parks.html).

45 Max Boot. 'The Andrew Cuomo Scandal Highlights Republicans' Appalling Double Standard', *Washington Post*, 8 Mar 2021 (www.washingtonpost.com/opinions/2021/03/08/andrew-cuomo-scandal-highlights-republicans-appalling-double-standard).

46 Shawn Cooke. 'Was Nancy Pelosi's Lectern Actually Sold on eBay?', *MIC*, 8 Jan 2021 (www.mic.com/p/was-nancy-pelosis-lectern-actually-sold-on-ebay-54854673).

47 E. J. Dickson. 'The Rise and Fall of the Proud Boys', *Rolling Stone*, 15 Jun 2021 (www.rollingstone.com/culture/culture-features/proud-boys-far-right-group-1183966).

48 Quoted by Amber Phillips. '6 Questions the Jan. 6 Committee Aims to Answer About the Attack', *Washington Post*, 9 Jun 2022 (www.washingtonpost.com/politics/2022/06/09/jan6-committee-questions-hearings).

49 Tommy Beer. 'Fox News Host Who Called BLM "Poison" Says Pro-Trump Mob Made Up Of "Solid Americans"', *Forbes*, 7 Jan 2021 (www.forbes.com/sites/tommybeer/2021/01/07/fox-news-host-who-called-blm-poison-says-pro-trump-mob-made-up-of-solid-americans/?sh=60ebdd6f6829).

50 Kanno-Youngs, 'A Battle'.

51 The US Attorney's Office, District of Delaware. 'Man Sentenced for Hurling Molotov Cocktail at Newark Planned Parenthood', 10 Mar 2022 (www.justice.gov/usao-de/pr/man-sentenced-hurling-molotov-cocktail-newark-planned-parenthood).

52 Danielle Sarver Coombs, Cheryl Ann Lambert, David Cassilo & Zachary Humphries. 'Flag on the Play: Colin Kaepernick and the Protest Paradigm', *Howard Journal of Communications* 31:4 (2020): pp. 317–336.

53 See e.g. T. Stenz. 'Radical Right vs Radical Left: Terrorist Theory and Threat', *Police Chief* 57:8 (1990): pp. 70–75; Manuela Caiani & Donatella Della Porta. 'The Radical Right as Social Movement Organizations', in *The Oxford Handbook of the Radical Right*, ed. Jens Rydgren (2018): pp. 327–347.

54 Tim Wu. 'Quantifying Liberal Suckerdom', *New York Times*, 26 Feb 2020 (www.nytimes.com/2020/02/26/opinion/democrats-sanders-appeal.html).

55 Kristen Underhill & Ian Ayres. 'Sunsets Are for Suckers: An Experimental Test of Sunset Clauses', *Harvard Journal on Legislation* 59 (2022): pp. 101–144.

56 Wu, 'Quantifying'.

57 James Slack. 'Enemies of the People', *Daily Mail*, 3 Nov 2016 (www.dailymail.co.uk/news/article-3903436/Enemies-people-Fury-touch-judges-defied-17-4m-Brexit-voters-trigger-constitutional-crisis.html).

58 Nicholas Goedert. 'Gerrymandering or Geography? How Democrats Won the Popular Vote But Lost the Congress in 2012', *Research & Politics* 1:1 (2014).

59 Kim Fridkin & Patrick Kenney. *Taking Aim at Attack Advertising: Understanding the Impact of Negative Campaigning in US Senate Races* (Oxford University Press, 2019): p. 80.

60 Jieun Shin & Kjerstin Thorson. 'Partisan Selective Sharing: The Biased Diffusion of Fact-checking Messages on Social Media', *Journal of Communication* 67:2 (2017): pp. 233–255.

61 Michael Alan Krasner. 'Donald Trump: Dividing America Through New-Culture Speech', *When Politicians Talk* (Springer, 2021): pp. 257–274, p. 269.

62 Ron Elving. 'What Happened with Merrick Garland in 2016 and Why It Matters Now', NPR, 29 Jun 2018 (www.npr.

org/2018/06/29/624467256/what-happened-with-merrick-garland-in-2016-and-why-it-matters-now).

63 George Lakoff. *Moral Politics: How Liberals and Conservatives Think* (University of Chicago Press, 2010): p. 100.

64 Lakoff, *Moral Politics*: p. 101.

65 Lakoff, *Moral Politics*: p. 101.

66 Wu, 'Quantifying'.

Conclusion

1 Sara Ahmed. *Complaint!* (Duke University Press, 2021).

2 Cai Wilkinson. 'Are We Winning? A Strategic Analysis of Queer Wars', *Australian Journal of International Affairs* 71:3 (2017): pp. 236–240.

3 Quoted by James Tyner. *The Geography of Malcolm X: Black Radicalism and the Remaking of American Space* (Routledge, 2013): p. 104.

4 Elizabeth Martínez. *De Colores Means All of Us: Latina Views for a Multi-Colored Century* (Verso, 1998).

5 Brittney C. Cooper. *Beyond Respectability: The Intellectual Thought of Race Women* (University of Illinois Press, 2017).

6 King Jr., 'Letter': p. 835.

7 Dale Antony Turner. *This is Not a Peace Pipe: Towards a Critical Indigenous Philosophy* (University of Toronto Press, 2006).

8 Turner, *Peace Pipe*: pp. 48–49.

9 Cordova, *How It Is*: p. 224.

10 Eric K. Yamamoto. 'Race Apologies', *The Journal of Gender, Race & Justice* 1 (1997): p. 52.

11 Annabel Crop Eared Wolf. 'Matsiyipáítapiiyssini: Káínai Peacekeeping and Peacemaking', PhD Dissertation (University of Lethbridge, Faculty of Arts and Science, 2007).

12 Turner, *Peace Pipe*: p. 50.

13 Quoted by Andrew R. Cecil. 'Economic Relations. Human

Relations', *The American Journal of Economics and Sociology* 18:3 (1959): pp. 259-276, p. 276.

14 Fainos Mangena. 'Hunhu/Ubuntu in the Traditional Thought of Southern Africa', *Internet Encyclopedia of Philosophy* (https://iep.utm.edu/hunhu).

15 Turner, *Peace Pipe*: p. 54.

16 Armour, *Negrophobia*: p. 31.

17 Quoted in translation by Marco Iorio and Ralf Stoecker. *Actions, Reasons and Reason* (Walter de Gruyter, 2015): p. 129.

18 Quoted by Susan Ratcliffe. 'Oxford Essential Quotations' (www.oxfordreference.com/view/10.1093/acref/9780191826719.001.0001/q-oro-ed4-00008541).

Acknowledgements

When Jaime Marshall reached out to discuss my research, we met for the first time in my office with a two-month-old Sully sleeping wrapped up in my coat. Monty was watching *Paw Patrol* next to us on the floor, and I was trying to say clever things through the soundtrack of 'Ryder Needs Us!' and the delirious mind-fog of very little sleep. If you'd told me then that – a mere five years (and hours of brainstorming) later – the agency JP Marshall was going to hustle my work out into the wider world, I never would have believed it. Jaime: please accept my endless gratitude in return for your endless patience.

Speaking of patience: the biggest slice of the 'thank you' pie goes to my ridiculously supportive husband Tom Sedgman, and the second to my work wife Kate Holmes, for collectively walking me back from the brink whenever I came close to throwing my laptop in the paddling pool. Many thanks too to my family: particularly my mum Carol, for helping me to proofread the entire manuscript! Also to my brother Davy and my sister Emma-Louise for all your cheerleading over the years, as well as Cynthia, Francis and Sam for always offering a sounding board if I need to work a particularly knotty problem through.

There's plenty of gratitude left for the whole Faber team for working so hard to usher this book out into bookshops and to get it into readers' hands. Especially my editors: firstly, Fred Baty for taking a chance, then the brilliant Emmie Francis for taking the project forwards and deftly supporting me on the long road to publication. To my 'palleagues' and fellow UoBaby-wranglers Jess McCormack and Ellie Rycroft – I love you both and never would have made it through the past few years without you. Nor would I have survived without the kind folks at Sweven Coffee. Thanks too to all my Bristol comrades – but especially the amazing feminist role models I've been lucky enough to find in people like Catherine Hindson, Elaine McGirr, Katja Krebs, Emma Cole, Nora Williams and Freya Gowrley – as well as to my CNF Club and Drag Them to Hell friends, and of course to everyone involved in Boredom Bites, where Furaha Asani, Leighan Renaud and Hannah Robbins nurtured the earliest seeds of this book idea. I am unbelievably lucky to know you.

Finally, to my children. Monty and Sully, my kind, fierce, sweet little boys – this book is for you. Thank you for teaching me what it takes to become reasonably-unreasonable, where necessary, in order to make the world a better place.

Index

INDEX